Sara,
I hope
this helps with
your helpless
hand raisers,
Fred Jones

POSITIVE CLASSROOM INSTRUCTION

POSITIVE CLASSROOM INSTRUCTION

Fredric H. Jones, Ph. D.

McGRAW-HILL BOOK COMPANY

New York St. Louis San Francisco Auckland Bogotá Hamburg
London Madrid Mexico Milan Montreal New Delhi Panama
Paris São Paulo Singapore Sydney Tokyo Toronto

This book was set in Times Roman by Compset, Inc.
The editor was Thomas H. Quinn;
the jacket and cover were designed by Laura B. Stover.
Project supervision was done by The Total Book.
R. R. Donnelley & Sons Company was printer and binder.

POSITIVE CLASSROOM INSTRUCTION

2 3 4 5 6 7 8 9 0 DOCDOC 8 9 4 3 2 1 0 9

ISBN 0-07-032782-3

Library of Congress Cataloging-in-Publication Data

Jones, Fredric H.
Positive classroom instruction.

Bibliography: p.
Includes index.
1. Teaching. 2. Teacher-student relationships.
3. Helping behavior. 4. Classroom management.
5. Motivation in education. I. Title.
LB1025.2.J663 1987 371.1 87-4128
ISBN 0-07-032782-3

CONTENTS

ACKNOWLEDGMENTS

I credit my wife Jo Lynne with much of my interest in classrooms. Throughout graduate school she was a teacher, and every night when she got home from work we had a 1-hour "debriefing"—like the astronauts have when they return from outer space. During our debriefings I got to relive every trauma and gratification of the day, and by Thanksgiving, the students were, for better or for worse, members of the family. After 5 years of debriefings you either get very curious about what goes on in a classroom or you get entirely turned off by the whole subject. When I began to do classroom management research, Jo Lynne was a collaborator, and she has been my partner in this endeavor ever since.

Jo Lynne was the kind of teacher who came home and did several hours of work in the evening to prepare for the next day. Knowing how hard good teachers work has been a crucial aspect of my awareness that has influenced every aspect of the development of the classroom management methods contained in this book. It is not enough for a technique to succeed. It must also be affordable in terms of time and energy.

I must also acknowledge my debt to my family. I come from a family of teachers. Not only was my mother a teacher, but also aunts, great-aunts, cousins, and my sister. Both parents taught me a lot about effective discipline before I ever got close to a classroom. Perhaps the most important lesson was that strength and firmness could also be gentle and loving.

I am grateful as well to my teacher, colleague, and friend, William Hansford Miller of the faculty of the Neuropsychiatric Institute at the UCLA Medical Center. Hans taught me the basics of behavioral management, supervised my clinical work with parent training, and collaborated on my first piece of classroom management research. Working together we came to understand limit-setting in the classroom and performance-oriented methods of teacher training. More importantly, Hans was available for hours of brainstorming during which time he helped me see how behavioral incentive systems worked at all times in both the home and the classroom. I am indebted as well to Michael J. Goldstein and Eliot H. Rodnick of the UCLA psychology faculty for teaching me to understand psychopathology in family systems from a psychodynamic framework. Together they supervised my dissertation in the area of developmental psychopathology.

I am also indebted to the Bureau of Cooperative Educational Services #1, Fairport, New York, for supporting much of the research necessary for perfecting the methods presented in this book. It is rare that a school system or educational center will undertake the basic research and developmental work required to perfect solutions to everyday classroom management problems. I am also indebted to the excellent students with whom I have had the pleasure of working in this and other settings: Robert C. Eimers, Ph.D.; William Fremouw, Ph.D.; Aden A. Burka, Ph.D.; Herbert Weis, Ph.D.; Richard J. Cowen, Ph.D.; Kenneth Docteur, Ed. D.; and Steven Carples, M.B.A.

And, finally, I am indebted to the many teachers over the years who have opened their classrooms to our work, who have tried new techniques, and who have enriched those techniques with their own ideas and feedback. I have never trained teachers without myself learning at the same time, and I always come home with several pages of notes that enlarge my understanding of classroom management and improve subsequent teacher training. Although I have spent a decade and a half in careful research and development, in teaching there is nothing new under the sun. To a considerable extent this book represents the collected oral tradition and professional wisdom of the teachers with whom I have had the good fortune to work.

Fredric H. Jones

FOREWORD

Dr. Fredric Jones, in *Positive Classroom Instruction*, emphasizes that "a professional most simply is a person with highly specialized skills—skills taking years to master which equip that person to do a difficult job that is far beyond the capability of untrained laymen."

To achieve this professional level, Dr. Jones makes program suggestions which range from basic instructional skills to teacher education. "Process skills" of instruction are addressed, including task analysis, lesson design and presentation, corrective feedback, and quality control of the student's work. These ultimately result in (1) a rapid reduction of teacher stress and exasperation, (2) a rapid increase in academic learning time and time on task, and (3) an elevation of standards. Stressing the preventative power of effective teaching, Dr. Jones focuses on the process of giving corrective feedback which all too frequently highlights error and produces discouragement. Dr. Jones replaces such negative techniques with teaching strategies that encourage and reward positive behaviors from students. "Be positive, be brief and be gone" is his credo.

One of the most important contributions of the book is Dr. Jones's incisive perception that "how to do it" is a matter of skill, practice, and supervision which rests upon a highly developed training plan—one which provides the structure for a broad-based, shared, long-term staff development effort that pervades the life of both the school site and the district. Educators, take heed, and may this book help all to eliminate the "quick fix" syndrome.

Madeline Hunter

POSITIVE CLASSROOM INSTRUCTION

SECTION ONE

INTRODUCTION TO POSITIVE CLASSROOM INSTRUCTION

INTRODUCTION

Positive Classroom Instruction is the companion volume to *Positive Classroom Discipline* and is the second volume in a two-volume treatment of the highly interrelated teaching skills that produce successful classroom management. Like *Positive Classroom Discipline, Positive Classroom Instruction* attempts to communicate effective management procedures to teachers and administrators in plain English. *Positive Classroom Discipline* focuses on the production of time on task and student cooperation within a positive classroom atmosphere at a price in time and energy that the teacher can afford. This book, in contrast, focuses on maximizing the rate of learning and students' desire to learn.

The subject of this book is the basic building block of the entire educational enterprise—a single lesson well taught. Be it direct instruction, discovery, learning, or what-have-you, the fundamental objective of classroom management is always the same—to get a group of students to do what needs to be done diligently, conscientiously, and independently. Until we can consistently succeed in this basic endeavor, most other attempts to accelerate learning in the classroom rest on a foundation of sand. This book deals with lesson presentation at a high degree of detail and precision. It examines the moment-by-moment student-teacher interactions that determine whether the student understands what to do, has the motivation and confidence to try, and works independently in one lesson after another throughout the school day.

Conventional wisdom and folklore are repeatedly examined, and some of our most widely accepted assumptions and practices are shown to be the invisible causes of most classroom disruption, helplessness, apathy, and fear of failure. Yet at other times our analysis focuses on timeless basics that are often lost in the theoretical confusion of the scientific and professional literature. As in the case of *Positive Classroom Discipline, Positive Classroom Instruction* has been forged through a blending of theory and practice in the school of hard knocks over a period of a decade and a half in all kinds of educational settings.

This book begins with the anatomy of a structured lesson and a clarification of terms so that we understand exactly what part of the structured lesson we are dealing with in every subsequent chapter. The next section of the book deals with the subject of corrective feedback—exactly how you help a student who is stuck. We will find that this relatively unexamined aspect of instructional methodology is the invisible cause of most of the seemingly insurmountable obstacles of classroom management that perennially block learning and frustrate teachers to death. Indeed, the precision technology of giving corrective feedback presented here is the core of this book; this technology holds a central place in preventing discipline problems in the classroom, creating self confidence, fostering independent learning, and developing constructive interpersonal processes between teachers and students *and* between teachers and administrators.

The technology of giving corrective feedback presented here is all the more important because it is lacking in the consciousness of the education profession and is therefore lacking in the skill repertoire of the vast majority of practicing teachers and administrators. Although this technology is presented here in considerable detail, I must emphasize that giving corrective feedback properly is one of the most difficult skills for people to learn because of the negative transfer of lifelong habits which get in the way. Consequently, while this volume places the giving of corrective feedback in its proper context within the instructional process, it also alerts us to the extensive training that is needed to produce correct practice in the field.

From corrective feedback we follow a course of practical necessity which takes us to lesson design, lesson presentation, and the systematic management of the quantity (diligence) and quality (excellence) of work produced during a typical lesson in the classroom. In all these subjects *Positive Classroom Instruction* weaves together key elements of instruction that are often disjointed or missing altogether in teachers' understanding of the presentation of a structured lesson. Yet, although particular elements represent innovation, it is the overall pattern and the interrelatedness of the parts that places such an increase in instructional power within the teacher's grasp.

The final section of this volume deals explicitly with staff development. As with *Positive Classroom Discipline,* the methods so carefully described in this book work if done properly and fail if done improperly, just like any other skill. All the basics of teaching that apply to students in the classroom apply to teachers within the context of staff development. Consequently, the major part of this book, while being a guide to effective classroom practice, is also a guide to effective teacher training.

It is a vain hope to imagine that any great improvement will occur within the educational process if lessons are taught the way they have always been taught. And it is an equally vain hope to think that teachers will master new methods of instruction if they are taught through superficial in-service presentations as they have traditionally been taught. The final section of this book, "Creating Change in Education," provides both procedures indispensable for successful staff development and warnings of the easy compromises that lead to failure.

Most school districts are at the entry level in their understanding of systematic staff development. They have neither experience with nor training in the procedures needed for the kind of teacher training and institutional support that might lead to lasting change. I hope this final section of the book will keep us from wasting the preceding sections, for I have learned from experience that in staff development you get only one chance. Once teachers have attended a presentation dealing with some new technique, they have done it, and you will not easily get them back to do it again even if the first presentation was ineffectual. *Positive Classroom Instruction,* therefore, is an attempt not only to define some very important instructional terrain within the classroom but also to clarify methods of teacher training so that this book and its companion volume, *Positive Classroom Discipline,* as well as the training programs which have been designed to accompany them, may produce a maximum of good with a minimum of disillusionment.

CHAPTER 1

ANATOMY OF A STRUCTURED LESSON

The procedures of *positive classroom discipline,* described in the first volume of this two-volume treatment of classroom management, are not sufficient by themselves to produce a positive learning atmosphere within the classroom. If lessons are improperly taught, teachers will produce more discipline problems than they can possibly remediate. Yet worn-out bromides about relating to students and having interesting and relevant lessons no longer suffice. There is a technology to instruction, and teachers must do a technically proficient job of lesson presentation if students are to invest themselves in learning. If fundamental errors of instruction are embedded in the teaching technique of an otherwise caring and interesting teacher, the price of poor methodology will be both failure and frustration for everyone involved—a feeling that will eventually erode the caring of both teacher and students.

Positive classroom instruction describes only those basic skills of instruction that I have found essential to the full success of *positive classroom discipline*. This book, therefore, is not intended as a comprehensive treatment of instructional methodology. Rather, our focus is limited to the fundamentals of lesson presentation: the generic skills of pedagogy.

Positive classroom instruction, like *positive classroom discipline,* takes its name from the affirmative interpersonal process created by effective technique. We will take a *single lesson* as our object of study and will examine methods of instruction that minimize experiences of failure and discouragement for the student while maximizing time on task, learning, and the experience of personal adequacy.

THE STRUCTURED LESSON

Lessons properly taught have structure: a clear and explicit structure both at the level of (1) content and (2) process. When improperly taught, lessons tend to be both hard to follow and boring.

The structure of the *content* of a lesson can be either in terms of skill performance or concept expression, or both. Task analysis sets forth this structure to ensure that the steps of performance are carefully laid out in order.

The structure of the *process* of lesson presentation, however, is very general in nature, whereas content is highly specific. There are certain steps that a teacher must follow in teaching any lesson in order to get consistently successful results. If this "outline of a structured lesson" is not well understood within the context of many subject areas, vital parts will usually be omitted. Such omission leads to a dramatically increased probability of student failure. Before describing the outline of a structured lesson, however, it is helpful to clarify our objectives.

The Objective of a Structured Lesson

The objective of a structured lesson is to transfer a specific competency from teacher to student. The objective, therefore, is *performance*. Although concepts are part of a structured lesson, they do not by themselves transfer to the student either correct skill performance or adequate conceptual expression.

The objective of a structured lesson, therefore, always has a strong *physical* component. What do we want students to be able to *do* by the end of the lesson that they were not able to do at the beginning? If they cannot *do* by the end of the lesson, the lesson was very likely a waste. The sights and sounds will soon fade, leaving only awareness at best. And when even awareness finally dissipates, the student is left empty-handed with only the memory of having taken the course. Think of all the final exams you crammed for in college, and ask yourself where all that knowledge was a month later.

A structured lesson properly taught finds its fulfillment in performance, the transfer of a competency from the mind and body of the teacher to the mind and body of the learner. Yet performance, *correct* performance, is only the midpoint of mastery. Ultimately we must create the capacity for correct *independent* performance in which students are able to continue learning and correct their own errors by themselves. If not, we have failed in preparing students to leave the classroom and succeed on their own.

Outline of a Structured Lesson

The outline of a structured lesson was presented briefly in Chapter 3 of *Positive Classroom Discipline*. It was discussed at that time to emphasize the fact that classroom rules and routines must be taught as thoroughly as any other structured lesson. This three-phase outline of a structured lesson is representative of our current understanding of lesson presentation within the field of education.

The three-phase format for teaching a structured lesson will be discussed in much more detail in this and subsequent chapters than it was previously. We will need a thorough understanding of the nature and objectives of each step of the structured lesson to provide a foundation for understanding the ways in which specific teaching techniques either help or undermine learning. The steps of the structured lesson, largely derived from the work of Madeline Hunter, are presented in Table 1-1.

Setting the Stage Setting the stage is an umbrella term for the "preliminary business" of the lesson which precedes the explanation of new material. Teachers can take a great deal of liberty with the sequence and content of the component parts of setting the stage since different types of lessons call for varying types of introductory material. Typically, however, at least the following three components are needed to prepare the students both emotionally and intellectually to receive new learning.

1 Raising the Level of Concern Why should students wake up and give special attention to the lesson that they are about to be given? Why is the upcoming new material a matter of great immediate concern? Raising the level of concern is the motivational "kickoff" of the lesson, and it can be either brief and simple or lengthy and complex, depending on the circumstances.

A teacher of receptive and well-informed students who is presenting a series of skills in a clear sequence may spend relatively little time raising the level of concern for each successive skill since both motivation and a shared focus of attention already exist. Raising the level of concern is greatest when the teacher in dealing with students who have (1) preexisting misconceptions which would block or confuse new learning, (2) old habits that are incompatible with new learning, (3) defensiveness or resistance to new learning, and/or (4) apathy. Raising the level of concern may be the pivotal section of a lesson in which people are being asked to abandon old and comfortable habits in favor of new ways of doing things. This state of affairs is typical of teacher training. Chapters 2 and 3, for example, represent a portion of *raising the level of concern* for learning to give corrective feedback properly during teacher training.

TABLE 1-1
OUTLINE OF A THREE-PHASE STRUCTURED LESSON

- **A** Setting the stage
  - **1** Raising the level of concern
  - **2** Review and background
  - **3** Goals and objectives
- **B** Acquisition
  - **1** Explanation
  - **2** Modeling
  - **3** Structured practice
- **C** Consolidation
  - **1** Guided practice
  - **2** Generalization and discrimination
  - **3** Independent practice

2 Review and Background What skills from previous lessons will be needed today? What concepts need to be brought to mind? Any teacher who expects the class to remember all the key skills and concepts from previous lessons is asking for a rude surprise.

Review can range from boring repetition to a highly engaging activity. Though the review of previous learning all too often takes the form of a monologue, the most useful and engaging form of review for most physical or computational tasks is simply *the repetition of a portion of the previous day's structured practice.* Walking the students through a few exercises from the previous lesson as a warmup brings performance competencies as well as concepts back to life in a most efficient and engaging fashion.

"Background" is a term analogous to "review" which seems to give teachers in the humanities permission to review more global concepts and distant events as a starting point for today's lesson. Review and background are particularly seductive for teachers in the humanities, however, since, for those without training, they all too often give license for a lengthy monologue which produces conceptual overload and student passivity and boredom.

3 Goals and Objectives The goals and objectives of the lesson may be presented quite briefly, but they are most helpful to students in discriminating key concepts from corollary information during the following lesson presentation. The clarity of goals and objectives, however, probably serves the teacher at least as much as the students as a built-in safeguard against a "split-focus" lesson and as a deterrent against winging it.

Acquisition The second phase of the three-phase structured lesson takes the student as far as the initial acquisition of the performance component of the lesson. In "acquisition" the teacher presents the new material of the lesson to the students in all three major modalities of sensory *input* (auditory, visual, and tactile). And the teacher elicits performance in both major modalities of *output* (verbal and physical). During acquisition, therefore, the teacher completes a sensorimotor teaching cycle that, in conjunction with highly specific quality control procedures to be described later, ensures correct *initial* skill performance and concept expression on the part of the student. The acquisition phase of the structured lesson is described in much greater detail in Chapters 7, 8, and 9. The acquisition phase of the structured lesson has three separate parts corresponding to the three major modalities of instructional input. They are (1) explanation (verbal), (2) modeling (visual), and (3) structured practice (tactile or physical).

1 Explanation "Explanation" presents the students with *verbal* input for skill performance or concept building. Since short-term memory for the verbal modality of input is easily overloaded, explanation is greatly aided by any form of activity which can periodically wake the students up, draw a response from them, and help them to integrate new input. Asking questions of the group and having them give answers accompanied by motor activity if possible makes a dialogue rather than a monologue out of explanation and heightens the students' level of attentiveness while the teacher checks for understanding.

2 Modeling Modeling provides the *visual* modality for the input of new material as the students see the teacher either give a demonstration of a skill or present a conceptual outline or map of a new concept. Having visual imagery of a skill or concept to accompany the linguistic imagery provided by the explanation allows the students to form a picture of correct performance in their mind's eye. Modeling can be made permanent, of course, by providing permanent prompts in the form of a "performance model" (see Chapter 7). In practice, explanation and modeling often occur together as part of the teacher's initial skill demonstration or concept explanation.

3 Structured Practice Between the initial presentation of the information during explanation and modeling on the one hand and the semiautonomous performance characteristic of "guided practice" on the other lies "structured practice." Structured practice derives its name from the fact that the teacher takes complete responsibility for providing the structure needed for correct skill performance or concept mastery. That is to say, the *teacher carefully prompts* the students through the steps of the performance sequence, whereas during guided and independent practice the *students must prompt themselves* through the steps of correct performance.

The objective of structured practice is to provide initial skill practice and preliminary mastery within a context which simultaneously provides a high degree of precision and low performance anxiety. The only way to produce precision within a context of safety is for teachers to lift the burden of prompting from the students as they carefully walk the students through performance step by step. Structured practice of a skill typically begins very slowly. As the students progressively acquire mastery with structured repetitions of the skill sequence or the logic of a concept, the pace of structured practice quickens until correct performance becomes automatic or at least semiautomatic.

Structured practice directly and explicitly transfers correct performance from the teacher's mind and body to the student's mind and body with corrective feedback. The higher the degree of structure, the more accurately the motor patterns of skill performance and the logic of conceptual expression will be reproduced in the students. The teacher continuously checks for understanding during structured practice so that any deviations from correct performance can be immediately fixed with a brief "positive helping interaction" (Chapters 4 through 6).

Structured practice is the missing link of the structured lesson as typically presented in the classroom—the part that is least appreciated and most often omitted. Structured practice or drill has, in fact, gone out of style over the past few decades. Several generations of prospective teachers have all too often been taught at college that drill is boring, repetitive, and dull. Thus, we have tended to shortchange it in the classroom, particularly under the pressure of covering all of the material. As a result, students are often thrust into guided practice while still at the *acquisition* stage of skill or concept mastery. This shortchanging of structured practice all but guarantees a high rate of failure during guided practice and a high level of need for corrective feedback for any student who has not yet fully internalized the structure of the lesson.

Observing structured practice through our adult eyes, however, misleads us. Although structured practice may seem boring to an adult who has perhaps mastered the skill decades ago, it is not boring, repetitive, or dull to a student engaged in anything even remotely close to new learning. Quite to the contrary, structured practice is by its very nature highly engaging since it represents a most relevant activity—the preparation for autonomous performance. In addition, structured practice is typically welcomed by students engaged in new learning since it creates the safety and security that comes from a repeated demonstration of one's own competence. When structured practice is foreshortened or omitted, we are in effect requiring students to transfer an *entire* performance sequence from explanation and modeling to guided practice in one momentous step. We therefore systematically produce not only error but also the performance anxiety and task avoidance that are natural concomitants of being ill-prepared to succeed.

Consolidation Initial learning is quite fragile, and it will most likely be lost unless the structured lesson contains specific exercises to consolidate or solidify the material presented during acquisition. The consolidation phase of the three-phase structured lesson contains the exercises in which learning is made more permanent, in which it is placed within a context of similar skills and/or concepts and in which the student is made into a fully independent learner. There are three distinct parts to the process of consolidation: (1) guided practice, (2) generalization and discrimination, and (3) independent practice.

1 Guided Practice In guided practice students perform a *previously learned* skill or concept as a means of solidifying learning, with the teacher available for guidance as needed. That is to say, guided practice is *not* for the purpose of skill acquisition. Basic skill acquisition should be complete during structured practice *before* the onset of guided practice or else the teacher will be met with a sea of waving hands from confused and helpless students.

The function of guided practice is limited to overlearning and fine-tuning. *Overlearning* is simply skill repetition beyond the point of initial mastery. Overlearning provides insurance against rapid forgetting. The more practice students experience (up to a point of diminishing returns), the more likely those students will remember what they were taught when several hours later they attempt to do their homework as independent practice. Corrective feedback will typically be limited to *fine-tuning* rather than acquisition as students ask questions of clarification which focus on the fine points or nuances of performance.

Students should *not* be attempting to understand the skill or concept for the first time. A classroom having several students at the *acquisition* stage of learning during guided practice indicates an inadequate job of teaching the structured lesson before guided practice and, in particular, inadequate structured practice. Teachers "pay their dues" for skill mastery and concept mastery during structured practice. Any pieces that are dropped during structured practice must be picked up during guided practice at a considerable increase in cost to teacher and student alike.

2 Generalization and Discrimination "Generalization and discrimination" deal with the dimensions of "same" and "different." Once a skill or concept is learned within a highly structured context, the process of consolidation or solidification is greatly enhanced if the student learns the typical variations of the skill or concept that will appear during independent practice, be it on an athletic field, in a computational practice set, in a work of literature, or in real life. And, in addition, students must be taught to discriminate errors which typically occur with a high degree of probability during the performance of that particular skill or the expression of a particular concept.

Experienced teachers of a given subject often know in advance that certain steps of a given performance sequence will cause students to make a particular kind of error. Effective teachers anticipate these predictable "typical errors" and build the discrimination of correct from incorrect performance into the presentation of the lesson. Discrimination training may occur rather informally as asides during explanation, or it may be formalized into a carefully designed practice exercise during the lesson.

Discrimination training is not needed with every lesson, but many times classroom lessons have a need for generalization and discrimination which our textbooks often slight. Thus, for example, our texts often teach a type of mathematics problem in the main body of the lesson but then include minor variations on that general type of problem in the following practice set. Since we have not systematically taught generalization, some students will get it and some students will not. Those who do not get it, or who are either dependent or anxious about failure, will very likely wave their hands at the teacher during guided practice and ask, "What do I do here?" The rule of thumb in generalization and discrimination training is, as usual, if you don't teach it you don't get it.

Generalization and discrimination training, however, must be built on a firm mastery of the basic skill in order to minimize the chances of confusion. Typically the teacher needs a thorough guided practice exercise which consolidates performance of the simple or generic skill before dealing with variations on the theme. Generalization and discrimination may then require an additional guided practice exercise with examples including variations on the theme. Depending on the complexity of the skill or concept and its variations, generalization and discrimination may represent a section of a single structured lesson or the subject of separate structured lessons with separate guided *and* independent practice for both the generic skill and its variations.

3 Independent Practice "Independent practice" is practice by the student independent of any need for corrective feedback by the teacher and, typically, independent of its availability. Students are now truly on their own. Independent practice implies that a student is not only able to typically perform correctly but also to *discriminate error* during performance and to *self-correct*. During independent practice, therefore, the student is his or her own teacher. If students have not mastered the lesson to a high degree of proficiency during guided practice, they will not only lack the capacity to perform proficiently during independent practice, but they will also lack the capacity to self-correct.

Some people get better with practice and some people do not. Why do some people improve while others remain the same? Some people can play the same game of tennis or golf for 30 years, whereas others steadily improve. What conditions are necessary for continuing improvement?

To put it most bluntly, people who improve know what they are doing and people who fail to improve do not. Imagine, for example, someone who has been taught well to play a piece on the piano encountering an error during practice at home. He hits the wrong note, and he immediately discriminates error because he knows the tune. He stops and slowly goes over the phrase again to get it right. He checks his fingering sequence, and he checks his hand position as he repeats the phrase several times, picking up speed as he goes. He is teaching himself the lesson that he was previously taught by his music teacher. He is his own teacher now because he has internalized the lesson and therefore is capable of improving during independent practice.

Without such mastery students are doomed to *repeat* the error because they cannot discriminate it, much less correct it. During independent practice, therefore, they solidify the learning of bad habits which will either remain permanently or be corrected later at great expense in terms of reteaching and relearning. When thinking of the role of independent practice, it is helpful to remember the following saying: Practice does *not* make perfect. Practice makes *permanent.* Once bad habits have been learned they do not disappear from memory. Rather they are covered up by relearning so that, should any forgetting of the relearning occur, bad habits exhibit their nasty tendency to reappear.

One of the most consistent errors in classroom teaching is to send work home for independent practice that has not been thoroughly mastered, much less overlearned, in the classroom. Such sloppy teaching not only dooms many students to failure, frustration, and a desire to avoid homework, but it also dooms their parents to deal with discouraged and oppositional children who do not wish to do homework. As always, failure is built into the learning process just as systematically and predictably as is success.

THE PERSPECTIVE OF POSITIVE INSTRUCTION

The typical way of approaching the teaching of a structured lesson is from the beginning to the end in chronological order. The perspective one gets when viewing the success of a structured lesson in terms of *discipline management,* however, is somewhat different.

Most lessons in most classrooms appear to hold together fairly well *until guided practice.* During the earlier parts of the lesson the teacher's activity usually keeps the students' attention fairly well so that discipline problems are relatively few. And students typically give the impression of learning as they watch the teacher "work out" and as they keep their hands in their laps while the teacher asks for questions.

It is during guided practice that all the chickens come home to roost. The flaws in instructional methodology all come shining through when the teacher asks the students to work on their own. Hands immediately go up, and the teacher starts reexplaining the lesson to students on one side of the room while students on the other side of the room begin to fall off task and goof off. Soon talking is audible, several students are out of their seats, and the teacher is nagging. Another day in the life of a typical classroom.

Beginning the analysis of a structured lesson at guided practice provides a valuable perspective for the analysis of instructional methodology. How do you get students to the point in learning where they can consistently succeed during guided practice without your help? How do you eliminate discipline problems in the process? And what do you do with yourself during guided practice if students do not need your help and are not getting into trouble? The first by-product of this analysis was a "precision technology" for conducting guided practice. The second by-product was a fresh look at every other part of the structured lesson from the perspective of maximizing (1) rate of learning, (2) probability of success, (3) retention and transfer of learning, and (4) independent study habits.

TOPICS OF *POSITIVE CLASSROOM INSTRUCTION*

Positive Classroom Instruction is divided into five separate sections which cover those instructional skills that are basic to teaching a successful structured lesson. The topic of each section is the subject of one or more separate chapters. In addition, a final section, "Creating Change in Education," deals with the methods and pitfalls of disseminating innovation and change in education.

Topic 1 (Chapters 2 and 3): The Universal Helping Interaction

As mentioned above, most lessons go fairly smoothly during the initial presentation of new material to the class. If the lesson comes unglued, it usually happens during *guided practice*. Hands wave in the air and the teacher moves as fast as she can around the room to help those students who are stuck. While helping students who are stuck, teachers give "corrective feedback."

The process by which teachers give corrective feedback is one of the most predictable and unremarkable habit patterns of teachers at all grade levels—so predictable that I call it the "universal helping interaction." The universal helping interaction is also one of the oldest habit patterns in any teacher's behavioral repertoire and is therefore one of the most difficult to change. Unfortunately, the universal helping interaction is also the direct or indirect cause of most of the (1) chronic motivation problems, (2) learned helplessness and dependency, (3) discipline problems, and (4) failure experiences in the classroom. To put it simply, one of the most common and unexamined practices of teaching behavior is an unmitigated educational disaster.

During the first portion of this book we will become extremely familiar with the universal helping interaction not only as a means of raising the level of concern for the first lesson of positive classroom instruction (Topic 2: Corrective Feedback during Guided Practice), but also as a means of sensitizing teachers to some old habits that will need to be changed.

Topic 2 (Chapters 4, 5, and 6): Corrective Feedback during Guided Practice

How is corrective feedback given to students during guided practice of a structured lesson so that students are systematically taught to (1) read the instructions, (2) follow the directions, (3) work independently, and (4) consistently experience success? In addition, how can corrective feedback be given so efficiently that the amount of corrective feedback supplied by the teacher during a typical lesson can be increased up to tenfold or more while the path to success is made absolutely clear? How can the teacher be everywhere at once to provide help rather than putting most students on hold for extended periods of time while he reteaches the entire lesson to those chronic few most needy students who always have their hands in the air?

The key to giving corrective feedback properly is the "positive helping interaction," or "praise, prompt, and leave" as it is typically called. The positive helping interaction is essentially simple in that it is not a complex process having many parts. It is, however, an extremely difficult process to learn because of the negative transfer from the universal helping interaction. We have to break habit patterns that we have had all our lives.

Topic 3 (Chapter 7): Performance Models

Both skills and concepts are learned one step at a time. Yet as teachers explain skills and concepts to the class, they frequently fail to leave any permanent record of the steps which lead from the beginning of correct performance to the end. Without a clear and permanent record of the step-by-step building process, students are required to remember everything the teacher has said in order to perform correctly during guided practice. This demand on short-term memory is highly unrealistic, and it is not too surprising that many students become confused and raise their hands for help. Without a clear, permanent record of the steps of the structured lesson, not only is the demand for corrective feedback increased, but the teacher also defines him- or herself as the only readily available source of corrective feedback during guided practice.

"Performance models" make the structure of the structured lesson clear, visual, and permanent while training students to work independently. There are three major forms of performance models.

1 Illustrated Performance Sequences (IPS) Illustrated performance sequences provide clear graphics or illustrations for each step of skill performance accompanied by varying degrees of explanation and labeling.

2 Performance Outlines (PO) Performance outlines present the structure or content of a concept. Although graphics are often the most appropriate medium for representing the steps of a skill, a simple outline is often the most appropriate format for presenting the structure of a concept.

3. Conceptual Maps (CM) Conceptual maps are a hybrid of the pictorial emphasis of an illustrated performance sequence and the emphasis upon logical structure typical of a performance outline. They show in a single, easy-to-read diagram how to (1) organize an idea, (2) conduct problem solving, or (3) perform a series of operations.

Performance models not only make the structure of a structured lesson explicit and permanent, but they also serve as an exercise in lesson preparation which structures the teacher's "task analysis."

Topic 4 (Chapters 8 and 9): Trimodal Teaching

Trimodal teaching is the process by which a structured lesson is taught most effectively. Trimodal teaching stresses the fact that effective teaching always teaches to the three modalities of sensory input and output (verbal, visual, and physical) and always focuses on student performance as the primary act of physical and conceptual integration of the content of the structured lesson. Trimodal teaching focuses on learning by doing. The ultimate focus of the structured lesson, therefore, is on learning the input through output. Unless the students can translate the teacher's input into consistently correct output within the time frame of the presentation of the structured lesson to the class, the lesson has probably been wasted.

Trimodal teaching, like corrective feedback, teaches skill performance or concept formation one step at a time. Trimodal teaching and the positive helping interaction, therefore, are variations on the same fundamental process of instruction. That process is known as "shaping"—the prompting and reinforcing of successive approximation of task completion. Performance models represent simply the graphics or logical structure of the steps of shaping—a series of permanent prompts.

Topic 5 (Chapter 10): Motivation: Incentives for Diligence and Excellence

The effective teaching of a structured lesson may greatly increase the motivation of students to learn, but it cannot guarantee motivation. Unless teachers are in command of a technology of systematically managing the diligence (quantity of work) and excellence (quality of work) produced by students, they will always have to pray for the best and accept whatever the cat drags in. Incentive systems for diligence and excellence add to the teaching of a structured lesson a technology for quality control and the systematic management of motivation.

For incentives to produce diligence and excellence, however, they must be given only for work done correctly and on time. How can a teacher monitor the quantity and quality of work being produced by students *continuously* so that students are held accountable while simultaneously being given a reason to try as hard as they can? How can a teacher have all the papers checked by the end of the work period? To operate incentive systems on a classroomwide basis, the teacher must replace taking papers home to be graded with monitoring and corrective feedback while the work is first being done during guided practice.

Incentive systems, of course, gain much of their potency from rewards. We will, however, learn to reward learning with learning. Much of the focus of incentive systems for diligence and excellence will be on expanding our understanding of the ways in which learning can be made enjoyable in its own right.

OVERVIEW

The volumes *Positive Classroom Instruction* and *Positive Classroom Discipline* go together to form an interlocking and interdependent system of classroom management.

The procedures described in *Positive Classroom Instruction* and those described in *Positive Classroom Discipline* will achieve maximal results only when used together.

Whereas positive classroom discipline is necessary to remediate typical problems of goofing off in the classroom and for building patterns of cooperation within the classroom, it must be paired with a high level of student motivation and involvement in learning or else the teacher will continually have to cope with students falling off task. Thus, in the overall scheme of classroom management, positive classroom discipline represents *secondary prevention*: the early remediation of classroom management problems so that they will not recur.

Positive classroom instruction must, of course, rest on a foundation of effective classroom discipline, but it prevents many discipline problems by maximizing students' involvement in learning. Thus, one might think of positive classroom instruction as the *primary prevention* component of a classroom management system—the prevention of the first occurrence of classroom management problems so that remediation is not required.

Positive classroom instruction and positive classroom discipline together maximize the amount of time on task of the students while simultaneously maximizing the efficiency of instruction and the experience of success of all students. *Positive Classroom Instruction* and *Positive Classroom Discipline* contain a coherent set of basic, generic skills for teaching and classroom management. These skills apply to anyone engaged in teaching whether they identify themselves with the teaching profession or not. Basic classroom management skills, for example, are nearly identical to basic parenting skills, and the instructional methodology is as applicable in business and industry as it is in the typical classroom. For professional teachers, however, the books *Positive Classroom Instruction* and *Positive Classroom Discipline* represent the essential survival skills of the classroom that will allow them to relax and enjoy success.

SECTION TWO

THE UNIVERSAL HELPING INTERACTION

CHAPTER 2

THE UNIVERSAL HELPING INTERACTION: CREATING PATTERNS OF HELPLESSNESS, DEPENDENCY, AND FAILURE

After half a decade of continuous research and classroom experience, the major components of positive classroom discipline had been developed and were being field tested in both regular and special classrooms at all grade levels. At that time I expected to stand back and observe smoothly functioning classrooms with teachers who felt on top of things. To say that I was disappointed puts it mildly. In contrast to our vision of the productive classroom, we consistently observed classrooms at all grade levels in which teachers were repeatedly experiencing a high level of frustration and exhaustion. Although discipline was greatly improved, we were obviously still a long way from our goal.

Why were teachers who were able to eliminate most disruptions within the classroom still frequently feeling tired and exasperated? Why was improved classroom control failing to produce teachers who felt highly successful at the end of a working day? There followed a period of observation on my part that lasted nearly a year before the puzzle began to fit together.

THE UNIVERSAL HELPING INTERACTION

No Matter How Hard I Try . . . !

In almost every classroom I observed from kindergarten through twelfth grade a similar pattern of student behavior emerged. No matter how well the teacher presented the lesson and no matter how effectively he or she managed behavior, the teacher was faced day after day after day with the same students who didn't get it.

The scenario became uncannily predictable in all settings. The teacher would present a particular skill in the form of a structured lesson to the class. The teacher would explain and model the skill, the class would do several examples together, and the teacher would ask questions to make sure that all the students understood how to do the assignment. Then, at the point where students were to do some of the work *on their own* (imagine a math assignment), the teacher would give the time-honored transition into that portion of the structured lesson known as guided practice:

> If there are no more questions, I would like you to take out your books, turn to page 105 and do the first fifteen problems in the practice set at the top of the page. If any of you have any difficulties, I will come around as soon as I can to help you. Just raise your hand if you need assistance.

These words would have *barely left the teacher's mouth* before the first hands would go up. The teacher would go to the first student and give him individual help until she felt that the student was able to continue on his own. When the teacher looked up, there would be several more hands waving in the air. And there would be several students fooling around that the teacher would have to deal with. The teacher would then quickly go to the next student to help, then the next, then the next. The process of helping individual students who were stuck would continue for the *rest of the work period.*

> It's the same students day after day that need all the help! No matter how hard I try, they just don't get it. I never even get to the rest of the class!

During guided practice the teacher would have to reteach the whole lesson a half-dozen times while overcoming the student's apathy or confusion each time. Over and over again the teacher would repeat instructions and reteach the lesson on a one-to-one basis with those few students who predictably needed help lesson after lesson, day after day. And at the end of the work period, how did the teacher feel—great because her efforts were paying off? Wrong! She felt tired, frustrated, exasperated.

The only logical self-attribution for a teacher after such an experience is one of failure. "It is the same students every day!" Consistent failure exacts a toll. At the end of a day a typical teacher feels exhausted for three reasons: (1) he has been expending nervous energy all day for the sake of discipline in an attempt to be constantly on top of the situation, (2) he has worked like a dog running around the room teaching each lesson a half-dozen times to the same students every day during every class period, and (3) he is feeling the first preclinical symptom of depression—loss of energy. Burn-out at the end of the day comes from both physical and spiritual exhaustion. "No matter how hard I try, they just don't seem to get it!"

What consistency in teacher behavior could produce the same pattern of failure in a predictable minority of students in any classroom and in any subject from kindergarten through twelfth grade? Teachers' personalities are quite idiosyncratic, so where could the commonality lie? It must be some *basic flaw* in the way we go about teaching.

One evening after a day of classroom observation and teacher training as I tried to get my two preschool-aged boys to clean up their toys and get ready for bed, I heard: I can't find the rest of the puzzle, I can't find my pajamas, and Where is the toothpaste? Daddy, will you help me? Suddenly I had a numbing realization: My gosh, they're doing it to me too! Thereafter I watched my wife and myself with our own children as carefully as I watched my teachers with their students, and slowly I began to see the pattern. It was under my nose all the time—so obvious and ordinary that it never stood out as a clear-cut management problem.

Helping Students to be Helpless

Almost all the chronic motivation problems and overt helplessness in any classroom are a by-product of one simple thing—the way a teacher helps a student who is stuck. The way teachers typically help a student who is stuck is perhaps the most consistent piece of classroom behavior that I have ever observed. Everyone seems to do it the same way although apparently no one has ever been explicitly taught how. It is universally assumed that when students are stuck, you *explain to them what they do not understand and then help them to do it right.* This method of helping a student who is stuck is so common and pervasive that I have named it the "universal helping interaction." What could be more straightforward and sensible than reteaching a skill to students if they did not understand it the first time?

Unfortunately, this unexamined and ordinary piece of teacher behavior is an unmitigated educational disaster. The universal helping interaction has two major flaws. It is inherently *inefficient,* and it is inherently *negative.* This chapter deals with the inefficiency of the universal helping interaction that causes most of the chronic motivation problems in a typical classroom. The next chapter deals further with the inefficiency of the universal helping interaction, which produces most of the discipline problems in the classroom, and also with its inherent negativism, which produces most of the failure experiences in the typical classroom.

Anatomy of the Universal Helping Interaction How do you help students who are stuck? Teach them what they do not yet understand, of course! Explain it again, and help them to do it if necessary until they get it right. This straightforward process is followed by nearly every teacher I have ever observed in dealing with a student who is stuck. It is so sensible and ordinary, in fact, that it has never even been closely examined as a formal teaching method, much less pinpointed as a central problem of instruction.

The universal helping interaction has three basic parts, each of which is as ordinary as the next:

1 *Diagnosis.* Find out where the child is having difficulty. ("OK, Sue, where are you having difficulty?")

2 *Reinstruction.* Reexplain that portion of the lesson which the student does not understand. ("Sue, let's go over this again. Remember what I said at the beginning of the period when I explained that. . . .")

3 *Application.* You want to be sure that Sue understands the process and can do it right before you leave. After all, she did not get it right the first time, and you may not be overly confident that she will get it the second time either. Therefore, most teachers will do at least one example of the task with the student to nail it down. ("OK, Sue, let's do this next problem together to make sure you have it.")

When I ask teachers what makes them think that they can finally leave one student who needs help to go to the next student who needs help, their answers are sensible. They say:

When I'm pretty sure they've got it.
When I'm sure they won't make the same mistake on the next problem.
When I feel that they've gotten the concept.
When I have a sense of closure.

The universal helping interaction, in following this sensible progression from diagnosis to reinstruction to application, seeks to unstick a student who is stuck. It attempts to remediate the deficit in learning—to reteach what the student did not understand. The universal helping interaction follows a simple old formula: *Find the problem and fix it.*

Inefficiency Takes Time When some teachers help a student who is stuck, they pull over a *chair,* and you know that they will be there for the next 10 or 15 minutes while the rest of the class goes to pot. Most teachers, however, try to help students quickly so they can move on to the next student who is waiting for help. When I ask effective teachers to estimate how long each part of the universal helping interaction takes on a good day, assuming that the student is at the appropriate level of difficulty on the one hand yet has a real problem on the other hand, they usually guess conservatively as follows.

Diagnosis	½–1 minute
Reinstruction	2–3 minutes
Application	2–3 minutes

Our observations indicate that this teachers' estimate is very close to the mark. On a good day a good teacher can average helping one student about every 5 to 7 minutes.

Take a low figure, 5 minutes. This simple piece of data by itself *dooms* the teacher to a host of classroom motivation and discipline problems that require considerable background to fully appreciate and understand. We will carefully examine the way in which most of these problems are generated within the classroom as a by-product of the universal helping interaction. But first, let us take a look at some of the simple realities that are determined by the duration of the universal helping interaction. We will start with the good news and then go to the bad news.

The Good News Imagine a typical classroom of thirty students. And imagine a guided practice work period of 30 minutes. During the work period the teacher will help one student who is stuck on the average of every 5 minutes.

a How many students can you help? $30 \div 5 = 6$. The teacher can help approximately six students who are stuck during the work period. On a good day she might get to a few more and on a bad day she might get to a few less.

b How often can you help them? The six students that the teacher helps will typically receive help only once each. Thus, the student will have one midcourse correction per half hour and might conceivably do the work incorrectly for as long as 25 minutes.

c How many students predictably receive no help? 30 − 6 = 24. During a typical work period the teacher cannot get to most of the class. Twenty-four of the thirty students can be assured that the teacher will *not* have time for them. With them as with the students who receive help, it will be the same students every day. Yet many of them need help with their work in order to complete it correctly, and others of them are not all that motivated to complete it in the first place. After waiting and being frustrated with their work for a while, many fall off task and start fooling around.

The Bad News The bad news is reserved for the students who were *helped*! They are the recipients of the universal helping interaction.

a *Your ticket of admission.* In any classroom, even in high school, one of the most potent, predictable, and ever-present reinforcers in the classroom is the teacher's time and attention. Almost *all* the teacher's undivided time and attention during the guided practice portion of any structured lesson during every class period on every day of every year in nearly every classroom in the country is given contingent upon one state only; helplessness, dependency, and failure simply being stuck.

What must students do if they want teacher time and attention? If they want the teacher, *first they must fail*! Being *stuck* is their ticket of admission. Without it, they are on their own, and the teacher will give time and attention to someone else who is *more needy*. You could not, in a laboratory setting, design an incentive program that more consistently and systematically rewarded extreme helplessness and dependency in a predictable minority of the class.

b *Competition for the teacher.* The teacher's time and attention are in short supply, however. There is never enough teacher to go around. Many students may want the teacher, but only a few will receive help. The teacher's very presence, therefore, inadvertently structures a competition among the students for the teacher's time and attention. Only the winners of that competition will receive the teacher's help on a *regular* and *predictable* basis. The students who are most needy will succeed in capturing the teacher for themselves on a regular basis while the rest of the class will be left on its own. While the most needy may be the losers when it comes to learning, they are the winners of the *helplessness sweepstakes*. The losers of the sweepstakes will have to play other games in the classroom.

THE GENESIS OF CHRONIC MOTIVATION PROBLEMS

The universal helping interaction creates and maintains helplessness and dependency in all grade levels exactly as it does in kindergarten. The dynamics of life in the classroom, however, are more blatant in kindergarten and are therefore particularly instructive. Kindergarten will therefore serve as our laboratory for studying the dynamics of helplessness and dependency. Do not worry about relevancy if you teach junior high or high school, however, because nothing changes.

Ready for Kindergarten?

Looks Immature If you ask kindergarten teachers which students of theirs will not learn how to read next year, can they tell you? They are, in fact, the best predictors of the child's imminent failure. How can they predict a student's performance a year later after considerable growth and with a different teacher, especially after only a week of school? Are they clairvoyant or what? If you ask kindergarten teachers how they know that a particular student will probably not learn to read one year from now, they will typically respond, "Oh, she is *immature*."

What does immature mean? How can the teacher tell? Such a subjective description of a behavior drives researchers nuts because it is difficult to measure, especially if they don't know where to look. But if you live with it every day, there is nothing subtle about it. The kindergarten teacher usually knows who the "babies" are by the end of the first day of school, and most of the immature students will have distinguished themselves by nine o'clock in the morning. The teacher can often count them as they walk through the door: "Oh no, here comes one now. He's only walked from the car to here, and he's already lost a shoe."

Immaturity has many faces, but in its simplest terms, immature students do not *follow instructions* and do not *work independently*. Unless the teacher is standing over them directing or helping them, they are usually in the wrong place at the wrong time doing the wrong thing. The one statement that is most predictable in any EH (educationally handicapped) referral from any grade level is: *Timmy may be capable of doing the work, but he will only apply himself when I am working with him one-to-one. As soon as I leave, he stops working*. Why will this child probably not learn to read in the first grade? Because, if he is only reading when the teacher is standing over him helping him, he will not be on task long enough to learn how to read. And he will not be on task long enough to learn how to do arithmetic either.

How You Can Tell Immaturity Let me briefly describe some of the most blatant features of social immaturity. You can rate your friends and acquaintances because they too have probably not changed all that much since kindergarten. The major features of a child's social development can be pinpointed by asking the following questions:

- Whose attention do they want?
- Do they engage in parallel or interactive play?
- Do they share?
- Do they wait their turn?
- What do they do if they do not get their way?

Compare a 2½-year-old and a 5½-year-old child on each of these dimensions to see how they have grown.

Whose Attention Do They Want? Imagine you are home with only your 2½-year-old child. Which room of the house is the child in? More accurately, whose feet is she under? By 3½ she is playing in the sandbox for 20 minutes at a time. By 4½ she spends the morning with a playmate, and by 5½ she is off on her bike.

Do They Engage in Parallel or Interactive Play? Your 2½-year-old interacts with other members of the babysitting co-op when they trip over each other. By age 3½ things have progressed somewhat, and by 4½ the kids are deep into interactive play with make-believe characters and fantasies that can go on all morning. By 5½ some are beginning to play games with rules like football although most of the time they degenerate into "chase".

Do They Share? For your 2½-year-old, this question has a bit of humor. By 3½, however, you can already tell the children whose play has been supervised by a conscientious parent from those who have not. With supervision a thousand squabbles have already been mediated and the toy has been awarded to the child who had it first. Enough tears have been shed to float a battleship, but the child who is learning to share has been taught over and over again that you *will share!* With this particular lesson children are not exactly fast learners, but with each passing year they improve. Without effective parental supervision, however, *might makes right.* The first kid who wrestles away the toy truck so that he can mash the other kid over the head with it owns the truck—end of contest. The kindergarten teacher can tell on the first day of school who shares and who does not, from across the room with one eye closed.

Do They Wait Their Turn? Learning to take turns progresses along with learning to share and for the same reasons. Watch out for the child who whines or shoves and then cries or fights when forced to wait.

What Do They Do If They Do Not Get Their Way? In some homes, no means no, and in other homes no simply means keep nagging me, and sooner or later I will give it to you just to shut you up. Can the kindergarten teacher tell the difference? Do you think it is subtle?

Now imagine that you are the kindergarten teacher on the first day of school. You wait anxiously to see what the new year will bring. If you have five or six "babies," it will be a pretty good year. If you have eight or nine it will be rough sledding, and if you have 11 or 12, help! A student walks into your class in a 5½-year-old body with a 2½- to 3½-year-old social maturity. Any kindergarten teacher will have a larger or smaller group of these children depending on the luck of the draw. Now, let us ask our questions again:

- Whose attention do they want? Do they want peer interaction, or do they want mama/dada? They predictably want the teacher's undivided time and attention while ignoring peers. They even cling physically.
- Do they engage in interactive play? No. They engage in parallel or solitary play, which soon causes them to seek the teacher out of boredom. In contrast, the more mature children are actually *pulled away* from the teacher by the lure and excitement of peer play. They regard the teacher more as an activities director than as a parent.
- Do they share or take turns? More to the point, do they share mama/dada? No. They want your body!
- Fussing, getting upset, and crying when they do not get their way causes the babies to stand out boldly in the eyes of both teacher and peers.

In the microcosm of the kindergarten classroom some 5½-year-olds have a social maturity that is already lagging behind the core of their peer group by nearly *half their chronological age.* Most teachers will be patient and will do what they can to help compensate for this disparity of maturity. Most immature students, however, will try that patience to the limit.

One developmental change has occurred over the past 3 years that may cause immature children to look older than a 2½-year-old. This change often deludes us into thinking that these children have matured. During the past 3 years the child's brain has grown, and they are smarter now. Thus, when they fuss to get their way, while they used to simply cry and whine like a 2½-year-old, they may now use *strategies*.

The Squeaky Wheel Gets the Grease The classroom is a *behavioral ecosystem* just as nature is a biological ecosystem. In nature animals evolve to become specialists so that they can effectively compete for space and food. A species must successfully occupy a "niche" in the ecology in order to survive. In a classroom, students also specialize to occupy niches in the behavioral ecosystem. There is always a "goody two-shoes," a bully, a super jock, a neatest, a best, and a first-finished. There are students who distinguish themselves in a variety of predictable ways so that the same cast of characters emerges every year in almost every class.

In the ecosystem of the classroom, however, most of the niches which are defined by *deviant* behavior are occupied by the *immature* students. They will make a place for themselves and get what they want (your body) by being babyish or obnoxious. The one thing the immature student will always want from the teacher is mama's or dada's *undivided time and attention*. All the different gambits that *force* the teacher to give time and attention to the immature child to the exclusion of the rest of the children represent the "immaturity games" that children play in school. A cursory look at some of the more common forms of immaturity will clarify the pattern. Remember, of course, that it doesn't change in secondary school.

The Clinger All kindergarten teachers have their quota of "clingers," the kids who glom onto their legs like a growth as soon as they stand up. How many clingers will a typical kindergarten teacher have? *Hint:* How many legs does a kindergarten teacher have?

Remember, however, that there is competition for a teacher's body. If teachers stand stationary for any length of time, they will accumulate a third clinger—the one who had to settle for the hind quarter. At that point the niche is almost full although a fourth may occasionally attach to the front of a particularly sedentary teacher who stands still throughout recess. However, as soon as the teacher takes a step, the fourth clinger is kicked off, and the teacher is back to three. Walk faster and the one behind falls off. Now the teacher has one holding on to each hand. The niche for clingers will hold from two to four students only. Beyond this point a clinger would have to hang onto another clinger in order to cling, which would serve no purpose as far as attention getting goes.

Not Following Rules How about the student who never carries out instructions properly? (We're getting closer to secondary school territory now.) Imagine, for example, that the kindergarten teacher lines the students up to come in from recess, but Sally and Billy are out by the chain-link fence at the edge of the playground goofing off. What does the teacher say to him- or herself?

> Listen, I called them once. If they run off and get hit by a truck, it's their own fault. Besides, we're insured.

Not too likely. The teacher, being responsible for the well-being of the children, dutifully trudges out to the edge of the playground where he or she commandeers the students' attention and leads them by the hand back to the school building. As the teacher walks along, he or she passes the oral tradition of the teaching profession on to the next generation with some timeless teacher talk.

> Sally and Billy, do you see where the other children are lined up over there by the door? That is where you were *supposed* to line up to come in from recess. You know that when the *bell rings* it is time to line up! We have gone over this rule several times and you *should* know it by now. I do not want to have to come out here and get you again tomorrow. Do you understand?

What do Billy and Sally get for messing up? The answer, of course, is that they get the teacher—by the hand even. What do all the other little kids get for doing it right? Nothing. It makes you wonder why they keep lining up. If they were observant they would be lined up along the length of the chain-link fence.

Falling out of the Chair How about the student who leans back in his chair while the teacher is reading a story? He finally loses his balance and falls. Can the teacher continue a story while the child is screaming on the floor? More than likely the teacher goes to the child, examines his arm to make sure it isn't hurt, checks his head where it hit the floor to see that it is not bleeding, calms the child down, sits him in his seat, and reminds him that if he would only sit properly in his chair such things wouldn't happen.

What does the child who fell out of their seat get? The teacher, of course, complete with touching and soothing. What did all the other kids get for doing it right? Nothing!

Making Messes As the students are getting their materials ready for art class, the teacher says:

> All right, students, remember as you carry your jar of paint from the sink to your table, be *extra careful*. Hold it with *both hands* and watch where you are going because [splash]—Oh, no! All right kids, stand back! Stand back! Don't track through the spilled paint! Don't anyone get paint on your shoes! Jim, quick, get the sponge!

Who is standing closest to the mess? The kid who dropped the paint, of course. Who is mommy or daddy's little helper? You guessed it. And what do all the other kids get for doing it right?

Tying Shoelaces to the Chair Leg What about the child who, while the teacher is giving directions, whiles away her time in a semicomatose state by tying one knot on another so that her shoelace is hopelessly attached to the chair leg. Can the child walk down the hall to lunch dragging a chair? Can the teacher ignore the problem? Kindergarten teachers spend lots of time untying knots in shoelaces.

All these deviant behaviors represent a sickeningly repetitive pattern. It is the immature student's job to put the teacher *over a barrel* so that the teacher has *no choice* but to give such students his or her *undivided attention*. Anything that these children can devise that accomplishes this end succeeds for them. If they do not squeak loudly enough or cleverly enough, they get left out.

Of course, there is never enough teacher to go around. While the more mature children are competing for teacher approval or for each other's approval through *competent* behavior, the less mature children are competing for the time and attention of mama and dada through *incompetent* behavior regardless of the form it might take.

Some will be more successful than others, but competition will spur the most hard-bitten competitors to excel. The others will get left out. Only the most astute squeaky wheel will get the grease.

Playing Helpless in the Upper Grades

The Pediatric Fallacy Do children outgrow their immaturity? I refer to that timeless hope as the "pediatric fallacy." Just give them some time and they'll probably outgrow it.

Unfortunately, catching up in maturation becomes more unlikely with each passing year, especially when the environment is consistently rewarding immature behavior patterns. For the most part children will not outgrow their immaturity without a great deal of special help. Look at the adults you know, excluding your friends who are a select group, and ask yourself: Are they dependent or self-sufficient? Do they have parallel or interactive relationships? Do they share, or do they want more than their share? Do they wait their turn? Do they fuss if they do not get their way? The behavioral pattern in early childhood remains discouragingly stable.

Cleaning Up Your Act While the immature student is passing through the elementary grades, however, he will *seem* to mature. His overtly babyish behaviors of kindergarten tend to disappear. This loss of infantile behaviors, however, is typically less a function of true social maturation than a result of the child's cleaning up his or her act. Cleaning up your act is a result of the most predictable characteristic of peer group interaction: *brutality.*

Unkindness toward the deviant child has always been one of the most easily identifiable characteristics of peer group interaction. Let's face it, if you are a jerk, they will let you know. If, for example, you whine a lot or ruin games or take things from others or make animal noises during story time, the peer group will call you names, with "jerk," "weirdo," and "creep" being the nicest ones I can think of. They will tell you that you stink and that you have cooties, and they won't touch you. They won't choose you for their team either, and they will tell you why. By this "innocent ruthlessness" the peer group will punish the deviants until they drop most of their grossly infantile behavior patterns and at least act normal. The immature children will be *forced* to clean up their act.

The Helpless Gambit Cleaning up your act, however, is not the same thing as social maturation. Immature students can still play their squeaky wheel games in the upper grades just as effectively as before without paying as a high price.

How do you monopolize the teacher's attention in the fourth or sixth or ninth or twelfth grades and get away with it? When they do it properly, students cannot only avoid looking like a jerk to the peer group while avoiding offending the teacher, but they can even give the appearance of hungering and thirsting after knowledge. All these students have to do is sit at their desks with their *hands waving in the air and let their minds freewheel while they wait their turns.*

Early in such a student's career, he may sit with his hand straight up in the air, but if this behavior continues into the third grade, it is cause to worry about severe retardation. If the kid is not retarded he soon figures out why his arm keeps falling asleep, and he will lower it to half-mast supported by his other hand. As he waits for the teacher, he will sag until his head rests in his shoulder. Arm and head will slowly sink further until finally both may be lying comfortably on the desk, hand dangling over the edge.

When the teacher finally arrives to help, the student in need may well be semicomatose. When the teacher says, "Billy, what do you need help with?," Billy, upon waking up, may not be sure what day it is. By the end of the first grade Billy will have learned the standard response which extracts him effortlessly from this potentially embarrassing situation. Billy simply looks up at the teacher with pained facial expression and calmly says, "Uh . . . I don't get it."

At first glance it might sound as though Billy is indeed stupid. Far from stupid, he is shrewd. If he were to say, "I don't understand how to do step 3," he *would* be stupid. Then the teacher would explain step 3 and leave. It might take only a minute or two. If, however, Billy says he doesn't get it, the teacher has to reexplain the whole lesson from the top. This *maximizes the duration of the teacher-student helping interaction.*

Did Billy listen to or carefully read the directions? If Billy understands the directions, the teacher does not have to repeat them. This *shortens* the duration of the helping interaction. If Billy is confused, the teacher must reexplain the directions, and that *increases* the length of the helping interaction. So, why listen in the first place?

It has taken me years of watching and working in the classroom to fully appreciate the strength of the immature, dependent, and helpless student's vested interest in *not learning*. Not learning is the most needy student's ticket of admission to the inner circle of those who get individualized teacher help and attention on a daily basis. You have to be skillful to win the "helplessness sweepstakes." You can hardly expect a student to relinquish that privilege for nothing—much less the opportunity to learn.

Teachers are repeatedly told during their training that if their lessons are interesting and their presentations scintillating, students will be drawn to learning. When it comes to the chronically stuck student (substitute immature, dependent, and helpless), it does not make a bit of difference how interesting the lesson is. You cannot sell something to somebody unless they are in the market to buy it. The immature students are not in the market for independent learning. They are in the classroom to get special attention and to be taken care of. They are most needy for a reason. As soon as they learn, they lose the very reward that they have cultivated and learned to exploit since they entered kindergarten.

Does the game change with time? Does helplessness look any different in the fourth grade than it does in the sixth grade or the twelfth grade? It is identical! It was sadly hilarious to walk into a twelfth grade classroom and see the same gambits being played over and over in the afternoon that I spent all morning watching in the third grade. Do the students outgrow it? They'll never outgrow anything that the social system of the classroom continues to actively support.

Perversities of Classroom Helplessness

How Many Chronically Helpless Students Can a Good Teacher Produce? How many chronically helpless, unmotivated, and stuck students does a typical classroom contain? You will have approximately a half dozen, give or take one or two. Why? Because a typical teacher can service approximately a half-dozen students in a typical 30-minute guided practice work period. Teachers generate the number of chronically helpless children that they can service on a regular basis. They are your regular clientele for helping interactions—the most needy who have won the "helplessness sweepstakes." The classroom system as molded by the lengthy and time-consuming universal helping interaction literally demands it.

The number of helpless students in a classroom is more predictable at the elementary level since the distribution of students between classrooms is more or less random, whereas in high school they stack up in certain classes. You have relatively few in physics and fourth-year French and a whole roomful in remedial math and English.

Ironically, an effective teacher who can move fast, cut the verbiage, get to the point, and help *eight* students per period can generate *eight* chronically helpless students instead of six. A less effective teacher, on the other hand, who talks too much and only gets to four children may only generate four. Isn't that perverse!

Can Aides Fix It? What is the first, most predictable by-product of placing an *untrained* aide in a classroom? The first consequence is to immediately *double* the number of helpless students who can be serviced. Now at least twelve students can be richly rewarded with individual attention for being stuck and needing help.

The role of the untrained aide was richly demonstrated recently as a result of teacher training. One of the teachers being trained had an aide on Tuesday and Thursday afternoons. During training the teacher learned how to train the class to read the directions, follow the instructions, and *work independently.* On the teacher's first week back in the classroom, the aide was absent due to illness on Tuesday afternoon. By Thursday the class was functioning efficiently, independently, and productively.

On Thursday afternoon the aide returned. The teacher looked up during guided practice in a math lesson to see *twelve students* standing around the aide saying, "I don't get this. How do you do this? Can you help me? I don't understand the instructions. Is this right?" On the way out of class one of the students said, "We like Mrs. Smith better than you. She helps us. You don't help us anymore the way you used to." Don't expect gratitude from children for giving them no choice but to grow up.

Most people going into any of the helping professions, be it social work, psychology, the ministry, or nursing, have a strong desire to help people. Teachers, as well as their aides, fall into this category. Without specific training to the contrary, aides help as much as possible in the way that they know best. The way they know best is, of course, the universal helping interaction with plenty of individualized time and attention reserved for the most needy students. Just like their colleague, the teacher, they will, with the best of motives, ladle out chicken soup until a half-dozen additional students drown in it.

Unfortunately the response of most teachers to being overwhelmed by the needy students is both predictable and self-defeating in the long run: "You mean the government has given the district some extra money to help with instruction? Quick, get me an aide." Aide spells quick relief, and quick relief is all that you will get. Teacher stress goes down as student helplessness and dependency goes up. The short-term cure exacerbates the long-term problem. Training teachers to use advanced instructional skills, in contrast, is slower, more demanding, and less tangible.

Ask your colleagues who teach high school whether the student population has changed over the past few years. Most will reply, "Yes, It has! Many of them can't do anything for themselves. You have to repeat the instructions three times, and then you still have to show a bunch of them!" Those high school teachers have just inherited the first generation of students who came through the elementary grades with untrained federally funded aides. I am not opposed to aides, just *untrained* aides because in the classroom of a well-trained teacher they can destroy independent learning habits as fast as the teacher creates them.

Can Special Education Fix It? What happens if you take two of your chronically helpless and unmotivated students and refer them to special education at the end of the third grade? Are there fewer helpless students in the fourth grade? No.

There are perhaps ten or twelve or fifteen potential candidates for special help in any classroom who are more or less immature—who would love to have the teacher's undivided time and attention if they could get it. Unfortunately for them, the teacher can only service about a half dozen students on a regular basis. The rest must learn to play other games.

What happens when two students in the third grade are referred to special education for some type of disability? When two slots are vacated among the regulars by a couple of referrals to special education, are there really fewer needy students left? No. The next two most successful competitors for the teacher's time and attention in the classroom pecking order will *immediately* fill the vacated slots. If you send two more students into special education for learning disabilities at the end of the fourth grade, how many will there be in the fifth grade? If you send two more at the end of the fifth grade, how many will there be in the sixth grade? Are they all gone by junior high? Are they all gone by high school? Do they ever disappear?

The niche for helplessness and dependency in the behavioral ecology of the classroom will always be full as long as there is sufficient reward to sustain the species. Students come to school immature and dependent to varying degrees. Whether or not they stay that way during their school careers depends on events within the classroom. They will either be trained to become more independent and self-reliant, or they will be trained to become the most needy—our chronic cases of underachievement.

The students who compete successfully for the teacher's time and attention, those who distinguish themselves as most needy, run a high risk of ultimately being labeled "learning disabled," "educationally handicapped," "emotionally handicapped," "behaviorally handicapped," or any combination of the above. They will swell the ranks of special education while doubling the cost of their education, or lack of education as the case may be. Helplessness and dependency is the most pervasive learning disability in American education today. It cannot be cured by special education. It can only be cured by good regular education.

A major part of the cure is to learn to give help to the students efficiently. As long as a helping interaction takes several minutes to complete, teacher and student are doomed. The rest of the drama is foreordained.

OVERVIEW

The universal helping interaction is the totally unremarkable way in which almost any sensible person goes about helping anyone who is stuck: Find out what the person does not understand and reteach it. This simple strategy is so ordinary that it has never been regarded as a topic worthy of analysis much less a *major* problem of instructional methodology. The universal helping interaction, however, is the direct or indirect cause of most of the chronic motivation problems in the typical classroom. It is counterproductive because it is inefficient and slow.

In order to replace helplessness with independent work habits during the guided practice portion of a structured lesson we must learn to give corrective feedback properly. But before we begin to learn, there is more we need to know about the universal helping interaction. We must become sensitized to specific patterns of behavior inherent to the universal helping interaction which are habitual to us. These are the lifelong reflexes that may be the undoing of any effort to change. We must know the hidden faults and foibles of the universal helping interaction so well that they will grate on our nerves as we say them because we will be irrevocably committed to the universal helping interaction by the time our *first sentence* has left our mouth no matter what our intention.

In addition to causing most of the chronic motivation problems in a typical classroom, the universal helping interaction is also the cause of most of the discipline problems and most of the failure experiences in that same classroom. The next chapter examines additional facets of the universal helping interaction that cause it to be a consistently destructive force within the complex social system of the classroom.

CHAPTER 3

THE UNIVERSAL HELPING INTERACTION: CREATING DISCIPLINE PROBLEMS AND FAILURE EXPERIENCES

The universal helping interaction has two major and inescapable liabilities; it is inefficient and it is negative. We have examined the *general* anatomy of the universal helping interaction and the ways in which its inherent inefficiency creates a classroom social system that supports helplessness, dependency, and failure. It is now time to take a closer look at the universal helping interaction to examine the specific transactions by which it undoes our attempts to create a positive learning atmosphere even as we are trying to give help.

Apart from creating problems of helplessness, dependency, and failure, the universal helping interaction is also the indirect source of much of the negativism common to classroom instruction. That negativism is of two distinct types; *discipline problems* on the part of students and *failure experiences* delivered by the teacher. Both of these problems are related to the length and content of the universal interaction.

First, the universal helping interaction is the indirect source of most of the teacher's discipline problems. During guided practice in a structured lesson the teacher typically moves about the classroom to help students who are stuck while others simply wait. As the class period progresses, the amount of talking and time off task steadily increase as the students who are waiting for help begin to entertain themselves. Soon there is an audible din. Teachers in attempting to deal with the students' talking, fooling around, and out-of-seat behavior often reprimand or nag. Thus, many of the discipline problems and the resulting negativism of teachers' reprimanding, while destructive of a positive learning atmosphere, are in fact a by-product of instructional methodology.

In addition, the universal helping interaction is inherently negative in and of itself because its very content and wording are punishing to the student. As the universal helping interaction seeks to *find the problem and fix it,* it begins by focusing on the problem—the student's error. Most of the failure experiences in a typical classroom, therefore, are delivered by the teacher at the very moment he or she is trying hardest to help. The bottom third of the class receives most of the help, and they are the students who learn most thoroughly that they are deficient.

An examination of the universal helping interaction as it functions to produce and foster negativism and an expectation of failure within a classroom will be the subject of this chapter. In coming to thoroughly understand old habits of instruction that are counterproductive we will prepare the way for mastering a far simpler and more positive approach to giving corrective feedback.

CREATING DISCIPLINE PROBLEMS

Characters in the Classroom Drama

In any classroom there are roughly three groups of students characterized in terms of motivation and independence.

1 *The self-starters.* Self-starters are the students who listen to the directions, follow the instructions, and do the work correctly with good penmanship. They even double-check their work before they hand it in. They are the students we take credit for even though they do their assignments without us.

2 *The most needy.* The most needy are the winners of the helplessness sweepstakes described in the preceding chapter. No matter how hard we try to get our material across, they always manage to fail. They may seem to try when the teacher is helping them, but as soon as the teacher leaves, they typically become confused or start fooling around.

3 *The middle-of-the-roaders.* Sandwiched between the self-starters and the most needy is at least half the typical class, a group we will call "middle-of-the-roaders." The typical middle-of-the-roader is already settling into a nice, comfortable, chronic C+ lifestyle. To him or her the pursuit of excellence is something of an abstraction. For the middle-of-the-roader one question concerning education burns eternally in his or her mind. That question is, Am I done yet? It comes in many forms:

Is this going to be graded?
Are you taking off for penmanship?
How many words does this paper have to have?
Is this required?
Can I do this for homework?
Can I pass the course if I don't turn in a term project?
How many cuts before your grade is lowered?

Students on Hold—The Losers of the Helplessness Sweepstakes

As mentioned in the preceding chapter, there is competition for the time, attention, and individualized help of the teacher—a competition that only the most needy will win. What happens to the rest of the class—the twenty-four or more out of thirty who will *not* get help from the teacher on a regular basis? Some will work successfully and independently, while others will be on hold until help arrives. The losers of the helplessness sweepstakes who are on hold will find other games to play, and those games will probably not involve learning.

Can a middle-of-the-roader typically stay on task for 30 minutes of demanding academic work without input from the teacher? Are you kidding? The attention span of typical middle-of-the-roaders is between 10 and 15 minutes on a good day. When they reach the end of their attention span or frustration tolerance or simply become bored, they will usually lose interest in working and fall off task. At that point they will either stare at the wall or begin to entertain themselves.

The nearest entertainment is, of course, their neighbor. This explains why 80 percent of the disruptions in a typical classroom is talking to neighbors. As soon as a middle-of-the-roader talks to his or her neighbor, that student is pulled off task. Thus when you lose one student, you lose two. Most teachers report that as the work period progresses, the classroom gets noisier and noisier. For many teachers the termination of guided practice comes as a relief.

Yet teachers will never be able to service the middle-of-the-roaders as long as they use the universal helping interaction. The universal helping interaction is too slow and inefficient. It ties the teacher up for the too long with too few students, and it leaves too many students unattended and unrewarded for too much of the work period. The middle-of-the-roaders are not motivated enough to withstand such a daily extinction program for being on task. Thus, with discipline as with the teaching of independence, the universal helping interaction dooms the teacher. As long as it takes several minutes to unstick a stuck student, the die is cast. The rest of the drama is foreordained.

Thus, most of the *discipline* problems in a typical classroom are caused *indirectly* by the universal helping interaction. If the teacher cannot get to the middle-of-the-roaders one or two times during guided practice to give them intermittent attention and reward for being on task, these students will check out and be lost for the rest of the period. These students clearly demonstrate the interrelatedness of instructional methodology, time on task, and discipline management in the classroom. The teacher either structures time efficiently for learning, or the students structure it for their own amusement.

CREATING FAILURE EXPERIENCES

A Negative Diagnosis

The universal helping interaction can be summarized in one statement: *Find the problem and fix it.* A helping interaction which attempts to find the problem and fix it must begin with finding the problem—a clarification of the student's deficiency. What don't you understand? Where are you stuck? What do you need help with? The diagnosis of the universal helping interaction is a *deficit* diagnosis.

Yet finding the error in the student's work before proceeding with corrective feedback is a thoroughly natural process, not an issue of "negative personality." The visual cortex is designed to scan for recognizable patterns and to rapidly discriminate any deviation from the expected pattern. This is a survival mechanism that allows animals to quickly discriminate something that is awry in their environment—they are in danger. The animal freezes as it experiences a "fight-flight" reflex.

Similarly, in the classroom when looking at a piece of work that is partly right and partly wrong, which part catches your eye—the part that is right, or the part that is wrong? The error, of course. Does "correcting papers" have anything to do with marking what is correct? Rather, finding the error for starters is part of our professional heritage—our oral tradition. We find the error because it is natural to find the error, and the exasperation we feel in our gut is our vestigial "fight-flight" reflex.

And now we will speak. But beware before you speak! Because unless we train our eyes to look again and our mouths to say new words, we will begin the help-giving process by rubbing the student's face in his own inadequacy. And who will receive this feedback most often—the strong and self-confident, or the weak and vulnerable? It is the price the "most needy" pay for their dependency and learned helplessness. The immediate experience of the student is discouragement, but it is preceded by a similar experience on the part of the teacher.

The Teacher's Failure Experience

The experience of failure occurs first for teachers. It is teachers who must confront the destruction of their instruction before they even open their mouths to help.

Imagine, for example, that you have done a beautiful job of preparing and presenting a lesson to your class. With clarity and enthusiasm you have raised their level of concern, explained the new skill, and modelled it with plenty of time for answering questions and for students to practice a few exercises together before the start of guided practice. Finally you give the students the opportunity to work on their own while you are available to help.

> All right, students, let's begin the practice set at the top of page 110. It will give you the opportunity to do some problems just like the ones that we did together. If anyone needs help, raise your hand, and I will be around to help you.

Almost immediately the first hand goes up—one of your regulars. You go to the student, look at her work, and see one of two things. Either she has done nothing or has managed to botch up your lesson within the first few minutes. You look down and you experience the first symptom of the universal helping interaction: a sharp, stabbing failure experience to the gut! "Oh no, I don't believe it! She did it to me again. Arrrrghh!!!"

You stifle the primitive instincts rising within you. You remind yourself that you have dedicated your life to young people and their learning. You are a *professional.* Besides, you should be used to this by now. Swallow hard. They are not really doing this to you on purpose. The feeling of exasperation may be intense, but it may also be so muted by repetition that it has become background—part of the deep breath that precedes your opening remark.

The Student's Failure Experience

Transferring Failure to the Student The first failure experience belongs to the teacher, but the next one belongs to the student. Although the universal helping interaction begins for the teacher with a sinking feeling in the gut, it begins for the student with an *opening remark*. The universal helping interaction begins with a negative diagnosis—a description of error. Thereafter the die is cast. With the first words that leave our mouths we transfer the responsibility for failure from ourselves as teachers to the students as learners. We ask them in one way or another: What is your problem?

It is crucial, therefore, that we become *hypersensitive* to the first remark to leave our mouths when helping a student who is stuck. Once we utter it we place our feet in cement, and there is no turning back. Unless we become highly familiar with and sensitive to these opening remarks, they will be out of our mouths before we know it, and the universal helping interaction will have irretrievably begun. Although perhaps sounding trivial, they constitute the beginning of the experience of failure.

Openers There are *five* basic openers that begin most universal helping interactions. Each of them dissects and highlights the student's failure in its own unique way. The destructive elements of each must be seen in paraphrase because, as adults having grown up with them, we are so accustomed to these openers that we can no longer feel the pain the student does. So, imagine a *vulnerable* student on the receiving end.

Opener 1 *Ask the student where he or she is having difficulty.* This is the most common and straightforward opener for the universal helping interaction and sounds innocuous enough until you hear it paraphrased. I refer to it as "the confessional."

Example

Where are you having difficulty?
What don't you understand?
Where are you stuck?
What do you need help with?

Paraphrase

How did you screw it up this time?

Opener 2 *Tell the student where he or she is having difficulty.* Sometimes it is not worth asking students to tell you where they are having difficulty. It is obvious to you where they need help and/or it is equally obvious that they haven't a clue as to where they need help. At such times you may avoid beating around the bush and simply tell the student what his or her problem is.

Example

OK, Sara, our first job will be to find the common denominator in each of these problems. Do you remember what a common denominator is? Let's go over it again.

Paraphrase

Well, Sara, it looks like you screwed it up. Let me show you how you screwed it up *this* time. And, by the way, your short-term memory isn't so great either.

Opener 3 *A "yes-but compliment."* If teachers are sensitive to the needs of their students for praise, and if they explicitly point out to students what they have done *right* as part of the universal helping interaction, the best they can hope for in their attempt to be supportive is a yes-but compliment. Trying to focus on the student's strengths before fixing the problem produces a statement which always begins with the *good news* and ends with the *bad news*.

Beware tender, loving, caring humanistic teachers who are most concerned with providing the student with a success experience. Yes-but compliments are most common among good teachers since these teachers are the most conscientious about giving support during feedback. Being both an old habit and a well-worn verbal reflex, a yes-but compliment will repeatedly slip past you unnoticed and unappreciated.

Example

Well, Dick, you have done the first part correctly. You have remembered that a common denominator must be divisible by the two denominators in the problem. Your common denominator for 4 and 6 is 24. But, to be a *lowest common denominator,* it must . . .

Paraphrase

Well, Dick, it looks like you got the easy part correct. *But* when you got to the new material that I presented today, you screwed it up. Let me show you what I mean by *lowest common denominator* . . .

No matter how pleasant the teacher tries to be, the net result of a yes-but compliment is a candy-coated failure message. The second half of a yes-but compliment always erases the nice part and leaves the learner with a net loss—first the good news and then the bad news. To get a taste for yes-but compliments, look around you and yes-but everything you see. For example:

- That's a beautiful new car you just bought, but did you know that a lot of that model are being recalled for transmissions?
- That's a nice material in your new sport coat, but the sleeves are a bit short.
- Those are nice potatoes, but the gravy was burned.
- Those are nice new drapes. They go with the couch, but they clash with your carpet.
- That was a nice talk you gave, but the people in the back couldn't hear.
- That was a nice lesson you taught, but a quarter of your class failed to master the skill.

Opener 4 *Body language with signs and moans of martyrdom.* Disappointment can be communicated almost as effectively with the body as it can with words, especially when aided by a well-emphasized expression of exasperation.

Example 1

Pause, stand dumbfounded for a moment, and then with a sigh lean over and say, "OK, let's see here!"

Paraphrase

"Why me, Lord?"

Example 2

Pause, stand with arms folded looking at the work for a minute and say, "Hmmmmm . . ."

Paraphrase

"You know, Joe, I've been teaching for *15 years,* and I've never seen anything quite like this before. Where in the *world* did you get that answer?"

Opener 5 *Zaps and zingers.* Sometimes, because of the intensity of exasperation that accompanies the teacher's failure experience, the thin veneer of civilization finally cracks, and teachers, swept along by an emotional rush, may indulge their more primitive instincts and simply blast the student for being so stupid. These are the unadorned failure messages, the direct expressions of frustration, disappointment, and anger that have not been dressed up in any way to sound nice. We call these blows to the cranium of the young learner "zaps" and "zingers."

"Zaps" and "zingers," incidentally, are not limited to unkind people. The best of teachers in moments of despair may let fly with them. Zaps and zingers come in an endless variety, but all can be paraphrased with one statement: *I don't understand how you could be so stupid!*

The following examples are arranged from small expressions of exasperation to large. They range from impatience to incredulity to resentment to bitter resignation. They are listed to sensitize us to old habits so that we may better hear ourselves as we begin to retrain ourselves to do helping interactions properly.

Examples, everyday fare.

Watch the level of impatience slowly increase. Choose the one that suits your mood.

- OK, let's start at the *beginning*.
- OK, let's go over this *one more time*.
- OK, let's go over this one more time. Now, I want you to *pay attention*.
- I went over this at the board *step by step*. Now we'll have to go over it again because you obviously were not paying attention.
- Carl, we have been going over this same material for *3 days* now. Where have you been?

• You know, I get tired of coming back here day after day just because your mind is *out the window* while I am teaching the class!

Examples, variations on a theme.

- Who was your teacher last year?
- Well, your sister didn't have any trouble with this when I had her.
- If I've told you once, I've told you a thousand times.
- Where were you 10 minutes ago?
- I can't believe you could possibly get that answer.
- If you would pay attention to the instructions, this wouldn't happen.
- Is anyone other than Mary having trouble with the first problem?
- If I had a nickel for every time I have had to explain this to you, I'd be rich!

Examples, heavy duty.

Beware, secondary teachers! Junior high and high school peer culture is very "zappy" and "put-down" oriented. The students have just discovered wit, and they hone it on each other mercilessly. A teacher can easily be drawn into this aspect of peer culture and inadvertently start relying heavily on sarcasm and put-downs. Even without sarcasm, however, exasperation can turn brutal.

- This is an answer?
- Give me a break!
- Can't you learn?
- Are you for real?
- Earth to Mary, earth to Mary, do you read me?
- What is your basic malfunction?
- Where were *you*!
- Kim doesn't even know the language, and she can do better than most of you.
- You couldn't carry a tune in a bucket if you tried.
- Time's passing. Are you?
- Do I have to beat it into your head?
- If I could pour knowledge into your ear, I would.
- Are you still with us?
- Any idiot could understand this.
- If you had a brain, you'd be dangerous.
- I *have* to see how you got this answer.
- Were you behind the door when the brains were handed out?

Examples, a self-fulfilling prophecy.

As a particular student distinguishes him or herself during the school year by being repetitively out to lunch, the teacher learns to expect failure. Should success appear, it is likely to be attributed to either chance or cheating.

- Not bad. Where did you get that?
- Did you copy?
- If you could do work like that all by yourself, you would be passing this course.

Zaps and zingers are the ugly openers. A highly effective teacher may be aghast at such statements and may assert that teachers don't say things like that very often. Wrong. Walk through the halls and stand outside the doors and listen if you want to know.

It is difficult for an adult to appreciate the impact that she or he can have on a student by remarks such as the zaps and zingers listed above. During training I often ask teachers if they can remember being on the receiving end of such a remark when they were children. At least half can, and most get visibly upset while recounting the humiliation. By chance I started asking if those who remembered such an incident could also remember the teacher's name and grade. I rarely find someone who cannot, although they often have forgotten the name of the teacher they had the year before or the year after. A surprising number of trainees can trace a lifelong lack of confidence in, or distaste for, a particular subject to such an experience.

Sensitivity Training What good is a catalogue of openers? Aren't they all too painful and familiar? Indeed, that is the problem. They are familiar to the point of being throwaway statements that fall thoughtlessly from our lips before we are aware of having begun instruction.

But we *have* begun instruction. We have begun our *negative diagnosis,* the first part of the universal helping interaction. We have focused the student's attention on the problem, the deficit, the failure. To a greater or lesser degree of explicitness, we have informed that student of his or her inadequacy.

And now that we have done everything in our power to undermine self-confidence and motivation, we will reinstruct. The reinstruction will be built on the motivational quicksand of discouragement that we have inadvertently produced by our kindly or not so kindly attempt to point out or clarify the student's problem.

Before we can learn new skills, we must learn thoroughly to discriminate the opening statements of the universal helping interaction. They must become like blisters broken open and rubbed raw so that we can feel them every time we use them. Only then can we notice them, discriminate them from the backdrop of long-established habit, stop them, and begin again as we retrain ourselves.

OVERVIEW

The curtain rises on the universal helping interaction as the teacher's stomach sinks. The teacher's failure experience prompts his or her opening words to the student as the teacher attempts to find the problem and fix it. Whether a simple inquiry or a candy-coated yes-but compliment or a straight zap or zinger, the opener not only commits teachers to the negative diagnosis of the universal helping interaction but also rubs students' faces in their deficiency. In so doing, ironically, teachers have bought themselves a measure of comfort. They have formally transferred responsibility for failure from themselves to the students. If you want to know the impact of a negative diagnosis, watch the students' faces and ask if they are encouraged or discouraged.

Negative diagnosis is followed by *reinstruction* of the concepts and skills that the student has failed to master. The reinstruction typically covers *too much* material to be remembered and applied with confidence—a whole skill or concept in most cases. Teaching too much guarantees cognitive overload for the student. The teacher may stay longer for *application,* walking the student through a sample exercise to help compensate for the overload he or she has created. Teachers keep going until they get "closure" because they know they will probably not have the opportunity to return to the student before the work period is over. The teacher's experience of closure occurs concurrently with the student's experience of cognitive overload. The teacher struggles as the student struggles, and the clock ticks. Those who are helped regularly become the most needy, while the middle-of-the-roaders who are on hold gradually fall off task and find other games to play.

Our efforts to solve problems of discipline management ultimately forced us to look at instructional methods in careful detail. We looked at the giving of corrective feedback first, since most discipline problems occurred during "independent work" or guided practice. As soon as we were able to see how certain common instructional methods were continuously generating discipline problems, we realized that improved instructional methodology would have to serve as the primary prevention component of a comprehensive classroom discipline management program. Thus, as mentioned earlier, positive classroom instruction represents *primary prevention* because it prevents the initial occurrence of most discipline problems. Positive classroom discipline represents *secondary prevention* because, as an effective first response to discipline problems, it tends to prevent their recurrence.

Primary prevention begins with a sophisticated replacement for the universal helping interaction. To give corrective feedback efficiently a teacher must be able to give all the input that a student needs and can absorb in a short span of time. Using the methods described in the following chapters, we will see how the teacher can give the student all the praise and encouragement, instructional input, problem-solving skills, learning-to-learn strategies, correction of error, and concept discovery while averaging approximately 30 seconds per helping interaction. Using additional skills, the duration of an efficient helping interaction will drop further to an average of 10 seconds while the need for helping interactions becomes infrequent. More important, we will eliminate the experience of failure from corrective feedback. And, finally, using these new methods, we will train the students, not as a separate management program but *as a by-product of effective instruction,* to (1) read the instructions, (2) follow directions, and (3) *work independently.*

The liabilities of the universal helping interaction have been carefully described so that we may have no illusions about them—no lingering notion that it may be all right after all. Yet the nastiest problem of the universal helping interaction is experienced only when you try to change. It is indeed part of us—to the center of our minds and to the marrow of our bones. It is one of the most difficult habits you will ever try to break.

CORRECTIVE FEEDBACK DURING GUIDED PRACTICE

CHAPTER 4

THE POSITIVE HELPING INTERACTION: GENERIC PROCESS

You may be glad to know, after having investigated the many hidden pitfalls of the universal helping interaction, that giving corrective feedback properly is relatively *simple* (at least on paper) since it has only three parts, two of which are optional. It is *brief*—10 to 30 seconds on the average—and it is always *positive*. In fact, it cannot generate a failure experience. Thus, we will refer to corrective feedback given properly as the "positive helping interaction."

The positive helping interaction is simple in its basic form, but it is not simple for teachers to learn to perform. Rather it is one of the most difficult single skills that teachers learn during training. As mentioned in Chapter 3, learning to deliver the positive helping interaction is difficult not because of its inherent complexity but, rather, because it runs cross-grained to so many habits and reflex patterns that are as old as we are. It is this negative transfer from prior learning that makes changing our habits of giving corrective feedback a process requiring a great deal of practice.

It is in the description of the positive helping interaction, however, that print is most limiting as a medium for communicating the nature of positive classroom instruction. To breathe life into the positive helping interaction during teacher training, a series of carefully designed and graduated training exercises from a variety of curriculum areas are practiced. Any one of these exercises, although it might take only 10 or 20 minutes of training time, would eat up a chapter of this book while appearing tedious. In a simplified form, therefore, this chapter and the following chapters attempt to explain and illustrate the positive helping interaction as well as possible.

The positive helping interaction has only three basic parts: (1) praise, (2) prompt, and (3) leave.

Praise. Tell the student *exactly* what she or he has done *right* so far.

Prompt. Tell the student *exactly* what you want her or him to do *next.*

Leave. Turn and walk away rather than standing to watch the student carry out your instruction.

Each of these steps presents the teacher with a simple task, yet each of these steps has many subskills and levels of understanding. We begin in this chapter with simple definitions, and then we proceed in the following chapters to elaborate on the nature of *praise, prompt, and leave* more fully.

PRAISE

Focus on What You Want to Teach

Imagine that a student has attempted to perform a particular skill but has made an error in performance. Imagine, for example, a mathematics problem in which a student has done the first part of the problem correctly but in which he has done the second part of the problem incorrectly, producing the wrong answer. Looking at his performance, which is part right and part wrong, which part would you want him to remember?

Most people on hearing this question instinctively answer, "The part that is right." And which part of his performance would he do just as well to forget? Most people answer, "The part that is wrong." Indeed, our first perception of the situation is clear and sensible. It is useful to remember the part of a skill sequence or performance sequence that you *can* perform correctly, and it is useless to remember a part of your performance that you do incorrectly.

In any skill sequence or performance sequence, even one as simple as adding two numbers or tying a shoe, there are at least a million ways to do it wrong. If we spend our time during corrective feedback talking about the error, we focus the student's attention on the "throwaway" portion of his or her performance. We make the error and the failure experience that it represents the best-remembered portion of their effort.

Ironically, teachers, and all other people for that matter, tend by habit to look for and focus on *error* when giving corrective feedback. We find out where students are having their difficulty, and then we spend our time during reinstruction explaining to them how they should have done it right. The universal helping interaction follows the formula "Find the problem and fix it," and we spend much of our helping interaction focused on repairing the error which has been produced by a student's inadequacy. It is odd how our focusing on the part of the student's performance that is *correct* seems sensible one moment, and yet how automatic and sensible talking about what the student has done *wrong* seems when we get in touch with our lifelong habit patterns.

Review Correct Performance

Now imagine that a student is performing a mathematics skill sequence of eleven steps. And imagine that the student has done most of the performance sequence correctly. The student has done six of eleven steps correctly, and she has made an error on the seventh step which makes the remainder of the problem incorrect. Typically we look

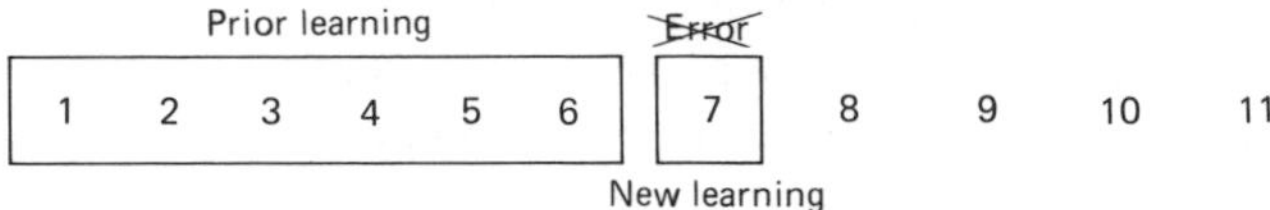

FIGURE 4-1
Focus on what is right so far.

at step 7, the error, and attempt to explain to the student how to do it right next time. It is natural for our eye to find the error. But when we do, we overlook the fact that she has done most of the performance sequence correctly.

To help us reorient ourselves, let us substitute for the term "error" the term "new learning." In the eleven-step performance sequence represented in Figure 4-1, steps 1 through 6 represent prior learning, and step 7 represents the beginning of new learning.

Looking at what is *right so far,* would we want to review everything that the student has done right so far? Probably not, since to do so would most likely produce *information overload* and confusion. What step in the performance sequence would be best for us to review to provide the student with a firm jumping-off place for new learning? Most people will take one look at the diagram and say, "Step 6, of course!" And what would be the *next* most relevant step in the performance sequence to review to provide the student with an even more solid jumping-off place for new learning? Most people instinctively reply, "Step 5."

Once again, our clear-eyed first impression is absolutely correct. Those steps of the skill sequence performed correctly just before new learning provide the best basis for taking the next step in skill acquisition. Consequently, reviewing what the student has done *right* just before new learning is the most instructionally useful thing to talk about at the beginning of a corrective feedback interaction. It not only reviews the most useful information for the student, but it also focuses his or her attention on that portion of the skill sequence that is the starting point for new learning. In addition to reviewing and properly focusing the student's attention, we talk about the student's adequacy rather than his or her inadequacy. Thus, the two functions of praise are (1) review and (2) focus.

Learning One Step at a Time

Initial instruction as well as reinstruction through corrective feedback might best be defined as the process of taking students from where they are to where you want them to be *one step at a time.* Since the performance of a skill sequence always takes place one step at a time, the initial learning and the relearning of a skill sequence would best take place one step at a time. Rather than *repairing* a flawed performance, we will simply *build* on correct performance.

As mentioned earlier, of the three steps of praise, prompt, and leave, two are optional. Praise is one of the optional steps. What if the student has done nothing right so far, or what if the student has done nothing yet at all? Are we blocked from giving corrective feedback? To the contrary, we are never blocked from taking the next step of a performance sequence. If you are on square 1 of the performance sequence, you can simply omit praise and go to prompt. Or you can praise as you normally would—focus on and review square 1 before telling the student what to do next.

PROMPT

Clear and Simple Directions

A prompt tells the student *exactly* what to do next. "Prompt" is a technical term in learning theory borrowed from the theater in an attempt to convey meaning without unnecessary jargon. Imagine you're a stage director with an actor who has forgotten his lines in the middle of a play. You have little time to provide direction; it has to be absolutely clear and simple. You don't use the universal helping interaction because you don't have time to point out the error, go over the reasons for the error, or review basic concepts. Such a strategy is absurd because the audience out there watching will soon realize that the actor has forgotten his lines.

If you want to get the actor unstuck and moving as easily as possible, you tell him exactly what to do next as efficiently as possible. It is hard to imagine the stage director saying more than a few words. He would probably just repeat the first part of the forgotten line.

A prompt in teaching is analogous to the prompt or cue used by the stage director. In a few simple sentences we tell students exactly what we want them to do next in clear, understandable terms so that they can perform the next step of the skill sequence with confidence. With prompts we proceed one step at a time. Our immediate objective is not to produce *mastery*. Mastery takes many steps, and a student can perform only one at a time. And many steps tend to produce cognitive overload. Our immediate objective is, rather, to produce *movement*. If we can consistently produce movement, mastery will take care of itself. A simple praise/prompt interaction is represented in Figure 4-2.

Avoiding Overload

The main enemy of clear prompting is *complex verbiage*. When explaining to someone what to do next, we rapidly reach a point of diminishing returns—usually after a few sentences. The more complex the instructions, the more likely we are to produce confusion and performance anxiety. Get to the point clearly and simply. Simplicity serves clarity, and clarity serves learning.

When a teacher reinstructs a student who is stuck, however, he or she usually teaches the balance of the day's lesson at one sitting. Most skills require several steps to perform, and the teacher will typically reexplain the remainder of the performance sequence to the student in the hope that the student will then be able to *complete* the task correctly. The teacher feels a necessity to complete the performance sequence since he or she will more than likely not have the opportunity to return to the student again before the period is over. Though sensible, this practice of extensive reinstruction is disastrous because it takes too much time and it presents the student with cognitive overload.

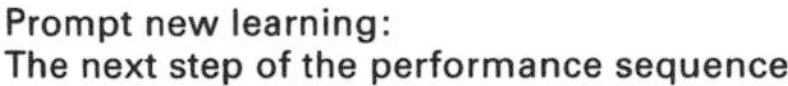

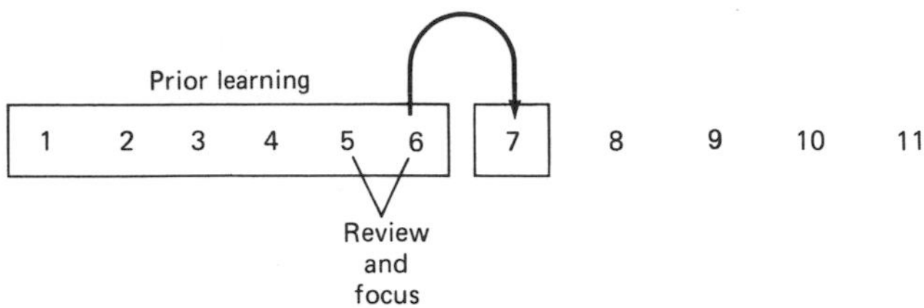

FIGURE 4-2
Praise and prompt: building upon strength.

To reexplain today's lesson, even a speedy teacher will need several minutes. The longer the clock runs the greater the risk of rewarding helplessness with teacher attention. And the longer the clock runs, the fewer other students will receive corrective feedback before the period is over. Teaching the remainder of the performance sequence if it entails several steps all but guarantees the production of a universal helping interaction by the teacher.

In addition, the more you explain to students, the less likely they will be to keep it all straight. Imagine that in the midst of an animated conversation with a friend, some weird person were to intrude, give you a paper and pencil, and say, "Write down verbatim exactly what was said in this conversation 2 minutes ago." Could you do it? Not likely—nor is it likely that a student can profit from an explanation of equal length.

How many steps of a performance sequence can the student accurately encode, store, decode, and translate into correct motor behavior on the basis of one teacher-student helping interaction? *The magic number is one.* To go beyond one step in the performance sequence when dealing with new learning guarantees a marked increase in the probability of failure—especially for a genuinely confused student who is struggling.

Effective prompting, therefore, conforms to a rule known as the "KISS principle." In most contexts the KISS principle means "keep it simple, stupid!" The more complicated a set of directions, the more likely it is that the person attempting to follow them will mess them up. In education "stupid" is a bad word, so our KISS principle means "keep it short and simple."

One of the most difficult behaviors for teachers to learn in prompting is to bypass old habits of talking too much while explaining complex concepts. It is difficult for anyone to review complex materials without using a lot of words and consuming a lot of time. In addition, repeating complex conceptual material typically focuses on the student's greatest inadequacy—understanding the concept. Thus, repeating complex concepts usually produces both conceptual overload and performance anxiety on the part of the student. The teacher, in effect, is saying, "Don't you remember what I just explained?" Although the explaining of complex conceptual material may provide intellectual closure to the teacher, the student tends to feel overwhelmed, inadequate, and helpless. The student needs to know *exactly* what to do *next,* so tell him or her.

The Affirmation Inherent in a Clear Prompt

In giving corrective feedback, there is one step that is *not* optional. That step is the prompt. Regardless of what else happens during the giving of corrective feedback, students *must* know exactly what to do next. Teaching is nothing more than taking students from where they are to where you want them to be one step at a time. With a good, clear prompt students can take that step. Thus, you can do an adequate job of corrective feedback by simply giving a good prompt and then leaving. While not as rich a helping interaction as the entire praise, prompt, and leave sequence, a simple prompt by itself is often preferable because of its sheer simplicity.

Ironically, one of the main emotional by-products of a good, clear prompt as far as the student is concerned is a sense of affirmation. If the prompt is clear, students will look at the next step in the performance sequence and say to themselves, "I *can*!" If students feel that they can succeed in the next step, they will feel adequate and encouraged, and they will have all the affirmation that they need even without the praise step of praise, prompt, and leave.

LEAVE

No Choice But to Leave

After you have given the student a clear and simple prompt which allows him or her to proceed successfully with the next step of the performance sequence, you have little choice but to turn and leave. We may want to stay to see how the student is doing, but if we stay, we will do more harm than good.

What does your body language say if you stay and watch the student perform after having told him or her exactly what to do next? Your body language is not too subtle in its expectation of failure. You are waiting to help the student again should she blow it. Students have an uncanny way of living up to your expectations, especially dependent students.

Waiting after giving a prompt also creates an incentive system for failure on the part of the student. If the student succeeds in carrying out your prompt, you immediately leave. If he or she fails in carrying out your prompt, you may stay and help again. The dependent student will typically respond to the incentive being offered by your standing around (in addition to your expectation of failure) by being helpless. We finally have no choice but to leave, for to stay offers a reward for helplessness which may seduce both the student and teacher into a prolonged helping interaction.

Discomfort at Leaving

But how can you be sure that the student will be all right? How can you deal with your own worry that the student may need you for just a little longer? Rather than being a function of the amount of time you spend with a student, the ability of the student to perform correctly is a function of the clarity of the prompt. As we master our prompting skills, our worry will subside. Our confidence that the student will be all right and the comfort that is produced by that confidence will only come from practice.

With the universal helping interaction we tend to *teach* too much and we tend to *talk* too much while giving help. This is our only chance to help, so we do a thorough job. After explaining too much during reinstruction—usually the remainder of the performance sequence—we often help the student do a sample exercise during the application phase of the universal helping interaction. Application is, I suppose, a rather sensible way to compensate for the cognitive overload that we have produced during reinstruction. It is also excess baggage.

It is hard at first to imagine that walking a student through an example is not only a waste of time but downright counterproductive. Yet the entire application step of the universal helping interaction is a no-win proposition. In the first place, it consumes too much time, and it is almost impossible to speed up. Second, the clarification that it provides is only necessary because of the complexity of reinstruction—a result of both teaching too much and, in most cases, verbosity. And finally, the teacher's staying with the student provides a built-in incentive for the immature student's continuing to be helpless and fail.

The teacher may leave the student with a sense of closure, having completed the reteaching of the entire skill sequence. The student, on the other hand, failing to perfectly integrate all the new input, will probably err on the next problem. The teacher says to him- or herself, "I got to help Sara, and I feel good that I was able to give her the help she needed." Sara, in contrast, may say to herself, "I *still* can't do this, even though the teacher helped me. I really *must* be slow." This discordance of perception between teacher and student helps to blind the teacher to one of the main causes of the student's continuing failure—cognitive overload. Consequently, the source of failure tends to be seen as lying solely within the student.

To put it simply, the universal helping interaction feels good. It helps to erase the teacher's exasperation with which the universal helping interaction began. It is the *self-reinforcement* which this final sense of closure produces for the teacher that perpetuates the pattern of verbosity and time-consuming "hand holding" as much as anything. While first using the positive helping interaction, you may experience a temporary decrease in closure and comfort at the end of a helping interaction until through experience you learn to trust in the efficacy of an efficient prompt.

Learning to Trust the Helping Process and to Try

As we leave the student after prompting, we will often conclude our prompt with the following words: "Do thus and so, and I will be back shortly to see how you are doing." When a teacher masters praise, prompt, and leave so that helping interactions are brief and clear, he will be able to keep his promise to be back shortly.

Indeed, the teacher may return many times during the work period. He may, in fact, give a student as much time with several positive helping interactions as he did previously with a single universal helping interaction. Since the need for helping interactions will decrease over time, it may be helpful initially to conceptualize our giving of time to needy students as the "repackaging" of help. We will give many short helping interactions that produce independent work habits as opposed to a single lengthy helping interaction that produces dependency. As students learn to trust their capacity to succeed one step at a time and to trust that you will indeed be back, they will learn to relax and *try.*

When to Leave and When Not To

As mentioned earlier, two parts of the positive helping interaction are optional, and one of them is leave. If you are tutoring a student, there is no need to leave. The only difference between group instruction and individualized tutoring is that tutoring is praise/prompt, praise/prompt, praise/prompt, etc. You are forced to leave only if you have somewhere else to go.

Actually, however, leaving is far less optional than is praise. We have found from experience that praise, prompt, and leave is, in a sense, too efficient for most small group instruction. When teachers are dealing with a group of six or eight students, even in a special education setting, they can help each student so frequently owing to the brevity of the helping interactions that they are, in fact, supplying almost continuous help. Continuous help almost always trains students to be helpless. Thus, as teachers master praise, prompt, and leave, they usually find that they have no choice but to leave the small group periodically to do something else for a while. Typically the regular classroom teacher finds that during small group instruction he or she has time to circulate among the rest of the class intermittently to give help to the middle-of-the-roaders and to check work.

OVERVIEW

In giving corrective feedback, teachers have a maximum of two instructional tasks to perform before leaving. They must tell the students exactly what they have done right so far, and they must show them exactly what to do next. Teachers must at most answer only *two questions* for the student.

- Exactly what have you done right so far?
- Exactly what do you do next?

If the student subsequently can answer both these questions correctly for themselves, the teacher has done his or her job.

With the positive helping interaction we take the students from where they are to where we want them to be *one step at a time.* With the positive helping interaction we are *building,* not *repairing.* We are producing *movement,* not *mastery.* We are proceeding one step at a time rather than rushing to closure by completing the performance sequence. We are specific rather than general, and we focus on performance rather than concepts. In giving corrective feedback, be positive, be brief, and be gone.

CHAPTER 5

PRAISE, PROMPT, AND LEAVE SUBSKILLS WITH TYPICAL SEATWORK

The technology of giving corrective feedback in its very simplicity sets a teacher free. Once "praise, prompt, and leave" has been mastered, effective teachers are typically far more focused in their efforts to help. They will therefore feel freed rather than constrained as they search for the right words in giving corrective feedback.

The more detailed description of certain basic praise, prompt, and leave subskills in this chapter should still be viewed as a generic description of the positive helping interaction rather than as a pat formula that sterilizes the teacher's language. Teachers are always free to choose the proper focus, direction, content, and complexity of the helping interaction. But in their creativity they must be ever mindful of both the passing of time, which may create dependency, and verbosity, which may create confusion.

It has often been said that teaching is an art, and it has just as often been asserted that it is a science. It is, in fact, both, and art and science meet in the positive helping interaction. Praise, prompt, and leave represents the simple technological basis for giving corrective feedback. Giving life to words that meet the needs of a specific student—that is the art of teaching.

PRAISE SUBSKILLS

The first step of the positive helping interaction is praise: tell the student *exactly* what he or she has done *right* so far. Praise, however, has some hidden complexities which become apparent only when one attempts to train a group of teachers to change after they have done the universal helping interaction all their lives. The subskills of praise do not represent any logical division of praise into its component parts. Rather, they represent the main habits that need to be broken by practice during teacher training in order for the positive helping interaction to replace the universal helping interaction in the teacher's classroom performance. During training, praise subskills must be practiced with many different kinds of lessons at varying degrees of complexity.

Subskill 1: Look for Adequacy

Imagine for a moment that you are an elementary school teacher who has spent many days teaching your class about subjects and verbs. Your assignment today is for the students to write six simple sentences in which they circle the verb and underline the subject. Soon a hand goes up from one of your least outstanding students, and as you approach his desk, you look down to see the following performance.

Looking at this sentence, what do *you* see? Did you notice the misspelling and the marks on the wrong words? If your eye was drawn to these blatant errors, it is simply because you are like everyone else. It is nobody's fault. It is simply the natural result of your visual cortex discriminating unfamiliar patterns from familiar patterns in conjunction with a lifetime of conditioning.

We instinctively look for the error—the *deviation* from correct performance. Our eye finds it effortlessly. Our eyes will betray us before we open our mouths.

Relax, clear your mind, and start over. Look at the student's work with fresh eyes. The first subskill of praise is a visual orienting reflex. What has been done *right* so far? The following is an incomplete list—the things most commonly noticed by trainees when they take a second look.

- a simple sentence as asked for in the instructions
- a clear thought
- proper capitalization
- proper punctuation
- good penmanship
- correct tense of the verb

The student has actually done quite a bit right so far, more right than wrong. What do you want him to remember—his adequacies or his failures?

Looking for errors also produces feelings within us. If we look at the failures and focus on them, we will probably feel frustration and exasperation—an exasperation that represents unnecessary self-inflicted pain. And if we talk about the failure, we will transfer that pain to the student.

First, we must consciously start over after having found the error. But, finding a student's adequacy will ultimately become our dominant reflex, and our self-inflicted pain will diminish and finally disappear. Learning to look for strength rather than weakness, however, is usually a struggle. The habit of finding the problem in order to fix it is one of the oldest and hardest habits to break. It is both a *visual reflex* and a *mind set* that afflicts nearly everyone both inside and outside education.

Remember, teaching is building rather than repairing. Prior competence is the foundation upon which we build. Prior incompetence is an accepted aspect of learning but of no immediate use. We cannot build on it efficiently and painlessly.

Subskill 2: Focus and Review with Simple, Specific Language

Once we have learned to find strength, our next job is to describe it. In describing what is right so far we focus the student's attention on critical features of prior learning and provide the review needed to form the foundation for new learning. In selecting the critical features of prior learning to describe to the student, the teacher exercises a degree of judgment which makes all positive helping interactions a type of *individualized* instruction. What is most relevant to this particular student?

Look at the list of things that are right about the simple sentence in the preceding section. We cannot rank-order them. We may have a student who knows her grammar but who typically writes sloppily. For her you may wish to focus on penmanship among other things, whereas for her neighbor with good penmanship, such praise would seem silly and irrelevant. For a student who typically omits punctuation, the period at the end may be the most relevant aspect of her achievement.

In addition, we will describe what is right so far, using simple language. The simpler the language, the more memorable it is. The more complex the language, the more confusing it is. If we learn to use simple language to describe the few steps of the performance sequence that precede new learning, we will perform several aspects of "focus and review" correctly and automatically.

Focus on the Highest Level of Achievement To praise in an instructionally useful fashion, we must pinpoint the extent to which the student has completed the performance sequence correctly. If we describe what students have done correctly immediately before new learning, we will typically describe their highest level of achievement (although other aspects of performance may also be relevant). One's highest level of achievement represents both new acquisition and real accomplishment. Its description is encouraging, useful in focusing at the starting point of new learning, and useful as instructional review.

Use Highly Specific Language Praise tells students exactly what they have done right so far. The key word is "exactly." Praise should typically be in the form of *simple declarative sentences* which describe those steps of the performance sequence which have been performed correctly immediately before new learning (i.e., error).

Specificity will remedy one of the most common errors teachers make when they are attempting to praise—the gratuitous and amorphous compliment such as:

Nice job.
You're off to a good start.
That's a good sentence.

I refer to such throwaway statements, which are so commonly used for openers, as "I'm glad to see you're still breathing" compliments. They are most common in the "yes-but compliment" form of the universal helping interaction: "Oh good, you have a pulse! Now let's look at your work and see where you messed up." Of course, such openers do not function as real praise for students in need of affirmation.

Gratuitous and amorphous compliments fail for two reasons:

1 They lack instructional content. It is nice to know that you have done something right, but what is right about it? Such general language does not specify, and consequently it does not review and reinstruct. With a few more words (usually one simple sentence) you can review the key concept from an entire previous day's instruction. You will probably repeat a catch phrase that has been repeated many times or a key definition that is well known to the class. With each repetition prior learning is solidified. At 20 seconds per helping interaction you can provide a lot of review "for cheap" during a half hour of guided practice. Compare the following:

General

That's a nice sentence.

Specific

That's a nice sentence. You have a subject, "Joan,' a verb, 'rode.' Subject and verb are the core of a complete sentence.

or

That's a complete sentence. Somebody [pointing to the subject] did [pointing to the verb] something [pointing to the remainder of the predicate].

2 They fail to reinforce. When you give an amorphous compliment such as "That's a nice sentence" to an "A" student, what is she thinking? "Big deal. I always write nice sentences." When you say "That's a nice sentence" to a "D" student or to any student with a poor self-concept as a learner, what is she thinking? "No it isn't. Not really." Or, "There's the good news. Now here comes the bad news: 'But—'."

Poor students immediately devalue or discount a general praise statement to match their self-images or their expectations. Consequently, the statement fails to function as real praise (i.e., reinforcement). Students are not fools, after all. They know that their performances are typically deficient, and they know that the praise statement is probably a meaningless, pro forma statement.

Specific language in a praise statement, in contrast, points to real and undeniable achievement. It therefore succeeds in reinforcement while generating self-confidence and encouragement.

Elaborate Judiciously In most positive helping interactions the teacher will want to describe one or two steps of the performance sequence—those that have been performed correctly immediately before error. Typically one or two steps represents the point of diminishing returns in preparing the student for the prompt that initiates new learning. Simplicity aids memory.

Sometimes, however, the teacher may opt to say more. Deciding how much to review during praise is a judgment call on the part of the teacher. It represents a creative decision point in the feedback process that integrates the teacher's understanding of the student's needs with the technology of the positive helping interaction. The teacher may wish to elaborate a concept or integrate two concepts. In these moments the teacher is both an *artist* and a *gambler.*

The teacher is an artist in his or her perception of the readiness of the student to integrate two previously learned concepts or in sensing the student's need for more information. And the teacher is an artist in her or his capacity to make the elaboration come clear. More talk on the right occasion can produce integration with no loss of clarity. In these elaborations, however, the teacher is an artist who is knowingly consuming instructional time that could be spent with another student while risking cognitive overload and the building of dependency. This makes the teacher a gambler. Teachers may elaborate, but they must elaborate judiciously lest they fall back into habits of verbosity which create confusion, helplessness, dependency, and failure.

Gambling is inseparable from teaching, and a good gambler can produce some artful teaching interactions. But beware of talking too much early in your mastery of the positive helping interaction. It is almost impossible to be artful while at the same time breaking old habits of verbosity. First learn to speak simply. Then, after you have learned to praise the student in one or two simple declarative sentences, you may begin to gamble more liberally.

A positive helping interaction, while it will eventually average 20 seconds or less, may take up to a minute on occasion because of elaboration. Corrective feedback is likely to be most lengthy on the *first* helping interaction with a student who is confused. It is then that you are most likely to carefully review key concepts and definitions. With every subsequent helping interaction, such careful and lengthy review becomes more redundant and unnecessary. Thus, praise is the elastic portion of praise, prompt, and leave—the portion that may be longer or shorter depending on the circumstances. The prompt is always short, simple, and to the point.

What If It Is All Wrong?

- How can you praise something if there is nothing to praise?
- Where do you begin if a student has done a whole page of work which is *all wrong*?

Questions about having nothing to praise inevitably come up during training as a result of all the foregoing emphasis on praise. The nature of praise, however, is always the same regardless of the degree of error. *Focus* the student's attention at the point of new learning and *review* whatever you need to review as the basis for performing the next step. You can always teach someone how to do something one step at a time. Simply focus on and review what this particular student needs. If you are on square one, teach square one. The basic job of instruction is never more difficult than taking the next step.

Subskill 3: How to Ask Questions

While giving corrective feedback, teachers frequently ask questions of the student. Some are useful, but many do more harm than good. How and why do you ask a question during a positive helping interaction, and how and why do you *not* ask a question?

Doing It Right: Check for Understanding A question has one major function during a positive helping interaction—to check for understanding. If you have the student's attention and if you make a clear and simple review statement, the student will usually understand. A question is, therefore, a setup for affirmation of the student's comprehension. The question also makes the student think and actively respond. It makes the interaction more kinetic for the learner and therefore aids attentiveness and memory.

When you ask a question, however, you make a gamble. If the student answers the question correctly, he or she has a success experience. But if he or she answers it incorrectly, he or she has a failure experience. How do you guarantee success? *Rule*: Only *ask questions that the student can answer.*

How do you know in advance that students will be able to give the right answer? Give them the answer just before asking the question, of course! Tell them what they need to know, and then ask them a question to make sure that they understood what you just told them. The result is a simple four-step process that all but guarantees success for everyone.

1 Tell them what you are going to tell them.
2 Tell them.
3 Ask them to make sure that they understood what you just told them.
4 Tell them again.

Doing It Wrong: Ask Leading Questions During practice of praise, prompt, and leave, one of the most commonly observed and tenacious bad habits of experienced teachers is the improper use of questions. The most common and most counterproductive form of questioning is the use of "leading questions." Leading questions are the sixth opener for the universal helping interaction in addition to the five mentioned in Chapter 2.

Leading questions attempt to draw out of the student knowledge that we believe to be somehow latent. They therefore make a demand for performance on a student who may be unprepared to perform successfully. The use of leading questions is often referred to as the "Socratic method." This label adds a sense of authority and correctness to the procedure (Socrates was no dummy, right?). Unfortunately, this label represents a poor understanding of Socrates and poor instructional methodology.

To get a taste for leading questions, try the following on for size. Would they predictably produce success and movement for a student who is stuck on square one of the lesson on subjects and verbs? Do you have an idea of the kind of answer you might get?

- OK, June. Can you tell me what a verb is?
- What is the first thing that we are supposed to do with the sentence?
- Do you remember what I explained at the board about finding the action word?
- Now, what did Joan do in this sentence? [The answer is usually, "rode her bike."]
- We were going to circle one word in this sentence. Which word is that?
- Who is the subject of the sentence "Joan rode her bike?"

My favorite leading question for this assignment is, "Can you tell me who is the recipient of the action in this sentence?" Such conceptual overload usually causes students to drop their pencils.

All leading questions have an absurd "Catch 22" quality: "Can you tell me what you would already know if you were not stuck?" If a student can somehow supply you with the correct answer, you were either lucky or not addressing the student's real problem. To help rid yourself of a tendency to begin helping interactions with leading questions, remember the following: *Leading questions are questions leading nowhere.*

When teachers ask a leading question, however, they occasionally do get correct answers out of sheer luck. ("They knew it all the time.") Such luck puts the teacher on a lean schedule of reinforcement for improper question asking. The use of leading questions thus becomes a tenacious habit pattern in which the teacher is fishing and the child is drowning.

Inquiry concerning the origin of this very common and tenacious habit reveals that teachers are almost never taught during their teacher training at college explicitly how to use questions during corrective feedback. Instead, almost all are taught never to *give* the student the answer. This directive is not spelled out procedurally, but most teachers assume you are not supposed to tell the student what to do next. This prohibition without further explication of method produces marked difficulty in dealing with a student who has done nothing right so far because review plus a prompt makes most teachers feel they are giving the student the answer. In lieu of being given a specific method for dealing with a student's ignorance during corrective feedback, a great many teachers develop, by the seat of their pants, the habit of teaching with leading questions followed, usually, by a relatively lengthy explanation of conceptual material—a sure-fire recipe for the universal helping interaction.

Can you ever use leading questions? There are no absolutes in teaching (except the one just stated). Yes, you can use leading questions in one specific set of circumstances: when you are sure of getting the right answer. Such a leading question as an opener for a positive helping interaction is simply a prompt for the student to demonstrate what she *does* know before the beginning of the helping interaction proper. It usually refers to some aspect of the student's performance that is obviously correct. Asking a student to tell you what the verb of a sentence is if she has indeed circled the verb is a simple example—a sure-fire praise statement that incorporates focus and review.

Subskill 4: Mark on the Paper

Praise is a visual, verbal, *motor* pattern. Marking on the paper is the motor portion of praise. We should learn to use our *hands* when praising and have a bright marking pen out at all times so that marking will usually accompany our words.

Why mark on the paper as you talk during praise, prompt, and leave? Is it a big deal, or is it just some little gesture which is not essential? The purpose of marking on the paper only becomes apparent when you have the luxury of returning to the student several times during guided practice. Marking as you praise does at least five jobs simultaneously.

1 The mark is a note which reminds you of *where you left off.* Such a note to yourself was not essential in the days of the universal helping interaction because you would probably get to the student only once during the work period. But as your new instructional skills develop, it will be possible to get back to students five or more times during the period. With training (plus skills to be described in the following chapters) it may ultimately be possible to give 50 to 150 positive helping interactions per period averaging 10 to 20 seconds each. If it takes you as little as *5 seconds* to find where you left off and to become oriented to what the student has done since you left, you will reduce the efficiency of a 10-second interaction by half.

2 The marks usually provide an explicit guide or "visual prompt" for a student to follow as he or she attempts to do the next step of the performance sequence.

3 The mark rewards the students. It is a visually explicit form of praise which increases the potency of the praise statement.

4 The mark eliminates the need to erase. The visual impact of a bright, heavy marker usually overrides the marks made by the student so that the combination of correct and incorrect marks on the paper does not make a confusing visual display. The resulting visual clarity eliminates the need to erase and the failure experience that often goes with it. Thus, such a directive should be omitted in most cases. If the student wants to erase to make the work pretty, fine. But erasing is optional, an option that is most often exercised by the most conscientious students. More easily frustrated students are likely to rip their papers when they erase, and at that point erasing has become more trouble than it is worth.

5 Marking as you praise checks the work as you teach. Checking the work rapidly as it is completed provides strict accountability for the quality of work being done by students, especially the work of the bottom third of the class who receive most of the helping interactions. Quick and accurate accountability and feedback is a precondition to providing powerful incentives for diligence and excellence during guided practice to *all* members of the class (see Chapter 10).

For right now, however, it is enough to realize that marking papers as you praise helps establish classroom standards while reducing your paper-checking load after school. Having the luxury to spend your time checking work during guided practice rather than constantly giving corrective feedback is, as we will find, a by-product of not only the positive helping interaction but also proper methods of lesson design (Chapter 7) and proper lesson presentation (Chapters 8 and 9).

PROMPT SUBSKILLS

A "prompt" is any message that tells someone exactly what to do next. A good prompt is brief, specific, and focused on the next meaningful step of performance. It should tell students exactly what you want them to do before you return, uncomplicated by instructional overload.

As with praise, there is more to a good prompt than meets the eye. In order for a prompt to be brief, effective, and supportive, the teacher will need to practice certain subskills to the point of comfort and fluency. These subskills are described below under the heading "Simple Subskills." The objective of the prompt is further clarified under the heading "Initiating and Terminating Requests (page 65)."

Simple Subskills

Four simple prompting subskills are discussed here, all of which are safeguards against common instructional errors.

The Transition Beware! The transition from praise to prompt is treacherous. It is not too late to slide into the *yes-but compliments* so typical of the universal helping interaction.

The old habit reasserts itself at the transition as we first give the good news and then the bad news. "You have done *A* and *B* correctly, but. . . ." But what? "But we still need to," "but you forgot to," "but remember that," "but instead of. . . ." To be supportive we will have to get the "but" out of teaching.

Fortunately there is a simple cure, a single pat phrase which sets you free of yes-but compliments if repeated conscientiously: *The next thing to do is. . . .*" This simple transition takes teachers to the point of saying exactly what they want the student to do next without tripping themselves up in the process. It is quick, clean, and "zap-free."

Teachers will invent many variations on this simple transition statement which carry a variety of unintended messages. Some examples include:

- The next thing you must do is. . . . (*Must* I?)
- The next thing I want you to do is. . . . (*You* want? Am I doing this for you or for me?)
- Next, I would like you to. . . . (*Like* me to? Are you asking for my permission? What if I say no, thanks?)

Although these transition statements are somewhat marred, they tend to work with most students most of the time as long as the praise step has been well done, the transition is fairly clean, and the prompt step is brief and clear.

Simplicity of Language Simplicity serves clarity, serves brevity, serves understanding. A prompt tells students *exactly* what to do next—what you expect from them before you return. It is a behavioral directive, nothing more. A good prompt will typically be one or two simple declarative sentences. Among the most common bad habits that teachers struggle with when learning to prompt are question asking with leading questions and reinstruction which repeats complex conceptual material. Both consume time, focus on inadequacy, and confuse the central issue, namely, what the student is to do next. When prompting, remember, get to the point and *get out*!

Structuring a Practice Exercise The prompt must structure the student's efforts *until you return*. Without such structure students may carry out a simple directive once and quit. At that point they may either lapse into a coma or start disrupting. More important, the issue of keeping the student busy while you are gone highlights the central objective of the prompt.

The main task of the prompt is to *structure a practice exercise* for the student that will yield continuing performance practice aimed at skill mastery. Whereas a prompt is a behavioral directive, it is an open-ended directive carefully chosen to provide structure for the student to work continuously and successfully in your absence.

The size of the task and the complexity of the task described by the prompt are highly variable and must match the student's ability to perform. Thus the prompt, like praise, represents an aspect of individualized instruction. If the task is too small, boredom may result and the student may quit. If the task is too large, the student may feel overwhelmed and failure may result.

The structure of the practice exercise may be quite simple and rudimentary—a simple reminder to keep working until you return. At other times the prompt may specify a particular type and frequency of repetition.

- Trace this letter five times and then copy it here until I return.
- Shoot free throws until you get ten in a row, and then shower.

Or the prompt could be far-reaching with an advanced student or professional, such as:

- Condense this chapter by one third. Keep the first half pretty much as is, omit the discussion of *X*, and condense *Y* and *Z*.
- Do a literature search on "classroom discipline." You can use grant funds to do a computer search if you think it is justified.

Are these last prompts too big—a next step that is so large that the students will be overwhelmed? That depends on the students. What are they already capable of? Asking them to live up to their capabilities without cognitive overload is the artful gamble of corrective feedback. The *next step* can potentially be of almost any imaginable size.

Altering Prompts That Fail Prompting like praise is, as we have said, an artful gamble. As we spell out the next step of performance, we make a judgment as to how much the student can do and how much structure he needs to understand the nature of the task. Thus, in prompting, there are really only two major dimensions along which we gamble: (1) the size of the next step and (2) the degree of explicitness or concreteness of the next step.

We are always gambling against the ability or *strength* of the student. We calculate what he can do and require him to do no less. To gamble well requires a thorough understanding of the student, the steps of skill performance, and art.

Once you have prompted a student to do a task that in all likelihood he or she can do and that requires continuing effort in the performance of a part of the task, you have done all that you can do for the moment. Yet no prompt comes with a guarantee of success. If you lose your gamble and the student fails, recycle the prompt with (1) a smaller next step and/or (2) more explicit or concrete structure.

Initiating and Terminating Requests

When you ask another person to do something, your request can take one of two basic forms. You can either ask a person *to do* something, or you can ask a person *not to do* something. An "initiating request" asks a person to do something—either to begin a behavior or to do it more. A "terminating request" asks a person not to do something—either to stop it or to do it less.

Prompts are directives. They must be either initiating requests or terminating requests. During instructional feedback, the psychological impact of initiating and terminating requests is *opposite*. Initiating requests are fail-safe assets, and terminating requests are pure liabilities. Initiating requests help, and terminating requests hurt.

A request to a student *not to do* something carries a judgment—the avoidable yet explicit message that she or he has done something *wrong*. In addition, the terminating request is devoid of information concerning what to do to make it right. Terminating requests are implicit, if not explicit, in the universal helping interaction. The net psychological result to the student is discouragement: "You messed it up, and now you must try again."

A request for a student *to do* something, in contrast, carries no evaluative message. On the contrary, when you tell someone exactly what to do, the request structures the path to success. Such structure provides *encouragement* while reducing performance anxiety. Initiating requests typify the positive helping interaction.

A prompt during instructional feedback should always be an initiating request. In a few simple declarative sentences the prompt should tell the student exactly what to do next, with no judgment as excess baggage. Using initiating requests you can tell anybody to do anything while being supportive, no matter how deficient their prior performance has been.

Examples of terminating (T) and initiating (I) requests may help to clarify and contrast the instructional and psychological impact of the verbal patterns typical of initiating and terminating requests.

Mathematics

T: You can't add the fractions until you have first found a common denominator.

I: First find a common denominator. Then add.

T: Don't hand in a paper like this unless you show me your calculations for each problem.

I: Recopy the problems showing all calculations. Then hand it in.

Typing

T: Don't go so fast. It causes you to make mistakes.

I: Slow down to half that speed. Focus on accuracy.

T: Don't run the line out into the margin. It looks sloppy. You'll have to type it over.

I: Retype this page for neatness, and be especially careful about the 1-inch righthand margin.

Home Economics

T: Don't pour in all the milk at once, or you'll get lumps.

I: First add a quarter cup of milk and stir until it is smooth. Then add the rest of the milk a quarter cup at a time while continuing to stir.

T: Don't cut the cloth until you have pinned the entire pattern on it or you will end up with odd-shaped leftovers that you can't use.

I: First pin the entire pattern on the cloth to minimize wasted material between pieces. Then you can begin cutting.

Physical Education (basketball)

T: Don't throw the ball to the post (center) until you see that he's open! You threw into the middle of a crowd.

I: Work the ball patiently until the post is open. Hit the post as he is coming toward you before the defense has set up.

LEAVE SUBSKILLS

When you have prompted the student, turn on your heel and *leave*! Leave *before* you see the student carry out your prompt. But you may hesitate.

What if she doesn't understand my prompt?
How do I know she'll get it right?
What if she still needs me?

At the beginning of the mastery of the positive helping interaction, the third step, leave, will typically be the most difficult step for us. We will want to *stay* and *verify* the effectiveness of our prompt in spite of the fact that to do so takes more time than it would to help two other students. But we *must leave*—not only for efficiency's sake but also for learning's sake.

As mentioned in the previous chapter, staying conveys an expectation of failure as it offers an incentive for helplessness. If the student succeeds, we *then* leave. But if he fails, he gets another helping interaction. Do not expect the "most needy" to pass up a deal like that! The dependent student would be a fool to become an independent learner under those conditions.

But leaving will create discomfort at first. We will worry. Does the student really understand what I want him to do? Leave anyway!

The antidote to our concerns about the student's failure is not staying but an *effective prompt*. As we master our prompting skills and subskills, we will gain the confidence to leave, knowing that the student can in fact perform correctly.

Movement and Motivation

Responding to Dawdling What do you do if the student is just sitting there doing as little as possible? Do you just praise, prompt, and leave?

Praise, prompt, and leave has an *informal* incentive component that is created as a by-product of the teacher's movement. Many dawdlers will be gradually co-opted into good work habits as they see that the teacher does in fact get around the room to interact frequently with students who attempt to do work. As one high school teacher stated:

> At the beginning of the year I had six do-nothings in the class. After several weeks of praise, prompt, and leave with some discipline thrown in, however, I had five of them working. I could afford to have the sixth one tested, although certainly not all six, and we found that this one student had a hearing disability that had never been diagnosed.

Soon after you establish a consistent movement pattern with praise, prompt, and leave, your students will learn to *trust* that you will indeed be back as you said you would, and the impetus to cling to you or play helpless in order to keep you will fade. With clear prompts and efficient movement a teacher fairly rapidly weans the "most needy" students away from their helplessness and dependency patterns while keeping the middle-of-the-roaders on task.

Responding to Nonperformance How do you respond in the midst of teaching to the student who simply refuses to work? Do you threaten or coax?

Quite the opposite, since attention is what students may, in fact, want, and nagging is what they certainly do not need. Rather, you will *starve them out*. With each circuit around the classroom your prompt to get started will become more brief. Your second interaction may be a single word such as "try," and the third interaction may be a silent look. Thereafter the nonperforming student is invisible until she or he produces some work. The classroom rule as far as teacher time and attention are concerned is: No work, no teacher. At this point the student has three choices:

1 Begin to work.
2 Look at the wall and bore him- or herself to death.
3 Entertain him- or herself by fooling around (usually by talking to a neighbor).

If you are good at limit-setting and responsibility training (see *Positive Classroom Discipline*), you can eliminate fooling around. That leaves (1) working and (2) boredom. In the majority of cases doing something to get *some* attention will eventually win out over doing nothing for *no* attention of any kind. This process of differential reinforcement is facilitated if you give generous attention for the efforts of a few students nearby to serve as a model.

As soon as the nonperforming student begins to do some work, the teacher gives generous attention. Thus the teacher uses the distribution of his or her time and attention as an *informal incentive system* (see Chapter 8 of *Positive Classroom Discipline*) for work completion—a simple variation of the movement pattern that is basic to praise, prompt, and leave as well as limit-setting. Most remaining motivation problems will be dealt with using *formal incentive systems* for work completion (see Chapter 10).

Mobility during Small Group Instruction Teachers pay a high price for their lack of mobility if they sit down during small group instruction. Not only does the rate of disruption increase among the majority of the class who are working independently, but those who are working independently receive no corrective feedback to provide help and increase motivation. The trade-off in teaching efficiency that causes many teachers to opt for small group instruction is that teachers gain more instructionally by their intensive work with the small group than they lose with the remainder of the class. For the present let us entertain the notion that in some cases the teacher's lack of mobility may cost more than it is worth—it may be detrimental both to the rest of the class and to the small group.

Let us take reading circle as our example of inefficiency through immobility since it is probably the most prevalent form of small group instruction in education. And let us look at the pattern of student performance that is produced by the teacher's immobility.

During reading circle students take turns reading aloud one at a time while the teacher sits and listens. This pattern of oral recitation so common to elementary classrooms produces two instructional problems within the small group: (1) minimum performance time for each student since only one at a time is reading out loud while others may or may not be concentrating and (2) the mixing of reading skill and stage fright so that students with performance anxiety come to dread reading circle. Because of anxiety they may block frequently during reading and receive giggles from peers and comments from the teacher which cause them to block all the more.

One simple solution for both dilemmas is for the teacher to have many students perform privately or semiprivately while the teacher moves to check student reading skills. The two most obvious performance formats for students are whisper reading by oneself or reading softly to a partner. In either case teachers can lean over a student's shoulder from behind to listen and give feedback just as well as they could during a normal reading circle. Teacher mobility, therefore, permits several students to perform at once while reducing the performance anxiety by making performance more private.

Once teachers are on their feet, they are free to circulate among the remainder of the class from time to time while the small group continues to perform. This intermittent help and attention will greatly facilitate the "middle-of-the-roaders" staying on task throughout the duration of independent work while providing a degree of quality control over the work they are doing. As far as movement is concerned, therefore, small group instruction need not be all that different from whole group instruction.

Eliminating Hand Raising One additional procedure related to the teacher's movement which further helps to eliminate helplessness and dawdling is a simple method of eliminating the hand raising that often occurs while students are waiting to be helped. Have students place an *X* on one side of a 3 × 5 card and place it clear side up on the corner of their desk during guided practice. Your rule is: If you need help, turn your card *X* side up and *keep working*. Stay busy until I get there!

You have just eliminated one of the most common occasions for students lapsing into a coma during guided practice: seeking "help" with the raised hand as an excuse for not working. At the same time you have provided a visual prompt for yourself regarding who needs help as you move about. You can therefore move rapidly *past* students who are not having difficulty since there is a signal to you that they are doing fine. This signal thereby further speeds up movement. You can, of course, spot check students' work at will—another artful gamble.

Speed and Efficiency The more skillful and automatic a teacher becomes at praise, prompt, and leave, the less time she will spend with each student and the more often she will get around to students needing help. The sooner you return, the easier it will be to pick up where you left off and the shorter will be your helping interaction as a result. I call this constant movement pattern of a well-trained and experienced teacher "floating" because she never seems to stop long enough to stay—like a butterfly that pauses but whose wings are never folded.

Movement and Discipline

A Single Movement Pattern for Discipline and Instruction The room arrangement and general movement patterns of "limit-setting on the wing"(Chapter 7 of *Positive Classroom Discipline*) and the positive helping interaction during either large or small group instruction—either during guided practice of a structured lesson or during a lecture or discussion—are identical. The teacher is out *among* the students, praising, prompting, and leaving; constantly monitoring the group as he or she moves. Teachers thereby suppress most disruptions by their sheer mobility and proximity. They are, indeed, limit-setting on the wing as a by-product of praise, prompt, and leave. Should a persistent disruption occur, terminate instruction *immediately* and begin limit-setting. With proper room arrangement a teacher will be only a few steps away from most of the class at all times.

Responding to Extreme and Disruptive Helplessness "But wait!" a student says, perhaps grabbing at your arm as you attempt to pull away. "I don't understand it! Is this right?"

Turn, take *two* relaxing breaths, look him in the eye, shut up, and wait. Any student who cannot read *this* message by now is indeed in need of special education. In the twinkling of an eye, the ballgame has changed from instruction to discipline; from praise, prompt, and leave to limit-setting (Chapters 5 and 6 of *Positive Classroom Discipline*).

This extreme wheedling and whining of dependency occasionally encountered during guided practice puts into bold relief once again the close interdependency of instruction and discipline skills in the moment-by-moment interactions of the classroom. Quick and skillful limit-setting will typically put an end to inappropriate help-seeking.

The attention of "camping out," should it come to that, is definitely not the kind of attention the dependent student was seeking. Outrageous help-seeking, of course, calls for stronger measures.

Gaining a Monopoly over Informal Incentives Providing informal incentives for work completion by the planned distribution of the teacher's undivided time and attention while moving among the students depends to a large extent on the teacher's limit-setting skills. Unless the teacher can effectively suppress or eliminate the nonperforming student's disruption, the reinforcing value of fooling around with a neighbor will often be greater than the reinforcing value of the teacher's time and attention for work. Thus in the marketplace of the classroom, the teacher's informal incentives for working will often lose out to the informal incentives for the student's goofing off provided by the peer group.

Only when teachers can gently suppress goofing off so that *their* time and attention is "the only game in town" will teacher attention have potency as a motivator for many unmotivated students. Effective discipline management gives the teacher a *monopoly* on informal incentives by eliminating the competition.

The movement pattern of teachers among students as they teach is, therefore, a fluid choreography of advanced management skills being used to simultaneously suppress disruptions, increase time on task, and accelerate independent learning. An understanding of the integration of discipline and instructional skills certainly underscores one of the most inescapable realities of group classroom instruction: You cannot teach a roomful of kids sitting on your behind.

OVERVIEW

The positive helping interaction achieves what the universal helping interaction sought to achieve: to help a student who is stuck to take the next step in learning. The positive helping interaction must be brief, but at the same time it must be instructionally rich. Little will have been gained if a stripped-down, sterile teaching interaction is substituted for one which was rich in content whatever other flaws it might have had.

And the positive helping interaction must be supportive. It must make learning safe. Students must *risk* in order to learn—risk stumbling and exposing their imperfections as they try. If this exposure is made painful, many students will learn to minimize the risk of failure by the avoidance of learning. Students cannot afford to attempt learning if they cannot afford to fail in the process. The first rule of gambling, after all, is that you cannot afford to gamble if you cannot afford to lose.

Thus the immediate objective of positive instructional feedback is not mastery of an entire skill but, rather, *movement*. Mastery is too large an objective for a given helping interaction. If you attempt it, you will teach too much, talk too much, and stay too long. In contrast, successful learning takes place one step at a time. Our job is simply to help the student take the next step in learning with certainty. Produce movement—movement that combines challenge with safety—and mastery will take care of itself.

CHAPTER **6**

THE POSITIVE HELPING INTERACTION: OTHER APPLICATIONS

In the preceding chapter we became familiar with specific subskills of the positive helping interaction with typical classroom seatwork. The positive helping interaction is, however, a fundamental, generic process that in learning forms the backbone of almost any skill-building endeavor. This chapter describes examples of the positive helping interaction in teaching situations as diverse as group discussions, art, and training teachers. Becoming familiar with many variations on the theme of praise, prompt, and leave will not only help us to appreciate the essential simplicity of the positive helping interaction, but it will also help us to generalize its use to many different subject areas.

INSTRUMENTAL LEARNING, OPERANT CONDITIONING, AND FORMAL INSTRUCTION

Types of Learning in Everyday Life

Instrumental learning is a broad term which covers the learning of all purposeful coping or problem-solving behavior. The term "instrumental learning," rarely used today in the social sciences, has for the most been replaced by the term "operant conditioning." Operant conditioning is, like instrumental learning, a blanket term which refers to all behaviors whose probability of occurrence is governed primarily by their history of consequences. For example, the use of a coping or problem-solving behavior would be governed mainly by its history of success in a particular situation.

In everyday life there are three processes by which instrumental learning or operant conditioning most commonly takes place as we learn coping skills. These processes are (1) trial and error, (2) modeling, and (3) shaping.

1 Trial and Error Trial and error, as the name implies, is the school of hard knocks. It is inefficient and often painful because of the errors which inevitably accompany figuring things out for yourself. However, it is all that is left in lieu of being formally taught. Trial and error is operant conditioning in which the natural environment provides the contingencies which tell us whether our behavior is useful or not. As we repeat successful behaviors and drop unsuccessful ones, we are "shaped" by the natural environment toward using behaviors consistent with social coping and physical survival.

2 Modeling Modeling is the process by which people learn most of their social behavior. We observe someone doing something that is particularly effective, and we imitate that behavior for ourselves. With modeling we might think of our eyes as a video camera that records everything that is going on around us, our brains as a tape library that stores all those experiences, and our bodies as the means by which we play back selected experiences.

Not all experiences that are recorded and stored in our brains are played back, of course. Rather, we choose from among the many behaviors that we have observed and play back with our bodies only those which we value—which we have observed to be successful for another person whom we look up to. Having observed someone else succeed with a particular behavior in a particular situation is known as "vicarious reinforcement."

Modeling, therefore, is operant conditioning in which someone else is doing the trial and error. Our behavior is vicariously shaped by the contingencies experienced by our model. The logic of learning through modeling is straightforward: If it works for them, it might work for me.

The capacity to accurately learn large chunks of behavior through modeling is truly uncanny. Indeed the complex social behavior of the human species would be impossible without it. One need only observe a 2-year-old child mimic the behavior of an adult to see how thoroughly she or he has internalized the walk, the talk, the gestures, and the mannerisms down to the most minute detail.

Our powers of imitation go beyond the learning of simple coping behaviors and include the feelings, attitudes, and values of the people we admire enough to choose as models. Thus within the classroom teachers are probably teaching as much about the purpose, nature, and value of formal education with their attitudes as with their instructional techniques.

3 Shaping Shaping is the term in operant conditioning which refers to the process by which skills are gradually and systematically transmitted from one person to another. Shaping can be defined most simply as "the prompting and reinforcing of successive approximations of task completion." Although we learn most of our social behavior through a combination of modeling and trial and error, most formal instruction is best done through shaping. The person who prompts and reinforces successive approximations of task completion is the teacher.

Shaping *should,* therefore, be the basic process by which the bulk of formal instruction in the classroom takes place. Shaping should also be the process by which corrective feedback is given should error occur. Unfortunately, in the everyday life of the classroom, shaping is *not* the primary means by which most teachers instruct and give corrective feedback. In fact, the vast majority of helping interactions between teachers and learners in any walk of life has no place whatsoever in any textbook on learning. Rather, the typical helping interaction is that homely hybrid known as the universal helping interaction.

Shaping and Classroom Instruction

Shaping, the process of systematically prompting and reinforcing successive approximations of task completion, embodies teaching one step at a time. Optimally, it is designed to maximize the clarity of the prompt and the precision of reinforcement for each step of the skill-building process in order to maximize the rate of learning.

The positive helping interaction is shaping. Praise, prompt, and leave as it has been presented thus far may best be thought of as a variant of shaping adapted to the teaching requirements of individualized corrective feedback in the classroom. In the hands of a talented teacher it is an amalgam of basic learning theory and artful gambling. Learning to improvise with this fundamental process through experience provides the capacity to adapt and fine-tune our teaching in order to maximize the efficiency of a single positive helping interaction.

Variations on a Theme

All instructional interactions and all corrective feedback interactions can, therefore, be viewed as simple variations on the process of shaping. The requirements of different lessons and different teaching formats call forth a variety of prompting subskills and reinforcing subskills which are tailored to the needs of the specific teaching situation. Nevertheless, the bedrock of instruction is always the same, the prompting and reinforcing of successive approximations of task completion.

In the following sections, we examine praise, prompt, and leave in teaching situations which are highly divergent from the seatwork typical of science and mathematics so that we may gain a more generalized and solid understanding of the positive helping interaction. *First* we will examine discussion facilitator skills—the skills by which a teacher produces idea sharing and concept building during the rapid give and take of a group discussion. *Second* we will examine some elaborated forms of the positive helping interaction that are most useful in lesson formats that emphasize self-expression, creativity, and brief dialogue between teacher and student.

DISCUSSION FACILITATOR SKILLS

The skills of facilitating a discussion are the skills of drawing people out and helping them to express themselves clearly and appropriately. As such, discussion-leader skills are a variation of the facilitator skills which might be used by the leader of a problem-solving team, a professional negotiator, or a group therapist. Failure to employ these skills of facilitation effectively will typically shut down the flow of ideas and feelings and, in a classroom discussion, cause students to stop talking.

Students' self-expression during group discussions is a vital part of concept building in the classroom. Although the subject matter of the discussion may be infinitely diverse, most discussions share the common objective of facilitating the active manipulation of ideas. Through the public sharing of thoughts and feelings students learn to be at ease with self-expression and to develop a point of view. From a Piagetian framework the group discussion serves as an important opportunity to facilitate the development of logico-mathematical thinking in which students go beyond associative learning to engage in the active synthesis of concepts via induction and deduction.[1]

Talk Formats

Many talk formats common to the classroom place the student and teacher in very different roles in relation to each other. Some specification of these talk formats and the roles which accompany them may help us become more clear about the teacher's job as a discussion facilitator. The main talk formats in most classrooms are (1) lecture or explanation, (2) oral examination, and (3) discussion.

1 Lecture or Explanation When a teacher is lecturing to the class or explaining as assignment or set of directions, he or she is for obvious reasons doing most of the talking. Although questions and answers may be solicited from time to time, a lecture or explanation is primarily a monologue in which the teacher is clearly the expert.

2 Oral Examination An oral examination is a question-and-answer format in which the teacher checks for understanding of material previously presented. The teacher typically conducts an oral examination by asking *specific* questions and by finding out who knows the specific answer. In this oral examination format, which may be fairly loosely structured and have the appearance of a discussion, students who know the answers typically wave their hands wildly while everyone else tries to disappear. In an oral examination, as in a lecture, the teacher is clearly in the expert role and reserves the right to correct student input once it is elicited.

3 Group Discussion A group discussion is an active give and take between students facilitated by the teacher in which the class actively exchanges information in order to build ideas, enrich understanding, share perspectives, and take a point of view. It is a creative, open-ended process in which students voluntarily risk in the sharing of their understandings and points of view to add to the group's collective pool of insight and information.

In a group discussion the teacher discards the *expert* role in favor of the role of *facilitator* in an attempt to produce frequent, voluntary participation. The discussion thrives as students speak at length and share their ideas and points of view in depth. Thus the teacher wants to produce a more elaborated form of sharing than the giving of specific answers, and it is the facilitation of this elaborated sharing that tests the teacher's skill as a discussion leader.

If the group discussion is succeeding, the students will be doing the vast majority of the talking while the teacher participates only intermittently to guide the proceedings. In successful discussions, a broad cross section of students will talk so that everyone contributes to the pool of knowledge while acquiring the ownership of a point of view. Without such active involvement by the total membership of the class, many, if not most, students become passive, with the exchange between a limited few of their fellow students tending to pass in one ear and out the other.

Shaping Idea Building with a Group

Praise, Prompt, and Leave Again The skills of facilitating a group discussion are variations on a familiar theme—praise, prompt, and leave. Our objective, as always, is to prompt and reinforce successive approximations of the desired performance. In the case of a group discussion, the desired performance is the spontaneous and elaborated sharing of viewpoints and the building of ideas among the students. We will see that the process of shaping idea expression during a group discussion is analogous in every respect to the process of giving corrective feedback during the guided practice portion of a typical seatwork assignment.

A group discussion differs from corrective feedback during seatwork primarily in the fact that discussion facilitation is a public, verbal version of the positive helping interaction. Teachers, therefore, *review* when necessary and provide a *focus* for idea building while they upgrade mediocre performance supportively. How can mediocre performance be transformed into superior performance within a public context—one which not only supports the participation of the struggling student but also creates a success experience as a net result?

Since discussion facilitation is a variation on praise, prompt, and leave, discussion leader skills will naturally focus on skills of praising (reinforcement) and prompting. In discussion facilitation leaving is often as simple as calling on a different student. During our analysis of the helping interactions of discussion facilitation, however, we will encounter our old nemesis, the universal helping interaction, complete with zaps and zingers.

Reinforcement Skills

Responding to Mediocrity If the students are holding a productive, orderly discussion, who needs corrective feedback? The test of the teacher's skills of correct feedback or facilitation are put to the test when she or he is hit in the face with student participation that is mediocre.

As with the universal helping interaction in any other situation, the first failure experience belongs to the teacher as he or she feels frustration and exasperation. As usual, however, the teacher's failure experience will be transferred to the student. For the sake of realism but with infinite possibilities for half-baked student responses in mind, let us imagine a group discussion during which the class is attempting to plan their room's booth for an upcoming school carnival.

Teacher: Okay, class, our job today is to generate ideas for building a carnival booth for the upcoming school carnival. Remember, it has to be something that we can do ourselves, and it has to be interesting so that people will spend their tickets at our booth. Each ticket costs 20 cents, so whatever we have people do cannot be too expensive. Does anybody have any ideas?

Jack: Yea, let's throw pies at the principal. [group laughter]

As you listen to Jack being his typical obnoxious self, your muscles tighten, your teeth clench, and you think to yourself, "Darn that little kid! Why haven't I learned never to call on him?"

Beware! We have just met the enemy and it is us. Our instinctive response to provocation or to the unexpected is, of course, the "fight-flight reflex," that sudden surge of anxiety and adrenaline which is the midwife of self-defensive behavior. While students always feel vulnerable when receiving corrective feedback, in a group discussion *we* feel doubly vulnerable. They can now frustrate, exasperate, and even embarrass us in public. Feeling potentially threatened or upset, how should we respond? What should we say?

Teacher: Jack, that is uncalled for! [snicker, snicker] We are not going to spend our time listening to silly ideas like that. Now let's get serious and think of some ideas for a carnival booth that we can *use*! Does anyone else have any *other* ideas?

Remember, almost everything you do in the classroom creates an incentive system. You have just taught your first lesson of the day. If anybody has an idea that I like, I will listen to it. But if anybody has an idea that I do not like, I will make you feel like a jerk in public. You have just passed judgment on a student's idea. You have just assumed the expert role, and in so doing, you have destroyed the safety of all but a few of your students.

"But that was a silly idea!" you say. Was it? Try to explain that to the more timid members of your class. They do not want to speak up and will avoid it in all but the most nonthreatening of situations. They know only that disapproval will quickly be forthcoming if you do not like their idea. We have just "zapped" the mediocre response. We have focused on the deficit portion of the student's performance as we always do at the beginning of a universal helping interaction.

Our tendency to zap at the beginning of a universal helping interaction will be even *greater* during a group discussion than during seatwork because everything that happens is *public*. Our anxiety about the discussion getting out of hand and our looking foolish will therefore be greater than during a private, one-to-one helping interaction at the student's desk. Beware, our tendency to buy quick comfort at the expense of the student will be greater in the discussion format than in any other instructional format.

How do we reserve judgment and negative feedback when faced with a mediocre or threatening response from a student? How do we avoid some kind of zap when the student:

- is off topic
- was not listening carefully
- is trying to be a "smart aleck"

- did not understand
- is being silly

If we cannot respond supportively to a mediocre student performance during a group discussion, we will be the primary punishing agent in our class during group discussions. By the universal helping interaction we will suppress student participation so that only a relative few will dare to risk self-expression.

Embracing the Problem The first response to hearing a truly mediocre answer from a student is to take two relaxing breaths. The second step is to *embrace* the very thing you wish had not happened—the student's mediocre response. If you are to affirm the student, you must affirm in some way her or his performance. You must take the verbalization that you wish had not happened and do something constructive with it.

At the beginning of discussion-leader training, teachers often fear that if they embrace the mediocre response, they will be stuck with it forever while giving the impression that mediocrity is acceptable. The discussion might then degenerate and get out of hand. While such a conclusion is logical, it will not happen because we will not let it happen.

The teacher is always in *complete control* of the discussion. No student verbalization is allowed to become a thorn in the teacher's side. But first we must relax and realize that we cannot make a student's mediocre participation go away by attempting to squash it. In the positive helping interaction, we must be wise enough to avoid beginning the helping interaction with a message that says: You messed up. We must *affirm* the *useful* part of the student's performance and *build* on it.

Selective Reinforcement Reinforcement during the positive helping interaction in discussion facilitation is analogous to reinforcement during the helping interactions of seatwork; the teacher describes what the student has done *right* so far. Praise is primarily review which focuses students' attention on their *adequacy* in order to produce a foundation for taking the next step in performance.

In discussion facilitation as in seatwork, reinforcement is selective. During a discussion the teacher focuses on the useful portion of the student's verbalization and ignores the useless or unacceptable portion of the student's participation (i.e., error). To put it simply, take the best and leave the rest.

What was useful about Jack's suggestion that we throw pies at the principal? If you allow yourself two relaxing breaths, you will probably have time to figure it out. Usually you can select a general idea or concept of which Jack's idea is a specific example. Then direct the conversation to the general concept.

Teacher: Jack says, "Let's throw pies at the principal." I imagine a lot of people would pay 20 cents to throw a pie. Carnival booths in which you throw something at a target seem to be very popular. At least real carnivals have a lot of them. Let's put the topic "throwing things" on the board and list the kinds of "throwing booths" that we might possibly have beginning with Jack's idea.

You write all ideas on the board including Jack's. During brainstorming all ideas are kept. Not to write Jack's idea on the board would be an obvious put-down or zap. Relax, you are still in complete control of the situation.

The Option to Stay or Leave You have controlled your emotions, you have relaxed, and you have selectively reinforced Jack's idea. At this point you can turn one of two directions. You may either prompt another student to give you another idea and thereby leave Jack, or you may prompt Jack to elaborate and develop his idea and thereby stay. Whether you leave or stay is dealer's choice, and the teacher is always the dealer. Leaving and staying might sound like this:

Teacher [*leaving*]: "OK, Jack has suggested throwing pies at the principal. How many of you would pay 20 cents to throw a pie at the principal? [laughter. Notice how "hanging loose" serves the teacher better during a discussion than any kind of enforcement which focuses on the quality of ideas being presented.] I'll put that idea on the board, and after we have generated a lot of ideas, we can come back and decide which one we like the best. Does anybody else have another idea about a carnival booth?"

Teacher [*staying*]: "OK, Jack has suggested throwing a pie in the principal's face. How many of you would pay 20 cents to throw a pie in the principal's face? [laughter, hands go up] Let me put it on the board. Now, Jack, let's talk about this booth some more. How would you operate the booth?"

Reality Will Protect You Why would a teacher ask a student to elaborate on such a stupid idea? You may in fact choose not to have Jack elaborate on such an idea, in which case you exercise your option to leave. But we will examine the elaboration of this stupid idea to demonstrate the utter safety and control that teachers have over the situation when they know how to function effectively as a group facilitator.

You, the teacher, perhaps without knowing it, are invulnerable. Nothing can hurt you because reality will protect you. *Any idea is a problem to be solved.* Your job is to make sure that the students address the key issues in problem solving. Their job is to solve the problem on which you have focused. If the problem cannot be solved, the idea dies of natural causes. If the problem can be solved, you have a viable plan. In either case the students learn problem-solving skills while building ideas and sharing points of view.

The only immediate tactical question of importance for teachers if they stay with this idea is the choice of the next problem to be solved. Most teachers, I imagine, would leave in this situation by simply placing Jack's idea on the board in order to get on to more brainstorming. But let us stay with Jack's idea a bit longer just to experience our sense of control.

By asking Jack to develop his idea, we cause him to own up to his idea. He gave birth to it, and now he must live with it. Describing what the booth would be like places the ball back in Jack's court, and as often as not he will respond with "Oh, it was nothing. Just forget it." But he may have some specific ideas to share about his pie-throwing booth.

Let us imagine that we continue to develop this idea. There are problems with throwing pies at the principal which can be used to teach the class problem-solving skills. Some of these problems include: (1) getting the principal to volunteer, (2) the cost of pies, and (3) cleaning up. All these issues are problems that need to be dealt with systematically. The teacher may use her or his facilitation skills to have the class develop a usable version of Jack's idea. Thus, for example, although the principal may not volunteer, the teacher may. How do you find out? Ask the teacher, of course! Who in the class will take leadership? You might ask for volunteers to form a committee. If no one volunteers, the idea dies for the time being of natural causes. Imagine the class simply asks the teacher. The teacher says no. Now who can we find? How about some of the students? OK, who will volunteer? Nobody? OK, we don't have any volunteers, so we will put that idea on hold for now. Back to brainstorming. See, reality has protected you.

How about the cost of the pies? What does a pie cost? Would your parents volunteer to bake a pie just so it could be thrown? How do you find out? If we can rule that idea out, then we can proceed to your next issue—what other kind of pie might we use and how much might it cost? How do we find out? How much does a pie at the grocery store cost? Does anybody know? Who will go to the store and find out? Let's form a committee to stop by the grocery store on the way home to price the pies so that we know how much they cost. Let's continue with some other ideas now and make the final selection after we have some more information.

Suppose somebody knows how much the pies at the grocery store cost. A frozen pie costs $2.50. Now, class, people pay 20 cents for a ticket, and we throw a $2.50 pie. What does that cost us? How do we find out? Can we afford to lose $2.30 on every throw? What else can we use for a pie? Somebody said shaving cream? Are there any problems with shaving cream? Shaving cream burns the eyes? Good thinking, so what could we use instead? Whipped cream won't burn the eyes. Good idea! How much does whipped cream cost? How do we find out? What will we use for pie plates? We can use chicken pot-pie tins for pie plates and get them for free at home. Very economical! Then we can fill them with whipped cream and throw them. Good idea.

Now we must calculate the exact cost of one whipped cream pie so that we may know whether we will be making or losing money with each throw. How many chicken pot-pie tins can you fill with a can of whipped cream? How will we find out? Is this idea worth taking up a collection to buy a can of whipped cream so that we can conduct an experiment? When you divide the cost of the can of whipped cream by the number of pie tins that we can fill, we will know the cost of one pie. If it is under 20 cents we make money, and if it is over 20 cents we lose money.

If you should care to pursue Jack's idea, which is admittedly unlikely, you may find that it is in fact possible to have a pie-throwing contest in which the students volunteer to be the targets, in which the students volunteer to clean up the mess, and in which the students find out how to make a pie that costs less than 20 cents. In the process you would be teaching the students something far more important—how to think and how to solve problems. If the problem can be solved, the idea can potentially be used. If the problem cannot be solved, the idea cannot be used. *Reality will protect you.*

Your job as discussion facilitator is to draw the students out by (1) making it *safe* to participate, (2) focusing on key issues, and (3) putting the ball back in their court so that they do the work of solving the problems. It is not your job as teacher to judge ideas or to solve the problems. Rather it is your job to point out the issues that must be addressed. By this simple mechanism you can point the discussion in fruitful directions at will while keeping it spontaneous. In leading a discussion, therefore, you are a free agent to choose the issues to be addressed, the way in which to address them, who addresses them, and how long they are addressed before you change topics.

Focus and Review When teachers choose what issue to address next, they focus the class's attention on a particular issue and thereby choose the vector that the discussion takes. "Focus" is the first part of "focus and review"—the praise portion of praise, prompt, and leave. By focusing we control the content and direction of the discussion, and by reviewing we supply enrichment at will. As with the positive helping interaction during seatwork, the teacher *focuses* on the most useful portion of the student's performance and then *reviews* relevant information as the basis for the students' taking the next step in idea sharing, problem solving, or concept development.

Prompting Skills As always, a prompt as part of the positive helping interaction tells students exactly what to do next. In a group discussion, the prompt is relatively simple. Whereas in seatwork the prompt must be specific concerning the nature of the next step of the performance sequence on which the student is working, in a group discussion the prompt is usually more general or open-ended.

Open-Ended versus Closed-Ended Prompts A closed-ended prompt asks for a *specific* piece of information whereas an open-ended prompt asks for *more* information. Thus if you were to ask who invented the electric light bulb, you would have given a closed-ended prompt. You did not ask the other person what they know about electricity. You only asked who invented the electric light bulb, and after they say Thomas Edison, they have answered the question. Closed-ended prompts by their very nature produce *brief verbalizations* on the part of the responder. Thus if you use closed-ended prompts, you will quickly *close down* a discussion. You will get a lot of short answers, and there will be almost no idea building.

An open-ended prompt literally opens up the topic for discussion so that anything of relevance can be said about it. All open-ended prompts can be paraphrased with one simple sentence: *Tell me more about that.* An open-ended prompt puts the ball in the other person's court and leaves it there. If you have been studying Thomas Edison and the invention of electric light, and if you want a student to expound on the subject, you may ask, "How did Thomas Edison go about inventing the electric light bulb?" It is hard to give a two-word response to a question like that. Or you might choose to be more narrow in your focus and ask, "What kinds of filaments did Edison experiment with before he found one that worked?" The breadth of the topic is your artful gamble. But the basic principle of prompting still applies. If you want students to talk a lot, use open-ended prompts.

Using Silence to Your Advantage After you give students an open-ended prompt, they may just sit there. Teachers with little training often begin to get anxious as the silence mounts. They think to themselves, "I'm not getting anywhere; this thing is dying; I had better say something quick to help the student out."

When in doubt take two relaxing breaths, shut up, and wait. Silence is one of the most productive times during a group discussion. Don't kill it with teacher talk. During silence people think. As soon as someone starts talking the rest of the class stop synthesizing their own ideas and passively listen to somebody else's ideas.

Thirty seconds of silence feels like five minutes to an untrained teacher. But if you can relax, the silence becomes the students' problem, not yours. Students too have a limited tolerance for silence. Sooner or later someone will start talking. A student may start talking because she too is uncomfortable with silence, but she may also conclude that what she has to say must be as important as anything anyone else has to say since no one else has started.

The Teacher's Role

The teacher's role in leading a group discussion, most simply, is to help the *students* do the work of idea sharing and concept building. The teacher simply guides the process of exchange. The teacher, therefore, is not the central figure in the discussion. That role belongs to the student who has the floor. The teacher, rather, is the person in charge of the process of verbal exchange.

Teacher Talk and Student Talk One very prominent error of teachers in leading a discussion is *talking too much.* In a typical classroom discussion the teacher does well over half the talking, and some teachers talk as much as 80 to 90 percent of the time. Teacher talk affects student talk in at least the following ways:

1 Teacher talk consumes the time available for student talk. Students are working hardest during group discussions when they are thinking and when they are talking. The time during which the teacher talks preempts the time during which the students can formulate and exchange ideas. Thus, if a teacher talks 50 percent of the time, he or she has reduced the potential time on task for students to synthesize and express ideas to a maximum of 50 percent of the class period.

Our research has indicated[2,3] that the amount of time that the students talk during a classroom discussion is extremely variable, ranging from as low as 2 percent with highly ineffective discussion facilitators to as high as 65 percent. On the average students talk about 25 percent of the time during a group discussion, a rate which is about half as high as it should be. Student talk ranging from 40 to 60 percent represents a lively discussion. Relatively few teachers, however, can produce that degree of student participation.

2 The more the teacher talks, the more passive the students become. The more the teacher talks, the more he or she defines the role of the student as one of observer rather than participant. Prolonged passivity will produce tuning out and a failure not only to talk but to think while others are talking.

3 The more the teacher talks, the more he or she dominates idea building. Dominating a discussion is antithetical to the role of discussion facilitator since the teacher's knowing all the answers shuts down the free exchange of ideas during which students construct their own answers. Why should students take the risk of exposing their ignorance when the teacher is going to correct them or give them the right answer anyway?

The more the teacher talks the more students perceive the so-called discussion as information giving in which they are expected to remember new input rather than to actively participate in information building. As the teacher dominates the discussion, the use of higher mental processes by the students disappears.

The Expert Role If talking too much is the first cardinal sin of leading a discussion, assuming the expert role is certainly the second cardinal sin. Teachers assume the expert role explicitly as soon as they pass judgment on a student's ideas.

Passing Judgment Teachers pass judgment on a student's idea when they criticize it, take exception to it, or change or embellish it to the point of replacing the student's idea with an idea of their own. In each case the teacher has said, "That idea is not good enough. It must be extensively changed to be acceptable." Do not be surprised if only the half-dozen brightest or most loquacious students in the class carry the discussion while the rest of the class falls passive.

In passing judgment on a student's verbalization by taking exception to it, the teacher is producing part of the universal helping interaction—a negative diagnosis. As with seatwork, focusing on the error consumes time examining the useless part of the student's performance while undermining self-confidence. In a discussion, however, the students' experience of discouragement and performance anxiety will be more acute because of the public nature of their effort, and the resulting task avoidance will be more pronounced.

Creating Safety Perhaps the most basic task of the teacher in facilitating a group discussion is creating complete safety for the participants. Only absolute safety will disinhibit most students to the point where they will share their ideas with their classmates. It is safe, after all, to be silent. It is only when you speak that you risk exposing your ignorance. Absolute safety will only come from a positive helping interaction—the skillful shaping of competent performance.

As adults and as teachers, it is easy for us to forget the magnitude of the risks that we are asking students to take in order to participate in a group discussion. We are, in effect, asking students to take the ideas that are private and safely hidden away within their minds and to lay them out on the table to be picked through and judged or even ridiculed by the rest of the class. It is not too surprising when one considers the vulnerability created by participation versus the safety produced by nonparticipation that most students are nonparticipants in most classroom discussions. Unless teachers can systematically produce absolute safety for all participants in the discussion, they will rarely engage more than a handful of students in the class in the task of idea building.

Pulling Teeth When fear is allowed to exist within the context of a group discussion, the avoidance tactics of students become predictable. It is far better for threatened students to appear detached or blasé in front of their peers than to prove their ignorance conclusively. Thus threatened students give you an absolute minimum of feedback in response to your probing. Students, in effect, put you on extinction for asking them to talk, with a response such as the classic "I dunno." Just as commonly, students will give a one-sentence response to a complex question and stop. You probe some more and get another one-sentence response. Obviously the student is protecting him- or herself, and soon you feel as though you are "pulling teeth" while getting nothing for your effort. Before long the teacher is doing all the talking or calling on the same eager few. Now the rest of the students can relax and listen rather than taking the risks of participation.

Discipline Management and Discussion Facilitation

Dealing with Put-Downs Although the teacher may be the primary agent in undermining the safety of participation in a group discussion by passing judgment on a student's ideas, the peer group will not be far behind. Peers can be cruel, and they can be particularly cruel when a classmate says something during a discussion that reveals a lack of understanding. Laughter is probably the most spontaneous and innocent form of put-down, but snickering and wise remarks are not far behind.

To the student who is not sure of him- or herself or to the student who is shy, the very possibility of peer put-down can serve as an adequate deterrent to participation. If one student can be unkind to another student in your class and get away with it, the likelihood of engaging all students in the process of idea building through discussion is slight.

To produce a safe environment in which group discussions can flourish, teachers must be *actively protective* of the student who is attempting to participate. They must not only avoid their own censure and judgment, but they must suppress the censure and judgment of the peer group as well while modeling supportive behavior themselves. Skills of discipline management (see *Positive Classroom Discipline*) such as "limit-setting" and "responsibility training," therefore, are critical elements in the repertoire of the classroom discussion facilitator.

Setting Limits on the Wing One of the primary tools of a teacher's controlling the potential disruptions, interruptions, and put-downs inherent in the give and take of a group discussion is by "limit-setting on the wing" (see Chapter 7 of *Positive Classroom Discipline*). Limit-setting on the wing exploits the room arrangement and continuous movement pattern of the teacher to keep small disruptions from growing without interfering with the flow of the discussion. By moving casually toward a potential problem while giving their undivided attention to the disruptors, teachers can use (1) body orientation, (2) physical proximity, (3) calm, and (4) eye contact to suppress most unwanted behavior.

Limit-setting on the wing can deal with a wide variety of problems during a group discussion including not only disruptions but also the occasional tangential digression by the young student who will talk endlessly if allowed to ramble. The standard cure for the endless tangential digression is for the teacher to walk unhurriedly to the child's desk, lean in slowly to "palms," and when the child draws her next breath, say: "Thank you, Karen. Now class [stand and turn slowly], as you remember, we were talking about . . ." [i.e., focus and review].

Taking Turns Taking turns and listening while others are talking are the two behavioral rules necessary for almost any productive discussion. Training the class to follow these two simple rules, however, faces any teacher with a difficult challenge that will constitute one of the primary agenda items of group discussions early in the school year. Although explicit methods of rule enforcement described in *Positive Classroom Discipline* are called for from time to time, an effective prompting mechanism (stimulus control) may be far more efficient in training the class to wait and attend than any kind of direct rule enforcement (contingency management).

Almost any clear visual or physical prompt that identifies the person who has the floor will help. For example, some teachers I have worked with have the students pass a bean bag early in the school year from the person who has just finished speaking to the next person to speak as a means of eliminating blurting out and everyone talking at once. Blurting out is a form of competition among students for the right to talk in a situation in which no more orderly transition has been well-established. The teacher's objective is to create a clear and orderly process of transition proactively so that she or he will not have to deal with interruptions reactively.

Prompting Errors and Reinforcement Errors Prompting errors and reinforcement errors take many forms in a group discussion which are often quite subtle. One of the prompting and reinforcement errors most commonly observed in the classrooms of teachers who have chronically disruptive group discussions involves the direct reinforcement of rule-breaking. The one behavioral rule common to all group discussions is that you take turns. If the teacher enforces the rule, a student should be out of order whenever he or she interrupts.

Many teachers, however, anxious that the discussion be productive (half-way intelligent and on topic), forget their own rule in their haste to find an intelligent answer. They recognize or give the floor over to any student with a bright answer. This creates competition to be "firstest with the mostest," and soon students are blurting out comments in an attempt to be recognized. The teacher is recognizing students on the basis of *content* rather than *rule-following,* thereby destroying rule-following. He has literally implemented an incentive system that rewards interrupting. This system favors a bright kid with a big mouth. Soon the students who have failed to get the floor start entertaining themselves.

Poor discussion facilitation will quickly translate into mental disengagement by students or "wheel spinning" which ultimately becomes boring. Rather than remaining bored, students seek some handy form of entertainment—like talking to their neighbor. When time is not effectively structured for learning, we get discipline problems by default. Unless led properly, classroom discussions can rapidly degenerate into a free for all, characterized by interrupting, side conversations, clowning around, or just staring out the window. Thus, discussion facilitation skills are directly related to discipline management since the effectiveness of discussion facilitation will determine the rate of disruption during group discussions.

Overview of Discussion Facilitator Skills

Ideas are built one step at a time during a group discussion just as other academic skills are built one step at a time during seatwork. It is always the teacher's job to shape successive approximations of competent performance. Thus, praise, prompt, and leave is as applicable during a group discussion as during seatwork.

Once the student performs, it is the teacher's job (1) to focus on what the student has done right so far, (2) to review the useful portion of the student's performance for the class as a basis for taking the next step in idea building, and (3) to prompt the next step in idea development. Skills of idea development and problem solving are skills which are built like any other skill. The major difference between seatwork and a group discussion is that in the discussion format everyone's performance is public rather than private. Since the teacher's vulnerability and anxiety level will probably be higher than it is during seatwork, his or her tendency to react judgmentally in response to mediocrity may be higher. And, since students' performance anxiety level is higher, they will be more sensitive to such punishment.

If teachers want to kill a discussion, they need do only two things: talk too much and judge or criticize the student's output. Once again, the verbosity and negativism of the universal helping interaction are our main enemies in giving corrective feedback to students as they perform. As in seatwork, the price we pay for our teaching errors is the destruction of the incentive and self-confidence needed for students to participate in the experience of learning.

Once teachers learn how to provide positive helping interactions during group discussion, they will be able to relax, experience their invulnerability, and focus on reducing the student's vulnerability in order to facilitate sharing. Praise, prompt, and leave, however, is only the beginning of learning to facilitate a group discussion. Facilitation skills at a more advanced level may involve questioning strategies in which different levels of questioning elicit different levels of conceptual integration on the part of the students. Focusing on levels of questioning, however, without *first* learning the more basic and fundamental skills of discussion facilitation places the cart before the horse. Once a teacher becomes comfortable in his or her ability to produce a productive discussion and to engage students in idea building at will, levels of questioning simply constitute more advanced prompting skills. All this structure, however, rests on the solid methodological foundation provided by the positive helping interaction.

ELABORATED FORMS OF THE POSITIVE HELPING INTERACTION

As mentioned earlier, the form which praise, prompt, and leave takes during a group discussion is highly analogous to the form it takes during typical seatwork such as mathematics, science, or English grammar. Further variations of the positive helping interaction, however, can be used within the context of classroom instruction for tasks which are more expressive or creative in nature—for tasks in which performance is more open-ended and in which there are no right answers. Predictably, within such lesson formats praise, prompt, and leave will also be more open-ended, and students will be given more choice as to the course of action they may wish to pursue. Yet although more varied and open-ended, the forms of the positive helping interaction which facilitate creativity represent a limited and predictable number of fairly simple variations on praise, prompt, and leave which resemble in many ways discussion facilitation skills.

When a teacher uses praise, prompt, and leave in a more *analytic* task in which the performance sequence is fairly predictable and predetermined, the choice of the prompt is relatively predetermined by the task analysis and is therefore supplied by the teacher. In more *expressive* tasks, however, choice of the prompt belongs most typically to either the individual student or a group of students. When the choice belongs to the individual student, the structure of choosing is highly analogous to the answer formats typical of formal testing.

Multiple-Choice Problem Solving

Imagine that you are an art teacher with students busily drawing or painting at their easels. As you approach a student who has been working for a while, you see that he seems to be having some difficulty. You begin a helping interaction by pointing out some strengths of his composition. He frowns, turns to you, and says, "I don't like it."

You may, of course, make a suggestion to the student which may help him out of his dilemma. Such a direct prompt, however, is an artful gamble which is a bit risky with a frustrated student. If the student is dissatisfied with his own performance, he will often reject your praise and be dissatisfied with your prompt as well. It is the student who must struggle with the options concerning what to do next, and it is the student who must choose.

If you do not feel in a position to successfully prompt the student, *let the student prompt himself.* This can be done in one of two fashions:

1 Open-ended Choice The most judicious course of action for a student who is struggling with a creative decision is often to "put the ball in their court." Use the open-ended prompt typical of discussion facilitation and ask, "What do you think would be best to do next?" Relax and have tolerance for the silence that will probably ensue. Remember, silence usually means that mental work is being done. Wait patiently while the student reviews options and prescribes the solution to the problem to his or her own satisfaction. Affirm the solution ("Give it a try and see what happens"), and leave. This is no time to state an opinion.

2 Catalogue of Choices Sometimes students will seem blocked or stymied in the problem-solving process so that "giving them space" in which to work out their own solution, as in the previous example, produces little movement. At this point the teacher can serve as a facilitator by helping the student *brainstorm* the options available in a fashion highly analogous to the brainstorming of a typical group discussion. Teachers may have varying degrees of input as they focus the discussion on certain issues (rather than others) and on the best or most useful ideas generated by the student. Thus praise, prompt, and leave will employ the selective reinforcement and open-ended prompting typical of group discussion facilitation. Yet the choice of what to do next belongs to the student.

Forced-Choice Problem Solving

Imagine that your are giving corrective feedback during an English composition class to a student with poor grammar skills. She has written a sentence in which the number and the tense of the verb disagree with the subject. You could, of course, review those aspects of the sentence that are correct or review some grammar rules and then prompt the student to look up the form of the verb that would agree with the subject. The teacher may, however, wish to have a *dialogue* with the student in which the student chooses the proper form of the verb, thereby experiencing the affirmation of "having known it all the time."

The primary teaching error that is endemic to teachers attempting to engage a student in dialogue during corrective feedback, of course, is the asking of *leading questions* as discussed in Chapter 5. Rather than asking a leading question, a fruitful type of dialogue is the structuring of a forced-choice decision on the part of the student which contrasts correct and incorrect performance that the student would probably be able to correctly discriminate. In a forced-choice interaction the teacher might review critical aspects of the task (the subject-verb agreement in this case) and focus the student's attention on the critical dimension of choice. The teacher, for example, might have the following dialogue with the student who wrote the sentence, "My dad and me gone fishing."

Teacher: Mary, will you read your first sentence for me, please.

Student: My dad and me gone fishing.

Teacher: Listen to the following two sentences and tell me which one sounds best to you. "My dad gone fishing," and "My dad went fishing."

Student: My dad went fishing.

Teacher: Right! "My dad went fishing." It sounds right, and you *are* right. "Went" is the past tense, and you and your dad went fishing in the past. Let's keep "went" as the verb in this sentence. [Mark on the student's paper or have them make a note.]

Now let's listen to the following two sentences; "I went fishing," and "Me went fishing." Which sounds best to you?

Student: I went fishing.

Teacher: Right! "I went fishing" is the way we usually say it, and that is the correct subject to use in this sentence. Using what we have learned then, the subject is "My dad and I" and the form of the verb is "went." Let's rewrite the sentence with our new subject and verb.

A corrective feedback dialogue using any kind of questioning technique, particularly a forced-choice questioning technique, considerably lengthens the helping interaction. Is it worth the investment? You always pay a price for such lengthy helping interactions because you will get around to fewer students and risk playing into the helplessness and dependency patterns of certain members of the class. However, although there is a risk involved, there is also a potential benefit which may more than offset the risk. The richness of the dialogue in the helping interaction may facilitate learning far more than a simple praise, prompt, and leave interaction. The choice is up to the teacher—one of the artful gambles.

Group Problem Solving

Sometimes guided practice of a new skill takes place within a group context in which performance can be seen and judged by fellow students and in which corrective feedback is a public event. The coaching of athletics is such a context, although the need to give corrective feedback publicly is part of many instructional situations including teacher training.

When giving corrective feedback in a group-learning format, the vulnerability of the student is heightened just as it is in a group discussion. Although the teacher's main objective is to upgrade student performance, corrective feedback must be given within a context of safety and low performance anxiety. In such public situations a variant of praise, prompt, and leave may be used which simultaneously protects the learner while capitalizing on the perceptions and feedback of fellow students.

During teacher training the most common situation in which students perform under the public scrutiny of their colleagues is in the guided practice of limit-setting (see Chapters 5, 6, and 7 of *Positive Classroom Discipline*). Most performance anxiety and performance error is eliminated before guided practice, of course, by the careful teaching of limit-setting as a structured lesson and especially by thorough structured practice. Yet in guided practice the students (teacher trainees) are on their own for the first time as they prompt themselves through the performance sequence rather than being prompted by the teacher as in structured practice.

How do you maximize the probability of correct performance in a group situation, and how do you maximize the safety of feedback from the group? Imagine a practice exercise in which a trainee playing the role of teacher is setting limits on two colleagues playing the role of disruptive students who are talking to each other on the far side of the classroom. Imagine also that the students continue to talk until the teacher has gone through the limit-setting sequence as far as palms on the desk. Safety during performance and corrective feedback is created by the trainer as he or she structures guided practice according to the following four steps:

1 Set the Scene Describe the upcoming scene (performance sequence) so that the people playing the role of misbehaving students will know exactly how and when to disrupt and when to quit. Setting the stage is more for the sake of structuring the performance of the disruptive students than for the sake of the teacher trainee to prevent the students from becoming outrageous. Protecting the trainee is paramount.

2 Model As trainer or "coach," I model for the trainee exactly what he is to do as he responds to the disruption. As I model, the trainee will walk with me as I explain my moves. Thus, my modeling provides a dry run for the learner so that the full response to the disruptions will have been rehearsed immediately before his performance. I thoroughly choreograph the entire scene to ensure that the trainee gains confidence with the simple performance sequence of limit-setting rather than having to ad lib in order to cope with the unknown.

3 Prompt During the *second* walk-through of the scene, the trainee and I switch roles so that the trainee is now walking himself through the scene with me alongside.

As he walks through the scene, however, I am on his shoulder watching him closely so that I may *immediately* provide a prompt for correct performance at any point should it be needed. Through quick and precise prompting, I correct errors as they are occurring so that we "build it right the first time." The learner must make his own decisions, however, and must prompt himself through the performance sequence with me available to make midcourse corrections only as needed. To talk the learner through the performance sequence takes decision making out of his hands and reduces guided practice to structured practice.

4 Feedback It is during the feedback portion of the practice sequence that the group enters into the process of corrective feedback within a context created by the trainer that guarantees safety. The feedback process has four distinct steps:

a Praise The first job of the teacher trainer or coach upon completion of the performance sequence by the trainee is to describe the *strengths* of the trainee's performance. As is typical of the positive helping interaction, we will talk only about things that the student has done right so far and make no mention of any deficit in performance. This does not mean, however, that we will turn a blind eye to error and pretend that it does not exist. Rather we will keep two sets of books in our mind. One has to do with strengths of the performance which we will talk about immediately. The second has to do with deficits of performance which we will replace during the next practice cycle by focusing on and carefully modeling and prompting correct performance. For the time being the words that the learner will hear are words of affirmation that focus on those aspects of performance that we will want to keep.

b Ask the trainee (playing the role of teacher) how he experienced the walk-through Typically the "teacher" will experience satisfaction in his performance. Adequate modeling and thorough structuring of the specific practice situation render a strong performance most likely. Whether the trainee's opinion of his own performance is highly positive or not, however, we want *him* to be the *first* person in the group to comment on his performance. If the trainee is aware of some deficit in his performance, it is far better that he describe it to the group himself than that the group describe it to him.

Occasionally a trainee in the role of teacher will be self-effacing in evaluating his or her own performance—usually in spite of the fact that the performance was quite adequate. When the learner is self-effacing, the trainer or coach responds by repeating a portion of the initial praise statement to refocus the learner's attention on critical strengths of his or her performance.

c Ask the disruptive students how they experienced the trainee's (i.e., teacher's) performance Within a group feedback situation there are always experts in the group. It is important, however, for the trainer or coach to realize that the expert is *not him or her.* In this practice situation in which colleagues are playing the part of disruptive students, the experts are the disruptive students. The trainee may have an opinion about the performance, and the trainer or coach may also have an opinion about the performance, but the final readout will have to be supplied by the individuals who were the recipients of the limit-setting. If they say it was good, it was good, and if they say something has to be changed, they have provided much of the structure for the next practice cycle.

It is easy to imagine negative feedback on the part of one's colleagues after such a practice exercise. The probability of negative feedback, however, is ultimately in the hands of the trainer, who, in order to make group learning safe, must (1) teach the lesson well in the first place with adequate modeling and structured practice and (2) use proper corrective feedback procedures. Consequently, when the trainer or coach asks the disruptive students to comment on the teacher's performance, the result is typically praise.

The trainer or coach is, in effect, structuring a dialogue between the trainee and his or her colleagues in which the affirmation of adequacy is the primary focus. This affirmation from colleagues has a higher validity than any affirmation coming from the coach since it is based on a real, immediate, and unbiased experience. Although suggestions to improve performance may occur, they do not produce pain under normal circumstances because they come at the end of a feedback process that has been structured to create affirmation. In almost all cases the net result of peer feedback is confidence building.

d Feedback from observers and group members other than those directly involved in the interactions Often there are members of the training group who played neither the roles of teacher nor disruptive students. These observers, however, often notice aspects of the performance situation that were not seen by those directly participating. Their comments are usually highly enriching and affirming of the learner.

During teacher training this four-step process of carefully (1) setting the stage, (2) modeling, (3) prompting, and (4) eliciting feedback is practiced by coaches until it becomes second nature so that the coaches will be able to put their colleagues at ease during skill performance. If the process is carefully adhered to by the coaches, everyone in the training group soon picks up the rules of the game so that the reliance on the coach for structure diminishes. Soon the exchange becomes spontaneous—an excited give and take. But the give and take is supportive because the coach has trained the group to focus on the positive and prompt improved performance.

OVERVIEW

Shaping is the fundamental skill-building process of instrumental learning or operant conditioning, and the positive helping interaction is that variant of shaping used to give corrective feedback during the guided practice phase of skill acquisition. The positive helping interaction may take a variety of specific but highly related forms depending on the nature of the teaching situation. But the basis of all formal instruction is a single, safe, and relatively simple shaping transaction.

Corrective feedback in a group instructional setting can take place in the form of a dialogue which, to an untrained observer, would appear to be a free and spontaneous give and take. To the contrary, the corrective feedback process in such settings is carefully structured by the teacher and guided to ensure growth with safety through selective reinforcement and open-ended prompts.

Praise, prompt, and leave in a highly structured analytic seatwork assignment such as mathematics, and praise, prompt, and leave in the open-ended give and take of a group discussion represent the boundaries of the positive helping interaction in terms of dealing with differing degrees of spontaneity and unpredictability of student output. They do *not,* however, represent any great contrast in basic structure. In all corrective feedback situations the trained teacher has very explicit objectives, and in order to accommodate the nature of the interaction with the learner she makes only fairly minor and predictable adjustments to the praise, prompt, and leave sequence.

In the following chapters we learn how to further increase the efficiency of shaping both during the initial presentation of a structured lesson and during corrective feedback. The next chapter deals with lesson design, and the following two chapters deal with lesson presentation. Together these three chapters will further enhance our understanding of the process of shaping in formal instruction.

REFERENCES

1 Elkind, D., *Children and adolescents,* New York: Oxford University Press, 1974, pp. 105–127.

2 Burka, A. A. Procedures for increasing appropriate verbal participation in special elementary classrooms. Dissertation submitted in partial fulfillment of the requirements for Ph.D., University of Rochester, 1977, Ann Arbor, Michigan: University Microfilms.

3 Burka, A. A. and Jones, F. H. Procedures for increasing appropriate verbal participation in special elementary classrooms. *Behavior Modification,* 1979, 3, 27–48.

SECTION FOUR

LESSON DESIGN AND PRESENTATION

CHAPTER 7

PERFORMANCE MODELS

The positive helping interaction as described in the preceding chapters plays a major role in eliminating the inefficiency and negativism inherent in the universal helping interaction. Yet in many cases the level of performance initially achieved by teachers from extensive practice of the positive helping interaction during training has still been inadequate. Teaching too much and talking too much are old and tenacious habits which for some teachers are extremely difficult to break. Even with the help of extensive practice most teachers struggle with the learning of "praise, prompt, and leave" during teacher training, and many finally backslide into "praise, blah, blah, blah" and "prompt, blah, blah, blah."

After increasing the amount of practice time allotted for the positive helping interaction substantially during teacher training only to see uneven improvement, I finally had to conclude that I was blocked—at least temporarily. I would have to deal with the entire context of excess talking, not just the talking itself. *Positive Classroom Instruction* would have to go well beyond training teachers to use praise, prompt, and leave. It would have to deal with the presentation of the *entire structured lesson* in order to ensure consistently correct performance on the part of both teachers and students not only during guided practice but also during the portions of the structured lesson that precede and build up to guided practice.

In this chapter we extend our understanding of prompting to the initial presentation of the lesson in order to learn how to further simplify corrective feedback during guided practice. We take a fresh look at task analysis and lesson planning to see how to present the skill or concept of a lesson in the form of a clear, step-by-step "performance model." Performance models greatly (1) reduce the likelihood of error, (2) reduce the need for corrective feedback, (3) reduce the duration of corrective feedback, and (4) promote independent learning habits. In the following two chapters (Chapters

8 and 9), we closely examine the presentation of the entire structured lesson so that the likelihood of skill mastery before guided practice will be maximized.

WHAT IS A PERFORMANCE MODEL?

Learning takes place one step at a time, whether it be the building of a physical skill or the development of a concept. Since learning takes place one step at a time, the teacher's first job in lesson planning is to understand the steps of skill performance or concept development in their proper sequence.

Performance Sequences and Task Analysis

Most skills or concepts are sufficiently complex so that several steps or operations are required to successfully master them. We refer to the steps of skill performance or concept development arranged in consecutive order as a "performance sequence."

Most formal instruction teaches all or part of a performance sequence during a structured lesson. The starting point of lesson preparation, therefore, is to list the steps of performance or the parts of the concept in the order in which they will be taught and subsequently performed or expressed. This careful sequential analysis of the task is quite fittingly called "task analysis" by most educators.

Although a teacher's knowing the steps of a skill's performance before he or she attempts to teach it may seem rather basic to nonteachers, the experience of teaching a skill proves most humbling. The steps of performing a skill that we overlook or fail to take seriously enough to include in our lesson plan are the ones most familiar to us. As soon as teachers *assume* that everybody in the group knows some basic skill or bit of information, they set themselves up for a quick demonstration to the contrary. Any step that is omitted will trip up the new learner. Hence the first cardinal rule of task analysis: *Assumacy is the mother of all screw-ups.*

In addition, while some performance sequences may seem rather clear-cut and easy to see, others are quite subtle and elude all but the most experienced and skillful of teachers. Thus, for example, the steps of a given type of mathematics problem may seem straightforward and easy to find in a textbook. But as you attempt to help a student who is having difficulty finding a topic sentence for the first paragraph of an essay, what are the steps of beginning an essay?

Whereas thoroughness is the first imperative of task analysis, attempts to be thorough, divorced from the actual physical process of skill performance, frequently lead teachers up a blind alley in their lesson organization. An adequate task analysis is *not* a performance sequence that springs solely from the teacher's conceptual or logical analysis of the task. It is possible for an adult to parse any task into almost any number of steps depending on his analytic compulsiveness. I have seen task analyses of a simple long division problem promulgated by a county office of education that had forty-two steps! There is no logical end point for slicing with the conceptual microtome, and the pieces produced have no necessary connection to meaningful acts of skill performance by students.

One of the most difficult tricks of task analysis is to place yourself in the student's desk and see the skill with the fresh eyes of new learning. An adequate task analysis is a performance sequence that usually springs from the teacher's actually or vicariously *performing* the task while imagining he or she is a naïve or moderately confused student.

Clarifying the next step of a performance sequence comes from repeatedly asking yourself the question, "Exactly what must the student do next?" The key word is the verb "do." A task analysis divides performance of the task into a sequence of *coherent actions,* whether physical or mental. You must *do* the skill as you analyze the task in order to make the transition from the infinite possibilities of logic to the limited options of performance.

Task Analysis and Effective Prompting

A task analysis describes the steps of skill performance or concept development. A prompt tells a student exactly what to do on the next step of performance. Obviously a close relationship is at work here. If you were to present a performance sequence to your students clearly, you would present a *string of effective prompts.*

The proper design of a structure lesson, therefore, represents an extension of the prompting skills already described in the preceding chapters. We will build on what we already know about prompting to construct a lesson design that combines effective task analysis with maximum simplicity and clarity at each step. An effective lesson design, therefore, should present the student with a string of prompts that (1) increases the clarity of the expected performance and thereby accelerates learning while it (2) simultaneously decreases the tendency toward the excess verbiage of teachers during the corrective feedback of guided practice. Rather than having teachers struggle with words to produce clarity during corrective feedback, we will "prepackage" clarity so that few words are needed.

The Prompting Hierarchy The road to prepackaging a prompt with maximum clarity combined with a minimal demand for talk will be made easier once we understand the dimensions of prompting contained in the "prompting hierarchy" (see Figure 7-1). The information in most prompts can be conveyed in *three sensory modalities.* These input modalities form a natural hierarchy in the degree of clarity or explicitness of the information conveyed to students about what they are to do next. The three input modalities coinciding with the three levels of information that can be conveyed by a prompt are (1) verbal input, (2) visual input, and (3) physical input.

1 Verbal Input A verbal prompt tells the student what to do next. This level of prompting conveys the least information of any of the three levels of the prompting hierarchy and therefore represents minimal clarity and explicitness.

A verbal prompt requires students to imagine what correct performance would look like and feel like in their minds. If a student could supply perfectly accurate visual and physical (or kinesthetic) imagery on the basis of a verbal description alone, we would almost by definition not be dealing with new learning. With new learning the sights and feelings of correct performance are left to the student's imagination, and the student's imagining will almost surely deviate from "correctness" to a greater or lesser

Physical	—	guides	↑	increasing
Visual	—	shows		clarity and
Verbal	—	tells		explicitness

FIGURE 7-1
The prompting hierarchy (levels of prompting).

degree. Any such deviation represents information loss at input which places a cap on the ultimate correctness of performance and understanding. Such loss or imperfection limits the extent of subsequent mastery since performance during practice cannot surpass the student's cognitive ideal or model of correct performance.

2 Visual Input A visual prompt shows the student what to do—what the task would look like if it were done correctly. It leaves very little to chance as it helps the student see correct performance accurately in the "mind's eye." The greater structure of the visual prompt, therefore, provides a much more faithful or accurate model to serve as a performance guide than does the linguistic imagery of a verbal description. Through the visual modality, information loss at input is greatly reduced.

Written instructions are "bimodal" in that they provide instructions visually in the form of writing but not in the form of pictures as with the modeling of a skill. Whether written instructions represent linguistic or visual input and storage depends, therefore, on how they are processed by the learner. We typically convert input into our strongest modality whenever possible. So some people remember written instructions as they would verbal instructions, whereas others convert them to graphics as soon as possible before they become confused and forgotten.

3 Physical Input Whereas verbal tells and visual shows, a physical prompt actually guides the physical performance of a skill. Students can not only see correct performance; they can also feel it. Nothing is left to the imagination when prompting is done in all three input modalities. Not only is correct linguistic imagery and visual imagery provided, but correct kinesthetic imagery is provided as well.

Physical prompts not only clarify input, but they clarify output as well. When our body is guided to the proper position, a complete input/storage/output loop is generated with the body actually performing the skill correctly under conditions of strict monitoring and immediate feedback and guidance.

Multimodal Prompting Altering the level of prompting is one of the primary ways in which an effective teacher can preempt error and generate consistent success while teaching. By going up the prompting hierarchy, the teacher can add structure to any prompt so that the next step of the skill sequence will be more clear to the student.

Regardless of the relative strengths or weaknesses of various students' modalities of acquiring, storing, and expressing information, seeing in addition to hearing will almost always produce a dramatic leap in the precision with which almost any student can reproduce skill performance. In addition, most people remember things they see better than things they hear—the modeling of correct performance, for example, as compared with a complex set of instructions. In almost all kinds of formal classroom instruction, therefore, the most dramatic gain in the clarity of a prompt is achieved by *going visual.* Exploiting the visual modality of input during instruction dramatically demonstrates the truth of one of the most time-honored (yet underutilized) bits of teaching wisdom: A picture is worth a thousand words.

To put it somewhat differently, a prompt is more complete and therefore more powerful the more modalities of input it contains. Clear and simple verbal input is strengthened by visual input. And a verbal/visual prompt is strengthened by physical input. The teaching of a *physical* skill, for example, may rely heavily on physical prompting to ensure correct performance, but learners still rely heavily on their visual memory of the sequence as well as their memory of instructions for guidance during practice. Clear *multimodal* input, therefore, maximizes the clarity of the desired performance while it prompts performance.

Permanent Prompts and Performance Models

Typically the teaching of the first step of any structured lesson is followed by the next step and the next step and the next step until the entire performance sequence is completed. However, the teacher's explanation and modeling of a skill or concept are fleeting and impermanent. Memory is imperfect and forgetting immediately begins. With the passage of time the instructions and concepts and steps of performance begin to run together like the forms of a watercolor painting that has been held up too soon.

A "performance model" attempts to make permanent the performance sequence inherent within the structured lesson. A performance model is a permanent visual representation, either graphic or written, of the structure of the skill or concept being taught in the structured lesson. Once the teacher learns to make the performance sequence clear, step by step, and permanent, explanation and modeling will be transformed from conceptual overload into a permanent study guide—a set of plans to be used by students throughout the remainder of the lesson.

Types of Performance Models

Since there are many different types of lessons which occur during a typical day in the classroom, the construction of performance models is a creative endeavor in which the teacher is afforded a great degree of latitude. The performance models presented in the following section, therefore, are suggestive only. They do, however, illustrate the main objectives of performance models—*clarity* and *permanence* of the structure of the performance expected from the student.

Performance models are described under three headings: (1) "Illustrated Performance Sequences," (2) "Performance Outlines," and (3) "Conceptual Maps."

1 Illustrated Performance Sequences Illustrated performance sequences are most typical for tasks which involve physical performance or computation such as mathematics, science, athletics, shop, and home economics. As the name implies, the illustrated performance sequence makes the steps of a performance sequence clear and permanent by providing an illustration for every step.

2 Performance Outlines Performance outlines are more common for tasks which involve research, concept development, and self-expression. Whereas an illustrated performance sequence relies heavily on graphics, a performance outline is, as the name implies, a systematic presentation in outline form of the logic of a concept or the information which would constitute a complete job of research.

3 Conceptual Maps Conceptual maps clarify the process of concept development in the form of an easy-to-read diagram. Conceptual maps, therefore, are a highly condensed lesson design—a kind of hybrid of the pictorial emphasis typical of an illustrated performance sequence and the emphasis on logical structure typical of a performance outline. The scope of conceptual maps is limitless and encompasses almost any *single graphic* that shows someone how to (1) organize an idea, (2) conduct problem solving, or (3) perform a series of operations.

Performance Models and Visual Aids

Illustrated performance sequences, performance outlines, and conceptual maps depict the entire sequence of performance. They are, consequently, relied on most heavily during the *initial* teaching of a structured lesson. It is during initial learning that the student needs any device that can clarify as many details of performance as possible for every step of the lesson.

As students gain mastery of a skill, however, performance models can be simplified so that they serve only as *reminders* of the performance sequence rather than as a complete set of plans. The result is a class of visual aids which contain only the vestiges of the original task analysis in the form of a single diagram. It is important to discriminate a performance model from simpler visual aids which fail to depict the entire sequence of performance, since early in training teachers often tend to produce the simplified rather than the complete set of plans.

ILLUSTRATED PERFORMANCE SEQUENCES

Making a Permanent Record of Our Modeling

Covering Up Our Tracks Let's imagine, as a simple example, that a teacher is presenting to his or her class a lesson on long division at the board. The students are sitting at their desks watching and listening as the teacher explains how to divide a three-digit dividend by a single-digit divisor that is *larger* than the first digit of the dividend. In explaining the process of long division that is used on this particular type of problem, the teacher walks the class through an example. In this case the sample problem is $495 \div 6$.

Typically, as the teacher explains and models for the class the process of long division step by step, he or she uses a *single* example at the board. The teacher might, for example, begin by explaining that the 4 cannot be divided by the 6 because the 6 is larger than the 4. The first step of the division problem, therefore, is to compare the size of the divisor with the size of the first digit of the dividend. The teacher may then proceed to explain to the class that, since the 6 will not go into the 4, you have to take the 6 into the first *two* digits of the dividend, 6 into 49. Most likely the teacher will ask questions of the class as they go along, to check for understanding and to elicit group responding as a form of participation.

The modeling of the performance of the long division problem proceeds according to the normal sequence of (1) compare, (2) divide, (3) multiply, (4) subtract, (5) compare, and (6) bring down until all digits of the dividend have been brought down and divided. Step by step the students receive both verbal and visual input describing the correct method of computation as the teacher walks them through a sample problem at the chalkboard.

When the teacher has completed the demonstration he or she will have produced a picture or diagram—a graphic—of the long division process at the board that is a byproduct of the method of presentation. Typically the graphic produced by the teacher's demonstration of the performance sequence looks like Figure 7-2.

I will refer to the picture that is typically produced by a teacher as he or she explains and models the performance sequence to the class as a "summary graphic." It shows exactly how the long division problem should look if it were done correctly.

The problem with such a summary graphic is that *it obliterates the steps of task performance*! As the teacher does the sample problem on the board, each step of the calculation is added on top of the previous step of the calculation on the *same graphic* so that the previous visual prompt is covered up. Consequently, when instruction is completed, the only graphic that remains is a picture of how a student's performance would look when completed *if the student already knew how to perform correctly.* Such a graphic is of little use as a set of plans or study guide to any student who does not already know how to perform correctly. For the student who is engaged in new learning and is experiencing mild to moderate confusion, there is no way to look at the graphic provided by the teacher and reconstruct the steps of the performance sequence. If he is stuck on step 4, where does he look to find it?

Summary graphics, therefore, are almost useless as a means of clarifying the instructional process, particularly during guided practice. As I watch teachers constructing their summary graphics on the board as they explain and model the performance sequence of a lesson to their class, I am often reminded of the scenes in old western movies in which outlaws who are being pursued through the badlands brush over their footprints in the dust with a branch so that they will not leave a trail. With our summary graphics we also obliterate our trail just as effectively as did those outlaws. No student can possibly follow us after our lesson presentation has been completed.

```
   82r3
6 |495
  -48
    15
   -12
     3
```

FIGURE 7-2
Illustration of a long division problem after covering up your tracks.

Advantages of a Clear Set of Plans Imagine, in contrast to covering up our tracks, that we were to produce a *separate* graphic for each step of the performance sequence as we explained and modeled the skill. These illustrations would be arranged in the order of their performance so that a student could look up at any time to see how the lesson or skill was to be done. This series of graphics produced during the modeling phase of a structured lesson would be as though someone had taken photographs of our demonstration at each step and had posted them in front of the class so that the steps of correct performance would not be lost.

An illustrated performance sequence for the long division problem described in the section "Covering Up Our Tracks" (495 ÷ 6) might look like the first row of graphics in Figure 7-3.

Although this illustrated performance sequence may seem unremarkable at first—not unlike things we have seen before—in fact such simple, step-by-step graphics are lacking in most textbooks and in most classrooms most of the time. When students are given a good set of plans for a change, the increase in the rate of learning can be truly

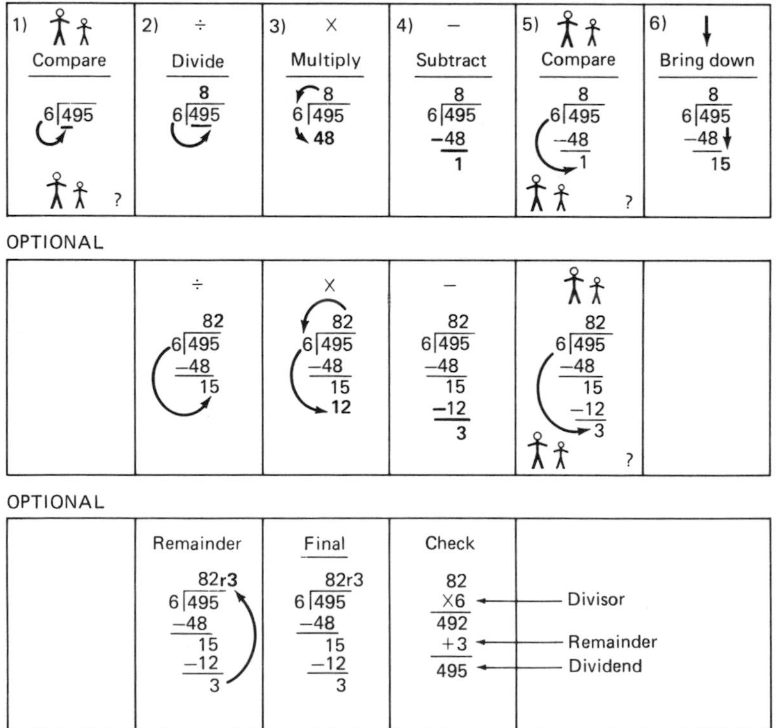

FIGURE 7-3
Illustrated performance sequence of a long division problem (495 ÷ 6).

remarkable, especially for the bottom half of the class. As one teacher remarked during training after having used similar graphics for long division:

> You know, last year I spent the whole first semester on long division for many of the kids in my class, and I still had a half dozen who couldn't do it. This year I had everyone doing it in 2 weeks—correctly!

Constructing an illustrated performance sequence for a lesson does several jobs simultaneously. Such graphics facilitate independent study during guided practice while reducing the need for teacher verbiage, and they help the teacher to do a more careful task analysis.

If you have a clear illustration for each step of the performance sequence, you do not have to talk so much when showing the student exactly what to do next. In fact, many corrective feedback interactions may consist of nothing more than pointing out the critical feature of one of the illustrations—a helping interaction which is often 3 to 10 seconds in length. Continual reference to each step of the illustrated performance sequence during lesson presentation teaches the class to use your lesson plan as a study guide and therefore further simplifies the job of giving corrective feedback later in the lesson.

An illustrated performance sequence also helps the students to know exactly what to do next in your absence. Now the students can look at the permanent prompt when they need help, and they do not need you to be with them. If you fail to supply the students with an illustrated performance sequence, you define *yourself* as the only usable form of corrective feedback during guided practice. By your failure to provide adequate graphics, therefore, you will inadvertently foster dependency rather than the independent work habits that you value.

With repetition the string of prompts and the skill performance which they represent will become internalized. To help students further, teachers will often have the students copy the illustrated performance sequence into their notebooks or pass out copies to be taken home to help with homework. Thus the teacher's illustrated study guide serves as an essential link between guided practice within the classroom and independent practice outside the classroom. In addition, an illustrated performance sequence can save the teacher a great deal of time when dealing with students who are absent. It can be sent home to sick students, and it can serve as the basis of effective peer tutoring once the student returns so that the teacher can be free to work with the rest of the class. An illustrated performance sequence, therefore, (1) clarifies each step of performance, while (2) freeing you to do other tasks during guided practice, while (3) training students to be *their own tutors* and *work independently*.

Building an Illustrated Performance Sequence

General Guidelines for Constructing an Illustrated Performance Sequence As you might imagine, there are many ways to produce an illustrated performance sequence for different tasks with varying degrees of verbal and visual structure. Although the building of an illustrated performance sequence leaves much room for creativity, all are constructed according to three guidelines:

1 One skill at a time.
2 One step at a time.
3 Illustrate every step.

One Skill at a Time The focus of a structured lesson is on a *single* specific skill. A common teaching error is to cram two skills into a single lesson. To do so actually crams three lessons into one in most cases: learning skill 1, learning skill 2, and integrating skill 1 with skill 2. Cognitive overload and confusion are the inevitable by-products for much of the class, especially for those students for whom *both* skills represented new learning.

Examples of "split focus" abound at all grade levels. Teaching a lesson in subtraction to young students which incorporates input on both regrouping and borrowing is common. Having students write essays while providing new input about both grammar and paragraph construction is equally common. Any lesson objective that can be stated in the form of a compound sentence is suspect and should be reexamined. Limiting the focus of the lesson is often the first by-product of a careful task analysis since an analysis of the steps of skill performance often reveals that the lesson is going in two directions at once.

One Step at a Time Place yourself in the desk of a naïve student, start with a blank sheet of paper, and begin your walk-through of correct performance one step at a time. Assume nothing and omit nothing. This task analysis from the *student's* vantage point will help clarify your starting point, the type and amount of review needed, and the steps of the performance sequence. Focus on the verb "do." Exactly what must the students do with their minds and bodies as each demand for thought or action confronts them? The result will most likely be a list.

Illustrate Every Step The final step in constructing an illustrated performance sequence is to supply the illustrations. Illustrations may take many forms, but though they tend to gain clarity as they go up the prompting hierarchy, they must also match the task. Thus although illustrations of a mathematics problem might be pictographic, illustrations of logic might be diagramatic. The term "illustration" was chosen purposely because its meaning is very broad. Though we may first think only of pictures as in the case of the long division problem depicted earlier, we may also illustrate Chaucer's writing style with passages from Chaucer. Nonpictorial illustrations are, naturally, most common in the humanities.

Simplicity and Clarity versus Complexity and Thoroughness Our attempts to develop a format for an Illustrated Performance Sequence (IPS) have produced two separate formats over the years, a long form and a short form. The long form which we call a "complete IPS" contains (1) complete instructions for carrying out each step of the performance sequence, (2) illustrations of each step, (3) a check routine, where possible, which describes a means of checking each step before proceeding to the next step, and (4) brief instructional aids or reminders where helpful. A complete IPS would be thorough enough to serve as a manual for self-instruction in many cases.

TABLE 7-1
TYPES OF ILLUSTRATED PERFORMANCE SEQUENCES (IPS)

- I Complete IPS
  - Instructions with each step
  - An illustration with each step
  - A check routine with each step
  - Instructional aids and reminders where helpful
- II Simplified IPS
  - Minimum written input (usually just labels)
  - An illustration with each step
  - No check routines or instructional aids

The short form, which we call a "simplified IPS," is an attempt to simplify instructions and graphics to only those visual components that would be of most help to a student who might need only review or clarification during guided practice. A simplified IPS usually contains only graphics and simple labels.

In constructing an illustrated performance sequence, a teacher must always make trade-offs between simplicity and clarity on the one hand and complexity and thoroughness on the other hand (see Table 7-1). A complete IPS is often thorough enough to serve as a guide for independent study in its own right. On a simple task it can be beautifully clear and complete, but on a long task it can be complex and confusing, especially for students with poor reading skills. A simplified IPS, on the other hand, is immediately visually comprehensible. It can make a long task simple and decipherable even to a poor reader, but much input is omitted. It relies heavily on the effective teaching of a structured lesson immediately before its use.

In our experience most teachers prefer simplified IPSs when they have time to thoroughly teach a structured lesson, whereas they prefer a complete IPS for an advanced student working independently or for a student who was absent for the structured lesson. As usual, simplicity seems to aid comprehensibility—especially for the slower student who would need to refer to the illustrated performance sequence most often during guided practice. Both types of illustrated performance sequences are presented here, however, to aid teachers in making the inevitable trade-offs between thoroughness and simplicity.

Examples of Illustrated Performance Sequences

This presentation of examples of illustrated performance sequences is an attempt to enrich teachers' understanding of the use of *graphics* in instruction. It is not intended to be a model of the world's best graphics for any given lesson—there probably is no such thing—nor is it a lesson on curriculum. Questions of curriculum development are beyond the scope of this book. Rather, the examples of illustrated performance sequences are intended to be typical rather than exemplary. They were all constructed by teachers during teacher training within a time frame of 15 to 30 minutes. They are representative of the kind of effort a conscientious teacher may ask of him- or herself on a daily basis.

Let us take mathematics as our starting point in becoming familiar with illustrated performance sequences since mathematics is so obviously step by step and pictorial. Figure 7-4 presents a complete IPS for computing the diameter of a circle. As a one-page handout for every student in the class, this study guide has proved most valuable. Figure 7-5 presents a simplified IPS. You may prefer to combine parts of both. The

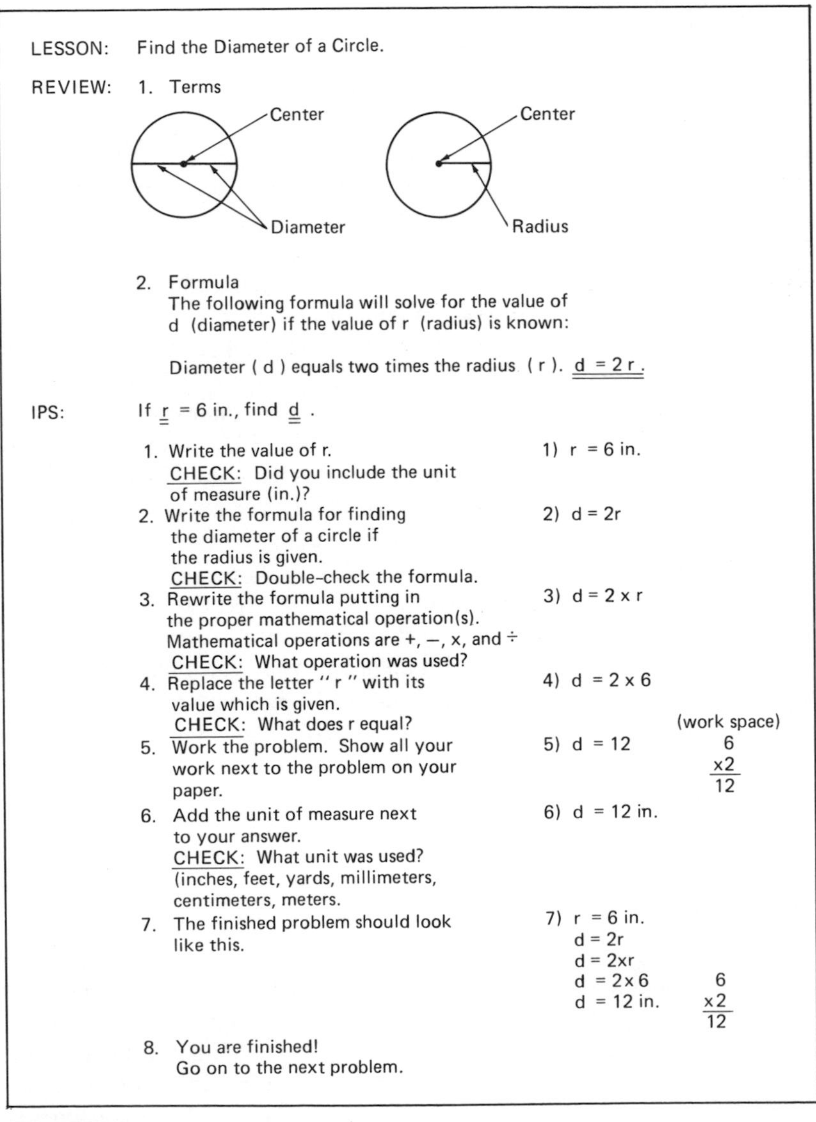

LESSON: Find the Diameter of a Circle.

REVIEW: 1. Terms

2. Formula
The following formula will solve for the value of d (diameter) if the value of r (radius) is known:

Diameter (d) equals two times the radius (r). d = 2 r.

IPS: If r = 6 in., find d .

1. Write the value of r.
CHECK: Did you include the unit of measure (in.)? — 1) r = 6 in.
2. Write the formula for finding the diameter of a circle if the radius is given.
CHECK: Double-check the formula. — 2) d = 2r
3. Rewrite the formula putting in the proper mathematical operation(s). Mathematical operations are +, —, x, and ÷
CHECK: What operation was used? — 3) d = 2 x r
4. Replace the letter " r " with its value which is given.
CHECK: What does r equal? — 4) d = 2 x 6
5. Work the problem. Show all your work next to the problem on your paper. — 5) d = 12 — (work space) 6 x2 12
6. Add the unit of measure next to your answer.
CHECK: What unit was used? (inches, feet, yards, millimeters, centimeters, meters. — 6) d = 12 in.
7. The finished problem should look like this. — 7) r = 6 in.
d = 2r
d = 2xr
d = 2x6
d = 12 in. — 6 x2 12
8. You are finished!
Go on to the next problem.

FIGURE 7-4
Computing the diameter of a circle—complete IPS.

A.	Write the "givens"	
	1. Formula	d = 2r
	2. Value of unknown	r = 6 in.
B.	Compute	
	3. Expand the formula	d = 2 x r
	4. Supply the value of the unknown	d = 2 x 6
	5. Multiply (2 x 6)	d = 12
	6. Supply the unit of measure	d = 12 in.
Good! You are finished!		

FIGURE 7-5
Computing the diameter of a circle—simplified IPS.

trade-off between thoroughness and simplicity is always an artful gamble that is largely determined by the preexisting skills of the students.

Figures 7-4 and 7-5 are helpful in illustrating the practical boundaries for the complexity of an illustrated performance sequence. Figure 7-4 is about as complex as you can afford to get with most groups of elementary and secondary students. To get much more complicated violates the KISS principle to the point where we are creating confusion rather than clarity. From experience the following rule of thumb has emerged to tell us when a complete IPS is too complete: If you cannot get a complete IPS on one side of a piece of typing paper, it is probably too complicated.

Sometimes the format for a simplified IPS can be expanded somewhat to contain an element of review and an instructional aid or two without sacrificing visual simplicity and clarity. Figure 7-6 is a simple study guide for a type of algebra problem that can give students a lot of trouble.

What if the student does not read at all? You do not need to use words! Figure 7-7 is an IPS for a typical kindergarten classroom routine—how to carry your chair. Note that you do not have to be a professional illustrator to get the job done. Remember also that classroom rules and routines are structured lessons that must be taught as carefully as any other lesson throughout the school year. Teaching classroom rules would therefore also include the presentation of an illustrated performance sequence in many cases.

Figure 7-8 shows a simplified IPS for a high-school level art lesson: making a line-perspective drawing. The graphics are not much more complicated than those of the preceding example, and the labels are simple, to say the least. Can you figure out from this IPS how to draw a house so that it looks three-dimensional?

Our final example for this section is an English grammar lesson (see Figure 7-9). This complete IPS teaches students how to scan a sentence systematically for the var-

I REVIEW

Multiplication Sign Rules

Same	Different
+ x + = ⊕	+ x − = ⊖
− x − = ⊕	− x + = ⊖

Rule: Same signs → "+". Different signs → "−".

II MULTIPLY

Example: (x+3) (x−9) =

Computation:

$(x + 3)\,(x - 9) = x^2$ — *F*irst

$(x + 3)\,(x - 9) = x^2 - 9x$ — *O*uter

$(x + 3)\,(x - 9) = x^2 - 9x + 3x$ — *I*nner

$(x + 3)\,(x - 9) = x^2 - 9x + 3x - 27$ — *L*ast

Memory Device: Remember "FOIL"

III SIMPLIFY

Definition: Add like terms.

Computation:

$$(x + 3)\,(x - 9) = x^2 \underbrace{- 9x + 3x} - 27$$

$$= x^2 - 6x - 27 \qquad \text{(Final Answer)}$$

FIGURE 7-6
The multiplication of two binomials—simplified IPS.

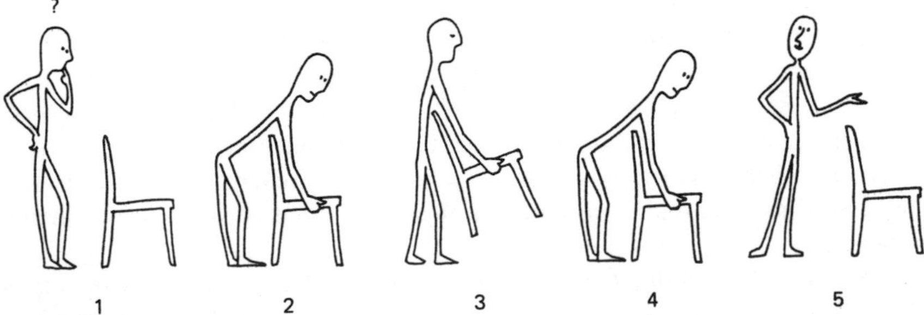

FIGURE 7-7
How to carry a chair—simplified IPS.

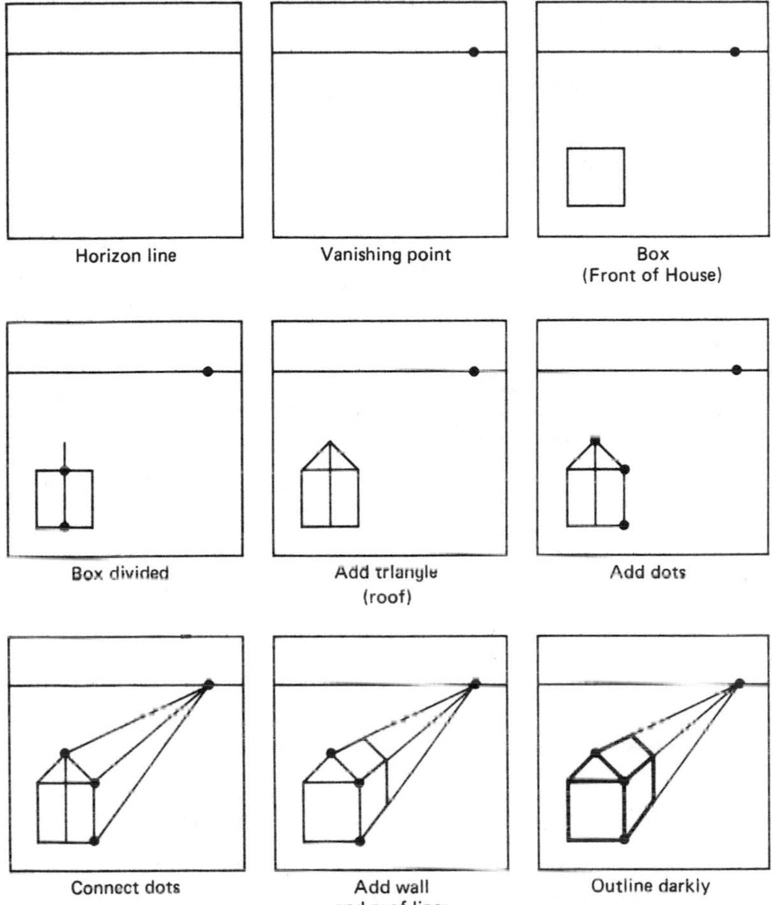

FIGURE 7-8
A line perspective drawing—simplified IPS.

ious kinds of adjectives that the class has been studying during the previous week. Rather than just giving the students an assignment, you can teach them the *process* for completing the assignment conscientiously with an IPS. What are the steps a careful student would perform in order to be sure of completing this assignment correctly? The review section greatly strengthens this particular IPS as a study guide.

Although the remainder of this assignment could be a ditto or a page out of the text, why not make it a team game in which everyone uses the study guide in order to win? A small team of three or four students would race with another team to identify all the adjectives correctly. Six teams would make three separate games. You would probably use a speed game format such as College Bowl (see Chapter 11 of *Positive Classroom Discipline*).

Space limits the number and range of illustrated performance sequences that can be

REVIEW

1. An adjective is a word that describes or adds to the meaning of a noun or pronoun.
   a. A noun: A person, animal, place, or thing (for example–John, zebra, building, Chicago, monster, kindness, girl, fear, mountain).
   b. A pronoun: A word that can take the place of a noun (for example–it, she, they, me, them).
2. There are several kinds of adjectives (underlined words below).
   a. Descriptive adjectives tell what kind.
      Example: Tall green grass covers the mountain.
   b. Numeral adjectives tell how many.
      Example: Two girls won the prize.
   c. Demonstrative adjectives tell which one.
      Example: This boy, that girl, and those teachers are helping us.
   d. Articles are special adjectives.
      Example: The little girl saw an eagle in the tree.

PERFORMANCE MODEL

Underline the adjectives in the sentences below.

1. Look for the adjectives that tell what kind.

   A long, narrow road leads to that old castle.
   CHECK: Look at each noun and pronoun. Are there any other descriptive adjectives that tell what kind?

   A long, narrow road leads to that old castle.
   CHECK: Any more descriptors?
2. Look for numerals. Are there any? Yes or no?
   A long, narrow road leads to that old castle.
3. Are there any demonstratives?
   A long, narrow road leads to that old castle.
4. Are there any articles?

   A long, narrow road leads to that old castle.
   CHECK: Read the sentence again just to make sure.
5. You are finished! Go to the next sentence.

FIGURE 7-9
Where are the adjectives?—complete IPS.

presented here. It would take a text to present the illustrated performance sequences for a single course. It is hoped that such illustrations plus practice exercises may someday comprise the core material of your textbooks so that you can teach with them, rather than around them. But for now borrow what you can from your texts and invent the rest. The basic notion remains simple—a picture for every step.

PERFORMANCE OUTLINES

The illustrated performance sequences described in the preceding section emphasized the importance not only of the visual modality of input but also of making visual input permanent so that the teacher's step-by-step modeling of the performance sequence is not covered up and lost as he or she teaches. The notion that instructional models must necessarily stress the visual modality, however, often leaves social studies and English teachers wondering what kinds of pictures they could possibly use to illustrate a concept in government or the writing of an essay.

Modality Matching

A prompt is more powerful the more levels of the prompting hierarchy that it incorporates. Yet although multiple modalities strengthen a prompt, one other factor, apart from using as many modalities as possible, strongly influences the nature of the prompt. Prompts are strengthened by a *match* between the type of prompt that is given and the type of output that is being sought from the student.

Imagine, for example, that an English teacher were to ask students to write an essay, or imagine that a social studies teacher were to ask students to write a research paper. The type of prompting that would most closely match the written output would be a written prompt. The string of prompts for the entire task might be written instructions or an outline of the points to be covered in the essay or research paper. We will refer to that type of instructional model which specifies the content of a concept or of a written assignment as a "performance outline."

A performance outline structures the step-by-step development of the concept or the writing assignment. It may also incorporate guides to concept development, sample topic sentences for a simple essay, or even references to be used for specific portions of a research paper. Literally anything that tells students exactly what to do next as they engage in idea development can serve as part of a performance outline for written or even spoken output on the part of the student.

Simple Outlines for Essays

Sometimes the performance outline for an essay can be deceptively simple. The outline for a four-paragraph essay in a typical junior high school English class shown in Figure 7-10 is illustrative. In order to appreciate what this amount of structure can do for a teacher, you must observe the student passivity and dependency which characterize the helping interactions of guided practice as the teacher attempts to deal with the class "nonwriters."

- I can't think of anything to write.
- How are we supposed to start?
- I'm stuck. This is a dumb topic anyway.
- Can't I just take it home and do it?
- Well, that's all I have to say. I can't help it. I'm done.

As you look over the papers that were turned in—the paragraph fragments, the rambling thoughts, and the perfunctory four-sentence essays—you begin to see how the helpless students have the teacher over a barrel because of the teacher's own lack of

Composition: What would you like to invent, if you could, and why?

Model:

1. Your first paragraph will tell what you would like to invent and why.
2. Your second paragraph will describe your invention. (What colors? How large? What is it made out of? What does it look like?)
3. Your third paragraph will tell how you operate your invention. (How does it work? Do you push buttons? Do you insert something? How is the final result accomplished?)
4. Your fourth paragraph will give a definite ending to your writing and show your reader that you are finished.

EXAMPLES:

Summary:
This invention is something I hope I can someday build.

Question:
Don't you think the world would be better with my invention?

Exclamation:
What a surprise it would be if my invention dream came true!

Note: After going over the model in class, the teacher asked students what word was overworked. They saw right away that it was "invention." So they made a bank of other words to use for invention (e.g., creation, discovery, device).

FIGURE 7-10
Performance outline for a four-paragraph essay.

lesson structure. They can play dumb doing as little work as possible while, in effect, asking the teacher to write the essay for them.

- I can't think of anything *else* to say.
- Where am I supposed to go from here?

If the teacher helps these students develop clear thoughts and complete paragraphs, she gets drawn into lengthy universal helping interactions that further feed the students' "do nothing" helplessness. If the teacher does not help the students, they quit.

The simple performance outline shown in Figure 7-10 has the immediate effect of producing four-paragraph essays. The expectations are clear and the structure is adequate. It takes away the helpless students' license to say, "I don't know what to do next." And this simple performance outline shortens the duration of helping interactions to 5 to 25 seconds (where they should be). Most prompts refer to critical features of the performance outline or to a chart at the front of the class entitled "Parts of a Paragraph." The teacher can do quite a bit of instruction during brief helping interactions because so much of the information contained in the prompt is prepackaged. Most helping interactions, instead of dealing with "I don't know what to write," deal with brainstorming, sentence development, paragraph construction, and the organization of thought.

Although you may not wish to structure every writing assignment in this way, by far the greater problem in the teaching of writing in education today is "understructure" rather than "overstructure." Many educators feel that structure automatically thwarts creativity, but any artist knows that you must master a medium before you can be very creative with it. There is nothing creative about students who either don't know what to do next or know that they won't have to try.

Chapter 9 approaches the teaching of writing from the vantage point of the process of learning rather than the clarity of task analysis. It is possible to use a simple design for essay construction (as in the preceding example) as part of a dynamic, discovery-oriented writing experience. For now we will focus on the clear organization of expectations for student output. Later we will look at the process of instruction.

Playing Hide and Go Seek with Research

Research papers represent perhaps the most common example of an assignment without structure in many classrooms. Students are sent to the library with a topic and nothing more: Write me a paper about. . . . Students learn to hate writing papers because they have never been taught how, and teachers wonder out loud about the quality of the work they get back. Quality work is typically attributed to motivation and brains, whereas poor performance is attributed to laziness and stupidity. In fact, much of the variability in performance is a direct function of a lack of structure in the assignment.

My own teaching of English composition centered around the writing of term papers, theses, and dissertations at the graduate level while I was on the faculty of a highly endowed private university in which the graduate students are *bright* and *motivated*. When, during teacher training, elementary and secondary teachers complain about the quality of the research papers that they receive from students, I often ask, "What kinds of term papers do you think I got from doctoral students at a major university?"

"Oh, boy!" the teachers reply. "If I had bright, motivated students like that, getting them to do research would be a snap!" "Wrong," I reply. "The quality of writing by such bright and motivated students is almost anything imaginable."

The uncomfortable part of my receiving highly variable performance from my bright and motivated graduate students was that it was exceedingly difficult to blame poor performance on the students' stupidity and lack of motivation. If good term papers could be written by college students, these students would write them. Stripped of convenient rationalizations, I had to look at myself to explain the high degree of variability in quality.

One day I experienced a blinding flash of the obvious. Rather than teaching the students to write a good research paper, I was playing a game with them. I was sending them to the library with a topic and little more. I knew where the answers were, but they didn't. The answers were hidden in the library among the books and periodicals, and it was their job to find the relevant information. We were playing a game of hide and go seek.

To put it bluntly, most of the variability in the quality of student work was produced not by their intelligence and motivation but by my own lack of lesson structure. I wanted them "to do their own work." They did the best they could in finding their way without a map, but much time was wasted and much learning was lost in the process.

I decided that on the next term paper, rather than playing a game of hide and go seek, I would tell the students not only exactly what I wanted from them but exactly where to find it. I knew what the major issues where, what the subissues were that related to each of the major research questions, and who had written the most relevant books and articles on each one. I gave the students an outline of a term paper which would correspond to a thorough job of research, and I directed them toward the best sources of information for each topic area.

Previously I would have received term papers that covered some of the topic areas of the research paper beautifully while omitting other topics entirely due to lack of familiarity with the subject. This time I received a stack of consistently excellent papers. They showed plenty of evidence of individual style and creativity, but they all covered the material thoroughly so that every student learned what he or she needed to know about the research topic. Give students a road map, and they will probably reach their objective. If, on the other hand, you don't know where you are going, you are not too likely to get there.

In providing students with a performance outline for a writing or research assignment, newly trained teachers often have the feeling that they are giving the student the answer in a manner analogous to the way they feel after having given a clear prompt during the positive helping interaction. The question, however, is not one of who does the thinking. It is more one of how productive the student's efforts will be. The difference between a structured writing assignment or research exercise on the one hand and hide and go seek on the other hand is the difference between teaching a structured lesson and operating a contest. If you want to teach, provide the structure for learning. If you want to have a contest, provide a minimum of structure and see who does well in spite of it.

CONCEPT MAPPING

"Concept mapping" lies somewhere between the detailed guidance of concept development typical of a performance outline on the one hand and the graphics typical of an illustrated performance sequence on the other hand. A concept map is simply a diagram which shows the relationship between ideas, events, or people.

The graphic aspect of concept mapping allows teachers to depict in particular two aspects of cognitive organization that are partially visual and therefore difficult to depict in a performance outline, namely (1) the relative "size" or importance of related ideas or events and (2) complex or multidimensional relationships between ideas and/or events. Perhaps more important, the construction of concept maps aids students in the preliminary organization of ideas, particularly ideas gleaned from reading, as a preparatory step for writing.

Maryland Buckley Hanf and Owen Boyle of the University of California at Berkeley have written a booklet entitled *Mapping the Writing Journey* as part of the Bay Area Writing Project (Curriculum Publication 15)[1] which provides a variety of exam-

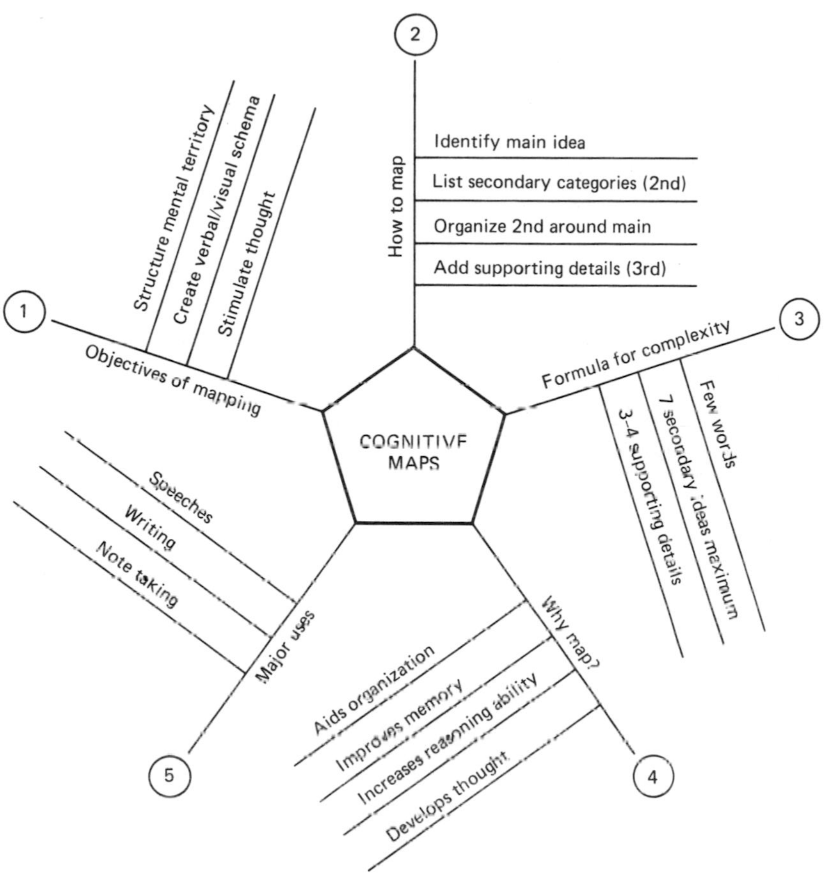

FIGURE 7-11
Map of "Mapping: A Technique for Translating Reading into Thinking," by M. Buckley Hanf.

ples of concept mapping. Dr. Hanf has also prepared a brief and clear explanation of the nature of concept writing in her article "Mapping: A Technique for Translating Reading into Thinking."[2] Alan Edwards, a high school teacher in Arcata, California, who has served as a trainer in both the Classroom Management Training Program and the Bay Area Writing Project, has mapped Dr. Hanf's article for use with his classes, and that map is presented in Figure 7-11 as both an example of concept mapping and a summary of Dr. Hanf's material. Figure 7-12 presents a summary of the more common types of organizational schemata used in concept mapping. They will probably already be familiar to you.

Concept mapping can be used as a means of organizing information in any subject area, but it is particularly useful in helping students collect their thoughts before beginning a writing assignment. The interrelationship of concept mapping, group discussions, performance outlining, and even student team learning is graphically represented in Figure 7-13.

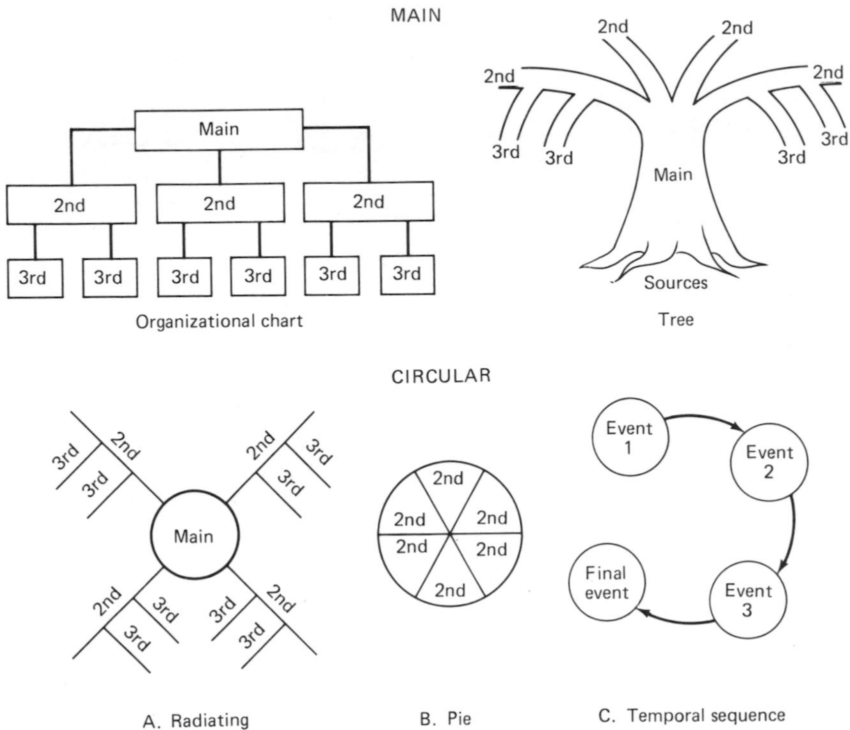

FIGURE 7-12
Typical styles of visual organization in maps.

OVERVIEW

The emphasis on the construction of performance models originally grew from a need to reduce teachers' verbiage as they gave corrective feedback during guided practice. My initial objective was simply to upgrade the teacher's graphics to the point where the teacher needed only point and speak a few words. This simplicity of language served as a safeguard against teachers slipping from praise, prompt, and leave back into the universal helping interaction through sheer verbosity.

To a greater extent than anticipated we found that performance models were crucial to the students developing independent study habits during guided practice. Performance models are the link between the teacher's presentation of the material to the students in class and the students' reteaching of the material to themselves while working on their own. You cannot expect students to become independent learners if, by covering your tracks, you establish yourself as the only source of needed information in the classroom. Students found that they could quickly answer their own questions by consulting the performance model rather than by asking the teacher. And teachers were trained to systematically frustrate dependency by briefly referring to their graphics whenever possible rather than providing lengthy explanations.

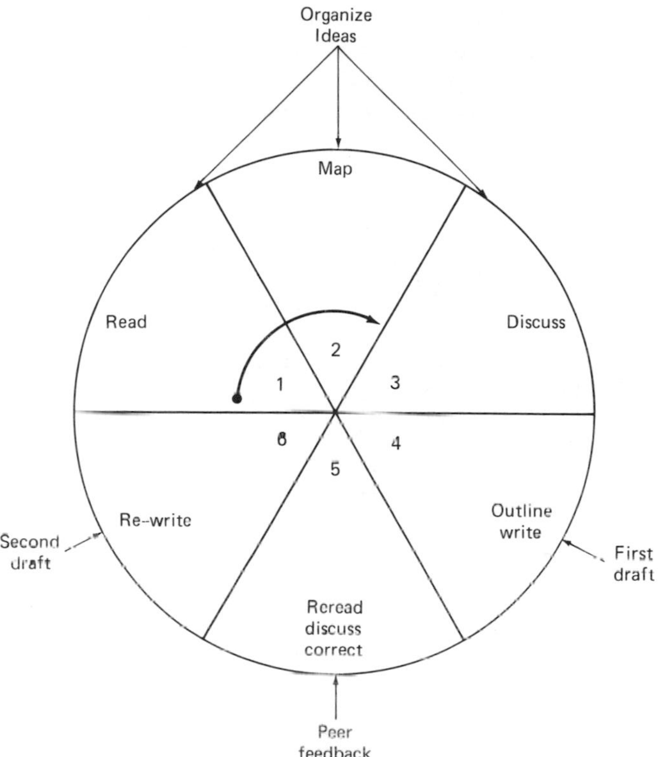

FIGURE 7-13
The use of mapping as part of concept development in writing.

During teacher training, which covered both positive classroom discipline and positive classroom instruction, a great many teachers, particularly at the secondary level, reported that the most important thing they got out of the entire training process was learning to make performance models. I was initially surprised by that feedback since I had regarded performance models in the beginning simply as a way of reducing teacher verbiage during corrective feedback. The emphasis on performance models had, in fact, produced in many cases a renewed focus on task analysis and an understanding of task analysis as an analysis of the *performance of the student* as opposed to an abstract exercise in "goals and objectives" which was of little utility in lesson presentation. Thus, although performance models have indeed paid large dividends in simplifying corrective feedback during guided practice and in promoting independent work habits for dependent students, they have made an equal contribution by upgrading the degree of preplanning and structure prior to lesson presentation.

Experience with training teachers at all levels and in all subject areas, however, has shown me how many teachers have great difficulty in organizing even a simple linear performance sequence into something that students can easily understand. It comes almost naturally to strong teachers, but these same strong teachers also have no idea of how their colleagues flounder in making a simple task appear simple until they become involved in peer teaching. Much more work is needed in the area of task analysis than teachers are presently getting, not only as part of their initial teacher training but also as part of their ongoing professional life.

REFERENCES

1 Hanf, M.B. and Boyle, O. Mapping the writing journey. Berkeley, Calif.: Curriculum Publication 15, Bay Area Writing Project, Dept. of Education, University of California at Berkeley.

2 Hanf, M.B. Mapping: A technique for translating reading into thinking. Berkeley, Calif.: Dept. of Education, University of California at Berkeley.

CHAPTER **8**

THE TRIMODAL CYCLE: GENERIC PROCESS

The focus of *Positive Classroom Instruction* up to this point has been on guided practice and, in particular, on the process of giving corrective feedback efficiently and supportively. By using the positive helping interaction in conjunction with instructional models, we can greatly reduce the *frequency* and *duration* of helping interactions while training students to work independently. Nevertheless, guided practice is one of the latter sections of a structured lesson. In this chapter we focus on those earlier sections of the structured lesson in which initial acquisition of a skill or concept takes place. How can the structured lesson be taught so effectively that teachers are freed from the giving of corrective feedback to focus their energies on more basic and important tasks during guided practice?

"Trimodal teaching" is a name given to a general approach to instruction that is both ancient and perennially new. At its simplest, trimodal teaching can be expressed in two timeless sayings: (1) We learn by doing and (2) we learn best by teaching. We learn by doing because it engages us thoroughly in two main modalities of learning—visual and physical. And we learn best by teaching because it combines all three modalities of learning—verbal, visual, and physical—along with the necessity of clarifying our thoughts as we explain.

When possible, therefore, trimodal teaching makes teachers out of students. And where the act of teaching proves impractical, we at least make "doers" of our students so that they learn through experience—through both input and performance in as many sensorimotor modalities as possible. Underlying trimodal teaching is a simple dimension: *activity—passivity*. Trimodal teaching is a term chosen to constantly remind us of our objective: to engage the student as thoroughly as possible in an active process of learning; a process of saying, seeing, *and doing*.

TEACHING THE STRUCTURED LESSON AS A CYCLICAL PROCESS

Mastery, Long-Term Memory, and Self-Instruction

The objective of the structured lesson is realized in independent practice. In independent practice students are not only able to reproduce and apply new learning, but they are also able to correct error so that they continue to improve with practice (see Chapter 1). The objective of the classroom portion of a structured lesson, therefore, is not only to produce initial mastery but also to commit that mastery to *long-term memory* insofar as possible and to make students *their own teachers*. It is of little use for a student to have initial mastery of a skill or concept, no matter how complete, which is lost before the beginning of independent practice. And it is of limited use for students to have initial mastery if they cannot reconstruct the performance sequence during independent practice to eliminate any error before the error becomes part of their practice. Thus, in addition to simple mastery, the structured lesson must be taught so thoroughly as to make students capable of self-correction and self-reinstruction hours after the end of guided practice in the classroom.

Fortunately the conditions required to produce not only initial mastery but also long-term memory and the capacity to teach the lesson are essentially the same. They can perhaps be best organized around a discussion of (1) multimodal integration and (2) kinetic integration—two processes which can occur side by side during the proper teaching of a structured lesson.

Multimodal integration refers to the integration or "welding together" of the various modalities of sensory input (auditory, visual, and kinesthetic) into a unified and stable memory pattern. Kinetic integration refers to the welding together of the various modalities of *output* (verbal and physical accompanied by visual) into a unified and stable *performance pattern*. The degree of integration of the modalities of input with the modalities of output into a unified and stable whole determines the ultimate success of the structured lesson.

Multimodal Integration Multimodal integration places at center stage the process of converting short-term memory to long-term memory. Almost anything we experience is placed into short-term memory, but for learning to be useful at a later time we must make these fleeting experiences permanent. We must convert them into a stable, long-term memory pattern that is overlearned to the point of being resistant to rapid fading.

How do we create stable long-term memory? Textbooks on memory are rather disappointing on this point. So we will have to rely upon some basic neurology and a lot of teaching experience to produce a useful heuristic model.

Different forms of sensory input are processed initially by different parts of the brain. The left temporal lobe is responsible for converting audition into language, the rear occipital lobe is responsible for vision, and the cerebellum is responsible for kinesthetic feedback. The result of this division of labor is three separate memory systems which are based on three phylogenetically different structures.

Of course, the three memory systems "speak to each other" so that we have a unified perception of experience. This process of speaking to each other is known as "cross-modal transfer." We can, for example, create visual mental imagery from either linguistic or kinesthetic imagery. Thus, I may explain to you how to do something, and you may be able to see it in your mind's eye. Or you may feel an object blindfolded and also see it in your mind's eye. There is a natural process of connection between these different data processing systems that is, of course, of varying strength from one individual to another. It can be either enhanced or ignored during the process of formal instruction.

The three memory systems are not all the same strength, however. Most people can visualize scenes from their childhood in their mind's eye, whereas they cannot accurately reproduce conversation that is but a few minutes old. Like visual memory, physical memory also seems to be relatively stable: Once you learn to ride a bicycle, you never forget.

Although the relative strengths of the different memory systems differ greatly from individual to individual, auditory memory seems usually to be the weakling. Simple instructions or data as brief as an address or a telephone number seem to slip our minds with unnerving regularity. Perhaps this type of loss should not be surprising given the recent phylogenetic history of language compared to the neurology for sight and kinesthesis.

How, then, can concepts expressed in linguistic imagery be made more permanent? From the viewpoint of multimodal integration the answer is fairly straightforward: The strong will carry the weak. Auditory/linguistic input will be remembered better if it is integrated into a memory pattern that includes visual and kinesthetic imagery. When all three modalities are welded together, memory in the strong modalities can prompt memory in the weak modality as an antidote to the rapid decay of linguistic memory. This welding together of the various memory systems is one of the major by-products of learning through doing.

A normal by-product of the relative fragility of auditory memory is its tendency to overload rapidly. Thus, when we give a single instruction to our class, it is fairly easy for everyone to follow. But when we give a whole series of instructions, we lose half the class. It is difficult to accurately store several bits of information that have been given to us auditorially in rapid succession. Avoiding overload is one of the major objectives of trimodal teaching.

Long-term memory, therefore, is maximized (1) if input takes place in small enough bits to avoid short-term memory overload, particularly in the auditory modality (i.e., one step at a time), (2) if input is in all three sensory modalities (auditory, visual, and kinesthetic) rather than in just one or two, and (3) if input is actively integrated not only through temporal juxtaposition but also through some kind of activity that forces the learner to *use* or *express* all the input in a unified fashion before it begins to fade or become confused in short-term memory. Thus, multimodal input must be linked to performance within a short time frame so that short-term memory may be "loaded," integrated, and then "cleared" to long-term memory through juxtaposition and unifying activity. Only when short-term memory has been thus cleared is it ready to be reloaded with the next bit or step of learning with minimal risk of overload and confusion.

Kinetic Integration The final objective of any structured lesson is performance. The only validation of input is output. Until a student can perform a skill correctly or express a concept adequately, mastery cannot be said to exist. Thus, while learning always implies an adequate level of cognitive understanding, mastery is ultimately a matter of doing.

The construction of a stable, integrated memory pattern for instructional input is obviously highly related to a unifying activity—the output or performance by which we form a stable, integrated *performance pattern*. In order to make each modality of input permanent, students must act upon each modality. They must input and output *each step* of the performance sequence in as many modalities as possible as soon as possible so that integration, memory, and performance are maximized one step at a time before forgetting fragments the memory pattern. Students must take a manageable bite of knowledge and then manipulate it, process it, chew it, and swallow it in order to both *internalize* learning as remembered understanding and *externalize* learning as correct performance.

If we want students to walk out of today's class period with any skills or concepts firmly in mind, we must consistently have them learn input via output. To quote an old truism: Teaching is not talking, and learning is not listening. Or, to quote an ancient Chinese proverb:

I hear and I forget
I see and I remember
I do and I understand

The Trimodal Cycle

Embedded within the structured lesson is an "input/output cycle" which, if fully exploited by the teacher, integrates all modalities of input with all modalities of output to form a stable memory/performance pattern (see Table 8-1). This input/output cycle incorporates three steps of the seven-step structured lesson, namely, (1) explanation which incorporates the verbal modality of input and linguistic mental imagery, (2) modeling which incorporates the visual modality of input and visual mental imagery, and finally (3) structured practice which incorporates physical prompting when necessary to create correct performance of the skill along with kinesthetic imagery or "body memory." This input/output cycle allows the student to *say, see, and do one step at a time*. We call this input/output cycle the "trimodal cycle."

The trimodal cycle contains an old friend in a new place—the prompting hierarchy. With multimodal input one step at a time, we provide an optimal prompt that tells and

TABLE 8-1
THE TRIMODAL CYCLE

1 Explanation (say)
2 Modeling (see)
3 Structured practice (do)

shows the student exactly what to do next. While the student knows exactly what to do, we will have him or her do it before short-term memory begins to fall apart. Learning one step at a time, therefore, is essentially the same during both acquisition and guided practice. Consequently, the skills of the positive helping interaction will transfer readily from guided practice to the acquisition phase of the structured lesson.

The Three-Phase Structured Lesson

When taught in a trimodal fashion the structured lesson falls into three distinct phases as described in Chapter 1. The first phase of the structured lesson is "setting the stage." The second phase of the structured lesson is "acquisition." During acquisition the skill or concept of the lesson is initially mastered one step at a time through a series of trimodal cycles. The entire performance sequence is then repeated several times so that the fragile and tentative mastery of first performance is solidified with additional structured practice. The third phase of the structured lesson is "consolidation" in which initial mastery is further repeated during both guided practice and independent practice in order to gain as much additional "insurance against forgetting" as possible. In addition, during consolidation initial mastery will be broadened and further solidified through generalization and discrimination so that the skill or concept can be used correctly in a variety of contexts. The consolidation phase of the structured lesson, therefore, deals directly with issues of retention, generalization, and transfer of learning.

Our understanding of the teaching of a structured lesson, therefore, has evolved over the years into the three-phase process outlined in Table 8-2. The central element, acquisition, incorporates the trimodal cycle. During acquisition initial mastery is produced with both precision and low performance anxiety because of the high degree of structure provided by the teacher. With structured practice tentative initial mastery is strengthened through repetition until it becomes routine and comfortable. Consolidation then follows acquisition and further solidifies and extends the process of learning.

The trimodal teaching of a structured lesson can be represented as a cyclical process

TABLE 8-2
THE THREE-PHASE STRUCTURED LESSON

A Setting the stage
- **1** Raising the level of concern
- **2** Review and background
- **3** Goals and objectives

B Acquisition: The trimodal cycle
- **1** Explanation
- **2** Modeling
- **3** Structured practice

C Consolidation
- **1** Guided practice
- **2** Generalization and discrimination
- **3** Independent practice

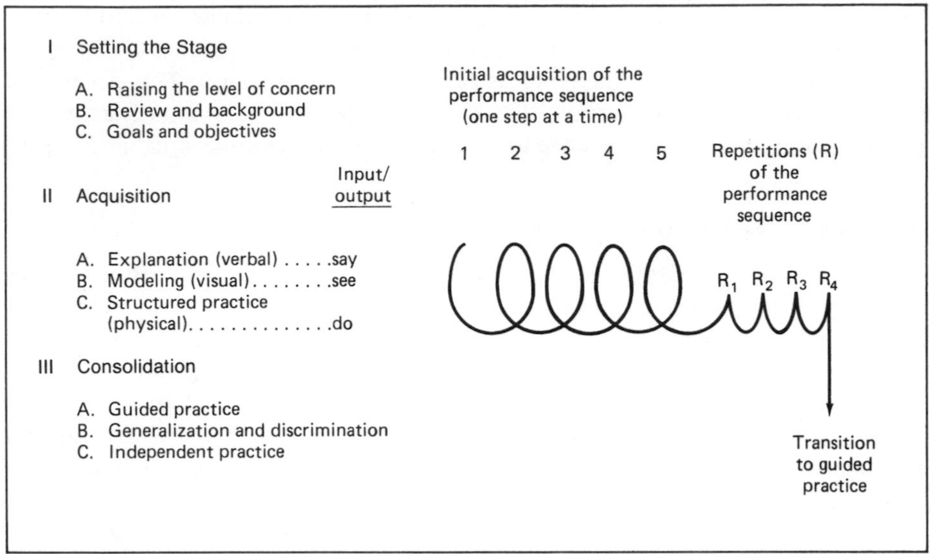

FIGURE 8-1
The teaching of a trimodal lesson as a cyclical process.

as in Figure 8-1. Each step of skill performance or concept acquisition represents a single trimodal cycle. Once the performance sequence has been completed during initial acquisition, the entire sequence is repeated several times during structured practice before the transition to guided practice.

Teaching the Structured Lesson as a Linear Process

On the basis of a decade and a half of classroom observation, I would describe the normative process by which teachers present a structured lesson as "linear." That is, the teacher takes the class from the beginning of the structured lesson right through to the end in an unbroken linear progression—from setting the stage to explanation to modeling right through to guided practice. In many cases, of course, certain steps are omitted altogether, such as adequate structured practice. And in other cases, the teacher leaps all the way from explanation and modeling to a homework assignment with no opportunity for practice at all. But in any case setting the stage is typically followed by the teacher's explaining and demonstrating the entire performance sequence all at one time.

The presentation of a structured lesson as a linear sequence tends to divide the lesson in half in terms of the student's activity and passivity. During the first half of the lesson the teacher is active as she or he present the lesson while the students are relatively passive even though they may be asked to respond occasionally. It is during the first half of the lesson that students are supposed to *absorb* the new input. During the second half of the lesson the students become more active in performing—*after* the teacher has completed the presentation of the lesson.

Although the presentation of new material all at once may seem normal because it is familiar, the linear presentation of a structured lesson produces several unavoidable problems of learning. These problems include (1) student passivity, (2) memory overload, and (3) a lack of conceptual integration.

Student Passivity If a teacher presents all the new input for today's lesson at one time in the form of explanation and modeling, the class will usually have been sitting passively for well over 10 or 20 minutes—long enough for half of them to tune out. To combat the tuning out that comes from an extended period of passivity, effective teachers use a variety of techniques to keep the students awake and aware during the first half of lesson presentation. Thus, as mentioned earlier, effective teachers may ask questions of the class or elicit a group response from time to time.

Yet, in spite of the teacher's best efforts, attempts to maintain student involvement throughout the *linear* presentation of a structured lesson are limited at best. Regardless of the nature of the teacher's "song and dance," a predictable portion of the class will typically tune out before the lesson presentation is completed. Although some of this tuning out is a by-product of the universal helping interaction (the most needy students know that they will soon receive individualized instruction), much of the tuning out is a by-product of *delayed and limited output*. The teacher will pay for that passivity by having to deal not only with a large number of confused or nonperforming students during guided practice but also with the disruptions that will inevitably come from tuned-out students who are placed on hold for corrective feedback.

Memory Overload The second problem with the linear presentation of a structured lesson is *memory overload*. When teachers present a performance sequence or a complex concept to the class in a linear fashion, they present all the steps of the lesson at once without adequate opportunity for skill practice or conceptual integration and expression one step at a time. Even the intermittent responses elicited by the effective teacher are not enough to transfer each step of new input from short-term memory into long-term memory. Consequently, the net result of the linear teaching of a structured lesson is the overload of short-term memory.

Our linear presentation of a structured lesson parallels the instructional errors of the universal helping interaction. In our initial instruction as with the reinstruction of corrective feedback, we typically teach too much and talk too much. We teach several steps of a performance sequence rather than one step at a time, and we then wonder at the confusion and passivity that is produced. In addition, if we produce a graphic on the board to parallel our linear teaching of a skill, we typically produce a single summary graphic in which we systematically "cover up our tracks" (see Chapter 7).

Conceptual Integration The final teaching error that is built into the linear presentation of a structured lesson is a *disjunction* of input and output. Typically the teacher explains a step of a performance sequence or a portion of a concept to the class, but the students do not have the opportunity to immediately explain that same material to anyone else. Thus, for the verbal level of input, there is no student output to match teacher input. In a similar fashion, the teacher models the skill or demonstrates the meaning of the concept to the students, but the students have no opportunity to immediately demonstrate that same material to anyone else. The teacher, once again, is active while the students are passive so that there is no matching student output. Table 8-3 shows the disjunction of input and output in the "linear" teaching of a structured lesson.

The net result of linear teaching is a lack of multimodal integration and kinetic integration one step at a time through participation in a unifying activity. It's not too surprising, therefore, that students have a tendency to forget the concepts contained in the explanation and to become confused with the nature and sequence of skill performance. Many students succeed as a result of a linear lesson presentation in spite of us. Nevertheless, the odds are stacked against mastery for those students of mediocre skill, motivation, or attention span.

Trimodal teaching, in contrast, attempts to have student output match teacher input at each step of the performance sequence. The teacher attempts to involve the students in explanation and modeling along with performance insofar as possible. Specific methods for achieving multimodal and kinetic integration are the subject of Chapter 9.

TRIMODAL TEACHING AND THE POSITIVE HELPING INTERACTION

It would be strange if instruction and reinstruction were fundamentally different. But for me the degree of parallelism did not become clear until the trimodal cycle was isolated as the primary process of acquisition in the teaching of a structured lesson. Trimodal teaching attempts to walk students through skill acquisition with effective prompting at each step so that a student always knows exactly what to do next. The positive helping interaction attempts to do the same thing in the form of corrective feedback. The only difference is that trimodal teaching during acquisition takes students through the performance sequence from beginning to end, whereas the positive

TABLE 8-3
DISJUNCTION OF INPUT AND OUTPUT IN THE LINEAR TEACHING OF A THREE-PHASE STRUCTURED LESSON

	Linear teaching		Cyclic (trimodal) teaching	
	Input	**Output**	**Input**	**Output**
1 Setting the stage				
a Raising the level of concern				
b Review and background				
c Goals and objectives				
2 Acquisition: The trimodal cycle				
a Explanation	X		X	X
b Modeling	X		X	X
c Structured practice		X	X	X
3 Consolidation				
a Guided practice				
b Generalization and discrimination				
c Independent practice				

helping interaction takes students from wherever they are stuck and tutors them with the next step in order to move them forward.

The explanation, modeling, and structured practice of the trimodal cycle incorporate the verbal, visual, and physical modalities of the prompting hierarchy as might an effective prompt during praise, prompt, and leave. Both the trimodal cycle and the positive helping interaction, therefore, use as many dimensions of input and output as possible, and both will strengthen the visual input modality with the use of an instructional model whenever possible. Verbal/visual prompts are the mainstay of typical seatwork, but an effective teacher adds the physical dimension as soon as the muscles of a student need guidance.

In praise, prompt, and leave, the job of praise is *focus* and *review*—to focus the student's attention on the material that immediately precedes new learning and to review prior learning in order to place it into short-term memory. The *prompt* then shows the student exactly what to do next as it creates an open-ended practice exercise. Then the teacher can leave. Affirmation for the students comes both from knowing what they have done right and from feeling that they *can* execute the prompt.

During each trimodal cycle of acquisition, the teacher is typically able to move among the students to see how they are doing and to give corrective feedback as needed. Thus the teacher is able to keep students from falling behind through constant monitoring and the giving of help. By teaching a lesson one step at a time in a cyclical fashion we therefore create the opportunity to give corrective feedback with each step of acquisition rather than later during guided practice when the whole performance sequence has become confused. With trained teachers, corrective feedback during guided practice is relatively rare—far less frequent than during the trimodal cycles of acquisition when the teacher circulates among the students.

The realization that the trimodal cycle and the positive helping interaction are essentially identical brings us back to basics in learning theory. There is one fundamental process of systematic skill building in operant conditioning known as "shaping." Shaping is, most simply, the prompting and reinforcing of successive approximations of task completion. That basic process emerges over and over again as the underlying process of formal instruction whether it be discussion facilitation, corrective feedback, or the initial teaching of a skill or concept. Thus, fundamental skills of the teacher's instructional repertoire will always be skills of prompting and reinforcing. Since reinforcement always focuses on what has been done right so far, it will always be supportive and affirming. Proper instruction does not produce pain.

OVERVIEW

The objective of teaching one step at a time is to produce errorless learning during acquisition so that corrective feedback will rarely be needed during guided practice. The trimodal cycle attempts to make input and output conjunctive at each step of the performance sequence so that students can learn by doing and, wherever possible, learn by teaching as well. Trimodal teaching, therefore, maximizes the likelihood of (1) mastery, (2) long-term memory, and (3) the capacity to teach so that students may work successfully during guided practice in preparation for independent practice. Having students perform each step of new learning during acquisition, however, slows down the pace of the lesson. Far from being a liability, this slowing of the lesson to allow time for performance creates not only the opportunity for adequate processing by students but also the opportunity for corrective feedback by the teacher before moving on to the next step.

CHAPTER 9

TRIMODAL TEACHING AND COOPERATIVE LEARNING

Trimodal teaching has as its objective "learning by doing" and, where possible, "learning by teaching." Its focus is creating the unifying activity by which multimodal integration and kinetic integration take place. It therefore attempts to make learning a process rather than a product. How can classroom teaching provide an experience that cannot be forgotten rather than information that must be remembered?

Trimodal teaching is a heuristic model of effective teaching rather than a specific method. The specific methods are all around us. There are an endless variety of ways of making even the most ordinary assignment into an experience. Creative teachers by the thousands experiment every day as they attempt to transform learning into an activity that engages the whole student one step at a time. Such experiences can cause learners to forget for a while that they are in a classroom as they become lost in the interplay of problem and solution.

This chapter describes some formats for making everyday assignments into activities. Some examples are specific to a given subject, but most of the activities described are general in nature and applicable to a wide variety of subject areas. These activities, however, are only a starter set to help get us hooked on trimodal teaching. By experimenting with activity-oriented lesson formats we will discover that "relevance," "motivation," and "mastery" are unavoidable by-products of doing rather than ideals that must be sought but never attained.

I am indebted to Bernice Medinnas and Janine Roberts of the Los Angeles Unified School District Teacher Center for sharing what they have found as we have all looked high and low over the past several years for activity-oriented teaching and learning formats. This chapter is divided into two major sections: "Experiential Lessons" and "Cooperative Learning." Experiential lessons tend to be more specific in format to a given unit of the curriculum, and interaction tends to be between teacher and student.

Cooperative learning formats, on the other hand, tend to be more formalized routines, and interaction tends to be primarily between the students themselves. The examples given are intended just to provide a nudge to get us all looking for activities that embody the ideas that we are trying to teach in the classroom.

EXPERIENTIAL LESSONS

Learning by doing is an open-ended category. The sky is the limit. But most teachers I interview cannot name five specific things they have done this year that elevate the notion of "doing" beyond doing the assignment. Coming up with good ideas is hard—a true leap of creativity. We all need a little help in order to have experiential lessons very often.

The Jocks and the Shop Teachers

I often find some of the best trimodal teaching at a high school site being done on the athletic field or in shop classes—and often in home economics. The varsity football coach teaches the new play one step at a time. The line coach models for each line position, and the backfield coach models for the backs. They walk through the play over and over until the players get it right. Then they speed it up and repeat the performance sequence until correct execution is comfortable and automatic (structured practice). Then they put the line and backfield together and run the play until it is so smooth that they are ready to try it against a defense. Kids who are barely passing their academic subjects learn the play book perfectly before the first game. It's one step at a time, watch me—now you do it, and practice, practice, practice.

Coaches often don't realize what good teachers they are, and they often regard in-service programs on instructional methodology as being irrelevant to the playing field. We tend to make arbitrary distinctions between one kind of teaching and another when, in fact, all teaching is essentially the same. By not knowing the fundamentals, we are deluded into thinking, for example, that coaching is different from the teaching of the humanities. So the coach stands up and lectures for 50 minutes in front of his or her social studies class.

In the same vein, the shop teacher uses the tried and true method of on-job training: Watch me. Now you do it. Good. Now here's the next thing to do. Look at how I am doing it. Now you try it.

Performing your way through the performance sequence teaches performance. Most home economics teachers have also discovered this as have many typing, foreign language, science lab, and math teachers. In fact we all tend to do our best job of trimodal teaching when we have something physical to teach, like assembling an engine or dissecting a frog. Why? I think it is because we can *see* what the student knows how to do. We get immediate visual feedback that warns us of overload or confusion, and we instinctively simplify the task by breaking it down into smaller steps, demonstrating what to do if we have to and having the student repeat it a few times until we can see that it is coming out right.

The difference in these "doing" lessons and "concept" lessons where ideas are the meat of the course is largely that we have not yet devised enough ways of learning concepts by doing. One of the most straightforward ways of teaching concepts through doing is by simulation games. Games stores are full of them, from the fall of the Roman Empire to the Battle of Waterloo. Once having played a good simulation game, you have a hard time forgetting the history lesson. Perhaps some day most of the social sciences will be taught by simulation, but until that day comes, teachers will have to supply experience-oriented lessons as best they can.

Relevance in Social Studies

The truly creative leaps in classroom instruction often come in a moment of desperation. High school history and social studies teachers are particularly prone to desperation given the apathy of the average high school student toward the nature and roots of what certain adults refer to as civilization.

For example, a high school social studies teacher who had become familiar with the objectives of trimodal teaching found himself confronted by a class that could not relate to issues of third world economic and political unrest. Apathy hung in the air as the teacher tried his best to relate current events to poverty, illiteracy, high birth rate, economic exploitation of peasants, and long histories of nondemocratic government. Finally, in desperation the teacher pulled out all stops in the name of relevance. He told the class that tomorrow's assignment was to skip lunch in the school cafeteria because he was going to bring enough food for everybody in fourth period. Shouts of approval resounded.

The next day the teacher ran out during his lunch break and bought one hamburger, one order of french fries, and one chocolate shake at a fast-food restaurant. Then at a Chinese restaurant he bought one large bowl of steamed rice to take out. When the students arrived for fourth period, the teacher gave one student the burger, shake, and fries. Then he told everybody else that for lunch they would have to split the steamed rice. The students looked at each other incredulously and then looked at the lucky student as she sheepishly looked down at the burger, shake, and fries—forbidden from sharing by the teacher, who instructed the students that sharing was not part of the experience.

Bitching and moaning filled the air. "This isn't fair!" "What a drag!" But soon a few students, stomachs growling, began to take some rice. Then some more joined in as the air was filled with snide remarks directed toward the "lucky" student. The classroom atmosphere turned dark as students got in touch with feelings of anger regarding their hunger and the unfairness of the situation. That demonstration with the hamburger, shake, and fries was worth 2 weeks of animated classroom discussion concerning the plight of the less developed nations of the world. Any form of doing is fair game. If you have never gone hungry, it is hard to understand the effects of poverty on the way people look at the world—at least until you have "done it" a little.

A Science Experiment

I remember a science lesson my wife, Jo Lynne, taught in fifth grade. Jo Lynne was the kind of teacher who volunteered to go to a special workshop every weekend for a month just so she could have access to a new science kit that the district was supplying to every school (one per school). This was in the mid-sixties after we had gotten over the trauma of Sputnik and before all the discovery-type science curricula that had been developed to close the technology gap had unfortunately fallen into disuse. Although there was a budget to buy the kit, there was no budget to replace the consumables. So you ended up with a booklet and some glassware.

In any case, the lesson was on protective coloration in fish. There was a large poster depicting an underwater view of a stream bed with four different habitats defined by the color and texture of the surrounding rocks, sand, mud, and plants. There were cutout plastic fish of various color patterns that would stick to the poster.

Jo Lynne would have the students put their heads down on their desks while she placed one of the fish in one of the quadrants of the poster. Then on a signal the students raised their heads and looked. One second later the poster was covered, and the students had to mark on their papers where the fish was.

After having repeatedly looked at all the possible combinations of fish colorations and backgrounds, the class tallied their answers to compute their "hit score"—the percentage of correct judgments. Then the class calculated the extent to which they were guessing with each combination. The closer the class average came to chance (pure guessing), the better the pattern of coloration protected the fish from being seen by a predator in a given habitat.

I remember the experiment because I was learning the same tachistoscopic observation technique in graduate school at the time. Given an adequate experience, fifth graders could understand the concepts locked away in the chapters of a graduate level textbook on experimental methodology. I never forgot that. Unfortunately, the marvelous curriculum that my wife used has been gathering dust on a shelf for many years now. But such experiences still exist should you care to dust them off.

Large Motor Addition

I was approached by a first grade teacher who was frustrated by the slowness of some of her students in mastering basic number facts. Some students seemed to have almost no concept of numerality. In desperation we resorted to something physical—a large motor adding activity. We went outside and helped the kids draw number lines on the playground with chalk (actually a string of ten squares with numbers 1 to 10 in the squares). Then we began counting and then adding by hopping up the number line. We all hopped together with the teacher being the chief number hopper. It went so well that we began to subtract (doing every addition problem frontwards and backwards, i.e., $2 + 4 = 6$ and $6 - 4 = 2$). Eventually we got so cocky that we made it into a game with kids from competing teams racing. Mastering math facts became an extra recess.

I read in a magazine a long time ago of a teacher in Boston who taught kids to spell by cheerleading the words. Kids were out of their seats moving and dancing to the spelling. Some of the most disadvantaged elementary students in Boston became super spellers through large motor activity. I have often wondered since then why the method never spread.

Learning to Alphabetize

A fourth grade teacher had just spent an entire period trying to teach the class to alphabetize a list of words, only to make the whole thing as clear as mud. As the teacher sat glumly looking over a set of incorrect papers, one of her students, a bright girl, came to the teacher's desk and said, "Would you mind if I tried to teach everybody to alphabetize after lunch?" Having nothing to lose, the teacher agreed.

During the lunch recess the little girl worked feverishly over a stack of 3 × 5 cards. First she put all the letters of the alphabet on separate cards and taped them on the wall all around the room in alphabetical order. Then she wrote vocabulary words on additional cards so that there were enough for half the class.

When the students had taken their seats following lunch recess, the girl (not being shy) stood up and said:

> OK, I'm going to divide the class in half. This side is Team A, and this side is Team B. I'm going to pass these cards out to Team A first, but leave them face down until I say go. When I say go, turn your card over and look at the first letter of the vocabulary word on the card. Then go line up in front of the letter of the alphabet that matches the first letter of the word on your card. I'll time you to see how long it takes you to line up alphabetically. OK, go!

The students looked at their cards and began scurrying to their places, asking for directions from each other as they went. When all the students found their places, the young teacher announced that it had taken them 26 seconds to alphabetize the words on the cards; then she collected the cards and had the students sit down.

Next, the girl passed the cards out to Team B, gave them the same directions, and set them loose. Having learned from watching the other team, they lined up correctly in 15 seconds. They were declared the winners. The first team complained. Team A wanted a second chance because Team B got to watch them before it was their turn.

"OK," said the young teacher, "but this time you will have to line up by the *second* letter of the word on your card. Turn your cards over and go!"

There is nothing quite like getting a methods course from a 9-year-old. Learning by doing isn't enough. Let's make it a team game while we're at it.

Going to the Chalkboard

> OK, class, lets all go to the chalkboard. We're going to learn our new list of spelling words for this week.

> Class, let's take our places at the chalkboard. Today we are going to learn to multiply fractions.

These vignettes of classroom life are flashbacks of mine. Teachers don't talk this way anymore (unless they are lucky enough to work in an old building) because they don't have enough chalkboard space for all the students.

We used to grin as we got out of our seats and headed to the chalkboards—free to move, looking for a good piece of chalk and an eraser that wasn't worn out. Then we got to write with chalk on the board. We could erase and start over as easy as pie. We looked forward to it.

> "All right, class, let's take the first word and write it together. Watch me, and I'll write it first as we all sound it out."

I rarely get nostalgic for the good old days until I remember how easy it was for the teachers in those classrooms surrounded with chalkboards to produce learning by doing one step at a time and make it feel like preferred activity time (PAT).

Summary

Trimodal teaching is not only a model of the instructional process but also an imperative to make learning an experience. How do you do that? Well, you don't—not by yourself. Nobody is creative enough to come up with good activity-oriented lessons to fit every major skill or concept that they plan to teach this year without a lot of help. You need a team of people working together for years to develop that kind of quality instruction. In one school district in which I was privileged to work, all the social studies teachers at the high school level are in their third year of collaboration in an effort to develop trimodal lessons for every major curriculum objective. Through leadership that was strong before I arrived (a committed superintendent and a teacher center staffed by experienced professional development specialists), they have long since surpassed what I was able to give them.

Yet, although not all teachers can be part of a collegial process at their school site which continually works on the improvement of lesson presentation, we can all be part of a collegial process in a larger sense. The following section shares trimodal teaching formats that have proved their worth over the years in a wide range of grade levels and teaching formats. They are presented here as a form of sharing so that we may all have some good "learning by doing" formats at our fingertips for everyday classroom work. With these formats, students get involved with each other to create a stimulating peer learning process. Consequently, we refer to them collectively as "cooperative learning."

COOPERATIVE LEARNING

Cooperative learning puts students to work helping each other while the teacher is freed to monitor the peer teaching and learning process that is created. Cooperative learning formats described in this chapter are organized under two headings, "Paired Learning" and "Small Group Learning."

Paired Learning

Paired learning has students work in pairs or as partners, an idea no doubt as old as teaching. What more straightforward way to have students receive feedback when performing a skill or to collaborate in problem solving when there is not enough teacher to go around? Thus students may read to partners during reading time so that half the students can be practicing while the other half listens and monitors (see Chapter 5). Or, we may have lab partners in high school chemistry, physics, or biology share the work of the experiment and help each other figure it all out.

Often paired learning is quite informal, simply putting two students together with a job to do, whereas at other times the process may be much more formalized in order to maximize speed and efficiency. We will begin with an example of a highly structured paired learning format.

Dyadic Teaching Dyadic teaching is one of the most highly structured forms of trimodal teaching and one which most closely replicates the heuristic model of cyclical teaching described in the preceding chapter. I first came to appreciate its power during teacher training as a means of speeding up the acquisition of praise, prompt, and leave, but it is highly applicable to a variety of typical seatwork lessons. Dyadic teaching would most commonly be used to teach complex sequential skills one step at a time. Its objective is to produce errorless learning with maximal opportunity for students to learn by teaching.

Let us use mathematics once again as a starting place since its performance is both sequential and graphic. Keep in mind, however, that the football coach teaching a new play to the team, a shop teacher training the class to use a piece of machinery, a science teacher in a laboratory, or an English instructor teaching grammar might all be using some version of the same step-by-step, cyclical teaching process.

Pairing Up for Output Imagine that we are teaching a mathematics lesson such as the multiplication of two binomials for which we have presented an illustrated performance sequence (see Chapter 7). We would typically explain the first step of the multiplication process to the students and we would then model it at the chalkboard. Now let us stop for a moment and make output match input.

As soon as we assign to ourselves the task of having students output every step of a performance sequence in every modality as soon as they receive it, we are almost hit in the face with the notion of pairing up the students into teaching dyads. If we explain and demonstrate the performance of a skill one step at a time, and if students then do the same thing, they are learning in the best way possible: by teaching. The most convenient person for students to teach, of course, is the student sitting next to them.

Dyads are often the most efficient form of grouping for initial acquisition of a skill since it makes teachers out of the largest number of students at any given time. Thus, in the teaching of the multiplication of two binomials, we first pair each student with a partner. Before explaining and modeling the first step of the performance sequence, the teacher may instruct the students as follows until the routine becomes internalized.

> I want you all to watch carefully as I teach. Then, as soon as I am done, the partner on the right side of the pair [pointing] will turn to the partner to your left [pointing] and explain and demonstrate the first step of the computation as I have explained and demonstrated it to you here at the chalkboard. Write the same graphic on your paper that I write here on the board as you explain to your partner.
>
> As you are teaching your partners, I'll walk among you to see how everyone is doing. As the first partner completes the teaching, I want you to teach the other direction. At that time the partner on the left—the one who has just been taught—turns to their partner on the

right and *repeats* the teaching to them. Both of you will repeat my explanation of the first step of the performance sequence, and both of you will reproduce the first step of my performance model on your paper as you demonstrate.

Before copying the first problem on the board, the teacher begins the lesson with review which may include multiplication sign rules. Let us imagine that the teacher also wishes to have the students create a performance model on the left side of their papers to serve as a study guide. The teacher may say:

Copy the problem $(x+3)\ (x-9)=$ on the left where we'll construct our performance model. Next copy the problem again on the right and label it "problem 1." Once we have our papers set up properly, we will be ready to begin. Explain the directions to your partner as you set up your paper, like this.

Model	**Problem**
$(x+3)\ (x-9)=$	(1) $(x+3)\ (x-9)=$

Now that the teacher has explained the nature of the problem, it is time to begin to learn the process of computation. The teacher may begin the next step as follows:

Let me have your attention again. We are ready to begin the process of multiplication. First we multiply the x in our first binomial times the x in the second binomial. Let me draw a line connecting those two numbers as a guide to remind you of the sequence of multiplication. Now, when you multiply 3 times 3, you get 3^2. And, when you multiply 5 times 5 you get 5^2. When you multiply x times x you get x^2 in the same fashion. X is a number even though it is unknown, and therefore you can square it just like any other number. Your first multiplication will look like this. Teach your partner.

Model	**Problem**
$(x+3)\ (x-9)=x^2$	(1) $(x+3)\ (x-9)=x^2$

As teachers explain the next step of multiplication, they may also explain the purpose of the graphics that they and the students are producing. It might sound something like this:

Let me have all your eyes forward, and I'll show you the next thing that we do with the multiplication of two binomials. First of all, however, as you teach your partner, I want you to review what we have done so far as you *recopy* the problem a second time on the left-hand side of your paper under the heading "model." You will produce a *second* picture of the problem with another curved line indicating the numbers to be multiplied. This diagram will be part of the study guide that we make as we teach. Watch and listen as I review.

Let's recopy our problem a second time here beneath our first graphic. Say it out loud as you recopy it when you teach your partner. x plus 3 times x minus 9 is our problem. x times x is x^2. Now that we have multiplied the x in our first binomial times the x in our second binomial, we'll multiply the x in our first binomial [pointing] times the minus 9 in our second binomial. I'll draw a line on my second graphic as a reminder of the sequence of multiplication. I want you to draw the same line as you teach your partner.

Now we have a plus x times a minus 9. What will our sign be? [pointing to the sign rule. "Minus," the class responds.] Good! Always compute your signs first [The teacher writes it on the board]. Next, x times 9 is written $9x$. Remember, by convention, we always put the digit before the unknown. [The teacher writes this on the board as well.] So, class, *plus x* times *minus* 9 is? . . . ["Minus $9x$" the class responds.] Good. Teach your partner as you copy the graphics onto your paper. Look at my graphic on the board if you have any questions.

Model	**Problem**
$(x+3)(x-9)=x^2$	(1) $(x+3)(x-9)=x^2-9x$
$(x+3)(x-9)=x^2-9x$	

To save space we will not complete the teaching of this lesson. A few cycles gives at least the flavor of this particular approach to paired teaching. At each step of the calculation teachers produce a new graphic as part of their performance model. The new portion of the answer produced on the performance model on the left side of the paper would then be transferred to Problem 1 on the right-hand side of the student's paper. At every step students would explain the computation to their partners as they wrote it on their papers. In this fashion the students would learn the lesson by teaching it while copying the teacher's lesson plan to take home for homework.

Dyadic Teaching and Quality Assurance Quality *assurance* in industry is the process of continually ensuring that a product is being built right exactly as designed. Quality *control*, in contrast, is the process of ensuring that the product works properly before it leaves the factory. Quality control, therefore, frequently involves costly repair as defective products are detected at some point in production and fixed. Quality control is analogous to the corrective feedback of guided practice in a structured lesson, whereas quality assurance is analogous to the process of learning it right the first time during acquisition. By far the cheaper way to build a perfect product or to learn a lesson is to do it right the first time in order to eliminate the need for costly fixing or corrective feedback later on.

During one cycle of trimodal teaching, one-third of the time is spent in *teacher* instruction and two-thirds is spent in *peer* instruction. Thus, most of the instructional time is spent in output by the students. In dyadic teaching teachers will find that, while the students are working much harder, the teachers have time on their hands. What do teachers do during all that time while students are teaching each other?

Dyadic teaching frees the teacher's time for continuous quality assurance. While the students are teaching each other, the teacher moves among the desks looking over the shoulders of the students while listening to their explanations to make sure that everyone is teaching the skill correctly. During a typical trimodal cycle teachers can double-check the teaching of almost every student in a typical class of thirty-five students at least once if they have an appropriate room arrangement and move continually. If any student is struggling or making an error, the teacher steps in with a positive helping interaction (typically just a prompt) and moves on. Thus there is constant checking for understanding as the skill is being built so that nobody falls behind.

The first quality assurance system during dyadic teaching is therefore the teacher. The second level of quality assurance is provided by the students themselves. Teachers will pair students in a highly pragmatic fashion in order to maximize the probability of correct peer teaching. The rules of thumb for pairing students are:

1 Avoid pairing best friends as well as enemies.

2 Pair fast students with slow (i.e., less motivated) students.

3 Use your judgment concerning the compatibility of various pairs of individuals (almost any compatible pairing will work).

4 Have the slower student teach first.

If the teacher pairs fast students with slow students, the slow students will be teaching someone who can correct them should they err. And the slower students will be taught by a peer who will probably teach the lesson correctly. Thus the fast students serve a quality assurance function for the performance of the slow students quite independent of teacher feedback.

When teachers pair the students, they should seat them so that the slow student is the *first* member of the dyad to teach each cycle of the lesson. Teaching first requires an active orientation toward the teacher's presentation, and it requires less short-term memory. Slow students have a greater tendency to slip into passivity and not listen to the teacher if they know that the bright student sitting next to them will repeat the input right away. Being the first one of the pair to teach forces the slower students to attend more carefully since they will immediately be responsible for performance.

In addition, the movement pattern of dyadic teaching tends to reduce the disruptiveness of all members of the class, both slow students and fast students alike. The most needy students and the middle-of-the-roaders are kept from tuning out by the constant necessity to perform. They are never on hold long enough to tune out. Problems of poor motivation and poor attention span tend to be reduced not only because of the inherent kinetics of the method but also because of the two quality assurance systems mentioned in the previous section.

And, while moving among students to monitor the quality of performance and to give corrective feedback as needed, the teacher is continually "limit-setting on the wing" (see Chapter 7 of *Positive Classroom Discipline*). Talking to neighbors and fooling around rarely even get started since the students are already busy talking in a productive way and since the teacher is always standing nearby or looking over their shoulders. Teachers rarely report having to use the formal limit-setting sequence during this particular format of trimodal teaching.

Quality Assurance and Guided Practice One of the most noticeable by-products of dyadic teaching as far as corrective feedback is concerned has been that most corrective feedback is now given during the *acquisition* phase of the structured lesson rather than during guided practice. By moving corrective feedback forward in the process of teaching a structured lesson, teachers are not only able to do a more rapid and precise job of quality assurance, but they are also freed even further from giving corrective feedback during guided practice so that they can do other more important tasks. Frequently almost no helping interactions are needed during guided practice when students have been adequately trained to use the teacher's lesson plan as a study guide.

During guided practice teachers continue to move among the students, but they will now be free to check work as a further part of their quality assurance system rather than being tied to giving corrective feedback. By the end of guided practice most of the students' work will be graded. It is hoped that this will free teachers from paper grading after class to a large extent so that they can now spend more of their nonclassroom teaching time in lesson preparation rather than in clerical work.

The quality assurance and work check which the teacher is able to provide during guided practice, however, is part of a much broader topic in classroom management, namely, incentive systems for diligence and excellence. The technology of incentive management for work productivity is the subject of the next chapter.

Values Implicit in Dyadic Teaching Teachers often ask about the bright students in the class. Won't they be bored if the instruction is slowed down and repeated as it is in dyadic teaching? One of the ironies of this format is that it tends to keep the brighter students engaged in the learning process to a heightened degree just as it does the slower students. The bright students have an important job to do throughout the lesson—teaching a slower classmate. Your gifted students will often understand the lesson when you are halfway through the explanation. The remainder of the lesson often seems tedious and boring to them, and they become restless and disrupt or complain.

During dyadic teaching, however, there is a more demanding task accompanied by an implied value system. It is no longer the task of the bright students to simply learn the lesson for *their* own sake, which is essentially a self-centered endeavor. Rather, students are responsible to *each other.* It is not the bright students' job to simply excel but, rather, to make sure that their *partners* succeed. Thus, the bright members of the class are their neighbor's keepers.

Yet, although explaining and demonstrating the lesson to a slower student is a far more exacting and therefore engaging task to most bright students than simply learning the lesson themselves, sometimes bright students become impatient because they do not care about the other student, or the ability spread of the group is simply too great. In the case of not caring, values clarification becomes an integral part of peer teaching. And, in the case of an awkwardly wide ability spread, teachers may consider either pairing students closer in ability level or ability grouping as they normally would. Dyadic teaching does not imply whole group instruction.

Dyadic Teaching and Task Analysis With this format of trimodal teaching in which students teach each other one step at a time, task analysis takes on a new dimension. In an earlier chapter (Chapter 7) we stressed that task analysis comes not from the logic of the teacher but from the performance of the student. For the task analysis to be useful it must match the functional steps of skill performance. Thus, to help themselves with task analysis, teachers might walk themselves through the actual task with one of their average students in mind in order to produce steps of appropriate size which match the actions that the students will be asked to do.

In dyadic teaching when students are each other's teachers during every cycle of a performance sequence, as in the previous example, the teacher is given an even more concrete and operational criterion for performing a task analysis: How much can one student explain and demonstrate to another student without getting confused?

Although there is no best or final task analysis for any task, analyzing the step-by-step teaching of the lesson in terms of students explaining it to each other helps greatly in making task analysis and, in particular, the size of each step something tangible and easily imaginable for the teacher. In any task analysis, of course, the teacher is an artful gambler, and she or he may in fact combine bits of performance for a fast class that she or he would separate for a slower class.

Just as important, during a trimodal cycle teachers can alter their task analysis in the heat of the moment as they read the feedback they are getting from the class. Thus, for example, a teacher might explain and demonstrate a trimodal cycle to the class only to find that several of the students either look confused or are becoming confused in their explanations to their partners. Before the cycle proceeds any further, the teacher can interrupt and say: "Class, let me have your attention for a moment. I've made a mistake here, and I want to fix it before we go any further. I think I've crammed too much information into that last step. Let's start over and break it in half. Watch me and I will reteach the next step. Just explain and demonstrate the material that I give you now."

As a general rule, dyadic teaching makes checking for understanding not only a continuous operation but also a precision operation. Typically teachers can get a very quick sense of when they have gone too far and have overloaded the students during a trimodal cycle.

Paying Our Dues in Structured Practice After the teacher has walked the students through the performance sequence one step at a time with peer teaching while producing a performance model as a by-product, the students will have a thorough *initial* grasp of the lesson. They do not, however, have a very well solidified memory pattern or performance pattern, since they have completed the performance sequence only once in their life. In order to solidify initial acquisition, we must repeat the performance sequence right away several times in the form of structured practice or drill before forgetting has time to set in.

As teachers repeat the performance sequence three or four or five more times, they pick up the pace as performance becomes more and more automatic. In order to pick up the pace, teachers typically *eliminate* dyadic teaching and simply walk students through the performance sequence one step at a time. They refer to the performance model with each step so that students become accustomed to using the performance model as a study guide. And periodically during each repetition of the performance sequence the teacher has the student team check each other's work as a quality assurance device since the teacher no longer takes the time to circulate among all the students with every step of computation.

After the students have walked through three or four or five more problems to the point where performance is becoming rapid and automatic, the teacher may have the following interaction with the class:

> OK, class, we are really getting good at this. We have completed four problems together, and we can see how the same pattern is repeated with each problem. Now, I want you to open your books to page 73 and look at the practice set at the top of the page. Our assignment today is the fifteen problems in this practice set. If you look at the first four problems of the

practice set, you'll see that they are the four problems that we have done together. Your answers are correct, of course, and we have double-checked them. So take your pencils and mark the first four of your problems correct. You are all "four for four" in this assignment. Congratulations! Now, start with problem 5 and continue. I will be coming around to see how you are doing.

Teachers get mixed results with dyadic teaching in the primary grades owing to the immaturity of some students and their hesitancy to verbalize to each other. If the teacher patiently instructs the students in how to teach each other, they usually become good at it in a few weeks. If you decide that the full dyadic teaching routine is impractical, however, use the routine described above for structured practice, and you will get most of the success which we have come to expect from dyadic teaching.

Limitations of Dyadic Teaching The preceding example is only one among an endless variety of lesson formats that enable students to learn by doing and, when practical, to learn by teaching. It should not be taken as synonymous with trimodal teaching. In fact, as lesson formats go, dyadic teaching can be rather tedious, a by-product of its very thoroughness. Yet it can produce an amazing increase in the rate of learning for complex tasks, especially for the bottom half of the class. Perhaps a quote from a trained teacher can help put the preceding example of dyadic teaching into perspective.

> I found that teaching in partners is really good, but I can't use it all the time. While everyone learns the lesson, and I mean *everyone*, nevertheless the kids just can't sit still for it, literally, lesson after lesson. So I only use dyadic teaching for key skills and concepts that we will be working with for a while. Then after they all have the basic skill down pat, I back off and use a variety of other lesson formats that I have become comfortable with over the years.

Informal Paired Formats One of the leaders in developing both paired and small group learning formats for classroom use, particularly in the area of teaching of writing, has been Julia Gottesman of the Los Angeles County schools. Her booklet, "Peer Teaching: Partner Learning and Small Group Learning, A Handbook for Teachers,"[1] provides a wealth of ideas for both the tasks that can best be accomplished in a paired learning format and the rules and structure needed to make each format work.

"Almost any learning activity in which students speak, listen, read to each other or share their written work" is appropriate for peer teaching, writes Mrs. Gottesman, including such things as:

- Evaluating written work based upon established criteria.
- Editing and proofreading written communications.
- Administering individualized spelling tests and quizzes.
- Practicing sentence combining and manipulation.
- Reading a short story.
- Discussing questions about a reading selection.
- Responding to written compositions.
- Recalling the sequence of scenes from a film or play.
- Making lists from observations as in a science project.
- Improvising dialogue or preparing a speech.

The real difference in the teacher's role in cooperative learning formats as opposed to most traditional teaching formats is that teachers become managers of a peer-learning process rather than dispensers of facts. Rather than standing in front of the class and addressing the group, they *move* continuously among the students monitoring their performance and giving brief input and corrective feedback as needed. It is therefore the teacher's job to maximize the students' opportunity to interact with each other around learning—to express thoughts, solve problems, share perceptions, and help each other.

Obviously cooperative learning rests on good discipline management since students are more active in many areas of the classroom. The opportunity to fully exploit cooperative learning might be regarded as one of the dividends of *Positive Classroom Discipline*—particularly in the classrooms of teachers who are presently afraid of peer interaction because "the whole class gets out of control in no time!"

Small Group Learning

Whereas paired learning gives students greatly increased opportunity to perform with much closer monitoring by both peers and teacher, small group learning greatly expands the range of interactions that students can experience in learning with their peers. In small groups students can receive ideas and feedback from many people, become comfortable in talking to a group, and develop a point of view based on the give and take of debate. Students also learn to share, to seek help, to give help, and to cooperate in group problem solving. They can learn to lead as well as follow. And they can help develop consensual rules for evaluating complex work, such as writing, that they can then apply to their own work.

Yet group learning requires structure in order to remain goal-oriented and productive. Simply breaking a class into groups and committees guarantees nothing except a quantum leap in opportunities for students to goof off. This section provides some small-group learning formats which, because of their well-developed structure, can make assignments that are commonly dreaded by students, such as creative writing or research reports, a joy. As in all cooperative learning formats, much of the motivation and activity of learning comes from a well-orchestrated peer process.

Leaders in developing cooperative learning formats for groups have been The Bay Area Writing Project[2] which began at the University of California at Berkeley and has now spread across the nation and the Student Team Learning Project[3] at the Center for Social Organization of Schools, the Johns Hopkins University. A few examples of group cooperative learning formats will, it is hoped, stimulate teachers and administrators to seek out more information and training in this area. The first two examples of small group learning focus on the development of writing and research skills.

Read Around Groups (RAGs) As mentioned in Chapter 7, the amount of structure for writing typically offered both elementary and secondary students by their teachers can be summarized as: I want you to go to the library and write a three-page paper about———.

Students procrastinate and fret and whine and cry as they sit at the kitchen table trying to grind out the report for tomorrow while their parents say, "You should have started earlier. Now you've let it all go until the last minute!"

The blank paper stares back at the student, waits him out, and finally defeats him. The student has been writing since first grade without being taught how to write. What is good writing? How do you brainstorm it, organize it, discuss it, generate a rough draft, analyze it according to well-understood criteria, and begin systematically to rewrite?

The aversion to writing generated by early experiences haunts our teaching efforts throughout students' schooling. Performance anxiety is expressed as negativism, procrastination, and an endless list of excuses that add up to "I'll sit and listen in class, but please don't make me write!" This resistance to writing hits us particularly hard around the teaching of concepts—for example, in a high school social studies class—as we attempt to convert one-way instruction (such as a lecture) and prolonged student passivity (such as listening to the lecture for most of the period) into a trimodal format.

This resistance to writing may ruin our best intentions of doing trimodal teaching, of making the students active learners rather than passive spectators. When we say, "All right, let's take pencil and paper and put our thoughts down while they are still fresh in our minds," we get:

- Do we *have* to?
- Oh, brother.
- Can we do this for homework?
- I don't have any paper.
- How many words does it have to be?
- I hate this.

This disheartening student response is enough to discourage the best of us. Many a potentially excellent teacher has been shaped into a chronic lecturer by the lack of satisfying alternative teaching formats. Enter Read Around Groups or RAGs.

RAGs offers the key ingredients of a group PAT—it is social, fast-paced, gamelike. It is a cooperative learning format that indirectly provides a high degree of peer tutoring. And it helps students to develop functional criteria of good writing at their age level as it generates revisions of increasing quality.

The UCLA Writing Project[3] has outlined the process for creative writing roughly as follows. This same process, however, can be used for both technical and creative writing. For technical writing substitute your favorite mode of presentation such as a brief lecture for "brainstorming" and "silent period" in Prewriting.

1 Prewriting
  a Brainstorming: Begin with a general concept and brainstorm. List all ideas on the board *around* the main idea. (Do not list ideas in columns, or many students will pick from items 1 to 5 on the list.)
  b Silent period: The group eventually falls silent. Wait several minutes if necessary to let ideas percolate during this "wait time."
  c Continue brainstorming: Change the color of your chalk and after a pause resume

brainstorming, allowing it to go far afield. Richer ideas with more emotion attached to them are typical of the second phase of brainstorming.

2 Writing
- **a** Have the students write for 10 minutes.
- **b** Give a 1 minute warning and be strict about the time limit.

3 RAGs Procedures (Organized in advance)
- **a** Have each student select a five-digit code number to be placed on the top of his or her paper.
- **b** Organize students into groups of four.
- **c** Designate a leader for each group. Seat them so that the leader can pass papers to the next group from a seated position.
- **d** Following the 10 minutes of writing, have each leader collect the group's papers and pass them to the next group. (Do not have students read their own group's papers.)
- **e** Have the group leaders pass out the four papers they have just received to the four members of their group.
- **f** Students read one paper (30 seconds for a half to one page) and then, on the teacher's signal, pass the papers to their right *within* their group. Repeat this process until all papers are read.
- **g** After reading all papers, the group decides which one is best, and the leader marks the code number on a record sheet.
- **h** The group leader then collects the papers and, on the teacher's signal, passes them to the next group. Continue this process until every group reads every paper *except their own.*

4 Discussion
- **a** The teacher polls the group leaders and lists on the board the code numbers of the papers selected by each group as best.
- **b** The teacher reads aloud papers that were repeatedly chosen to illustrate what the students consider to be good writing.
- **c** The teacher asks the students to explain what made these particular papers good. These qualities of good writing or good conceptual development are written down to produce criteria of good grade level performance. Such peer-based standards of excellence often seem to be more credible, compelling, and usable than those which come from a textbook.

5 Rewriting
- **a** Students revise their original papers according to the criteria of good writing and/or new information gained.
- **b** Second drafts of the material may take the form of either homework or a RAG the following day.

Limiting writing time to 10 minutes and allowing students to immediately read each others' papers does wonders for motivation. In addition, the fast pace and natural curiosity among peers minimizes "do-nothingness."

RAGs may have a very general focus in creative writing, as mentioned earlier, or a highly specific focus such as photosynthesis in a science class or colorful descriptive passages in English composition. Since teachers can use the same general format for either the development of writing style or the development of concepts, RAGs offers a direct route to helping a total faculty focus on the teaching of writing across subject areas.

Jigsaw Learning Jigsaw is a method of cooperative learning that is particularly applicable to classroom research projects and committee work. If teachers can provide a clear performance outline for a class research project, they can then organize the class into research or "expert" groups in order to maximize individual responsibility for doing research and for teaching their research findings to fellow students. In its original form described by Elliot Aronson[4] of the University of California at Santa Cruz in his book *The Jigsaw Classroom,* the teacher organizes the research project into roughly a half-dozen content areas. Students are then assigned to membership in two different groups, (1) a *research* or "expert" group and (2) an *integration* group. There are always as many research groups as there are integration groups, with students divided roughly equally among the groups. Imagine, for example, that there are twenty-five students in a class with five students assigned to each of five research and integration groups.

Each *research* group divides their topic five ways (with the teacher's help), and each student is responsible for a portion of the research group's report. After completing his or her research, each member of the research group then teaches the other group members his or her portion of the research topic complete with supporting written materials so that all members of the research group have access to the same information. Then each group member writes a final report incorporating all the group's collected material.

Once reports from each of the research areas have been compiled by each research group and written up by each group member, one member from each different research group is pulled together to form an *integration* group. Thus, an integration group has one person representing each of the five research areas with the collected information on each of the five research topics. Each integration group member is responsible for teaching the group what his or her research group had collectively learned. Then each integration group member is responsible for preparing a final report integrating information from each of the five research groups. See Figure 9-1.

Although the notion of jigsaw learning is often associated with secondary education and complex research projects, a simplified form of jigsaw can be used in almost any classroom. An "expert" group of five third graders, for example, could be given five parts of a story to read, with their task being to tell their part of the story to the other members of the group in sequence so that everyone would know the whole story. Each group could then act its story out for the class.

In the upper grades the use of peer groupings to teach both research skills and cooperative learning is in its infancy, but it is a safe bet that research skills will become increasingly important in our technological society and in our educational curriculum. Keep in mind, however, that the skills of jigsaw learning and other forms of cooperative learning rest on a foundation of more fundamental instructional and discipline management skills which require special training in their own right. Clear performance

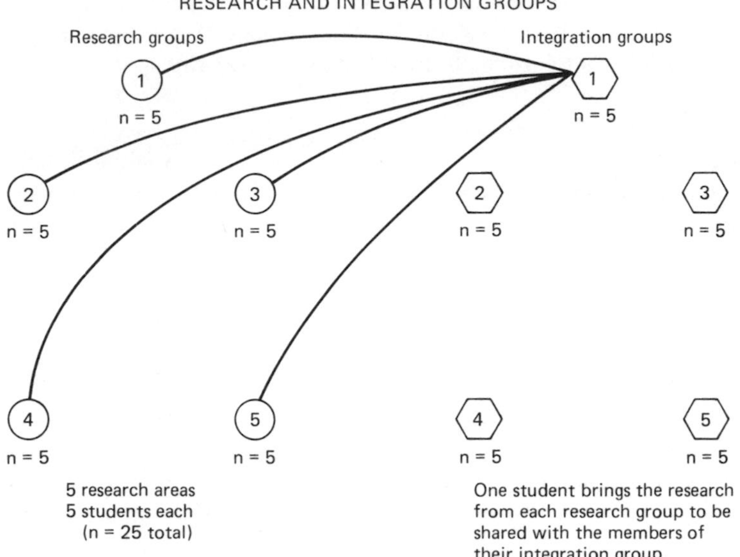

FIGURE 9-1
Student team learning: the jigsaw classroom.

outlines must be combined with constant movement, rapid helping interactions, and effective discipline management to produce consistently productive group work. When higher order teaching strategies such as jigsaw learning are laid on an inadequate foundation of classroom management, they predictably fail to deliver on their great promise as teachers are run ragged. Consequently they are *mis*labeled as fads.

Student Team Achievement Divisions (STAD)

Cooperation and competition can go together to maximize student motivation and learning if the class is properly organized into teams. We have already seen how team competition which focuses on learning can be enjoyable enough to function as a preferred activity in responsibility training (Chapter 11 of *Positive Classroom Discipline*). Team competition becomes a form of cooperative learning as soon as the teams are organized into study groups for such things as research, problem solving, review, and preparation for tests. Indeed, in the next chapter we will even give an example of using study teams to take care of paper grading so that teachers are freed to do more challenging and creative things with their time, such as lesson preparation. All that is needed to make team competition viable as a form of cooperative learning is simple and effective procedures that keep student motivation high while keeping extra work for the teacher low.

One of the perennial problems of learning-oriented team competition is the tendency of the slower students to become passive: "If the team is responsible for getting the right answer, let someone smart do it. If the first one with the answer wins, it won't be me."

How can you provide the same motivation and safety for slow students as for the more capable students? A variety of methods are available in team game formats, such as allowing the slower students to pick easier questions so that they have an equal opportunity to contribute to their team score. An example of such a team game format is "Baseball with a Lineup" which is described in Chapter 11 of *Positive Classroom Discipline*. An alternative way of organizing cooperative learning teams in such a way as to make everyone a potential winner is described by the Student Team Learning Project at Johns Hopkins University under the title Student Team Achievement Divisions (STAD).[5] For a detailed description of procedures, write for materials at the address provided in the chapter references.

STAD is designed to make a game of preparing for quizzes. Briefly, students are rank-ordered by the teacher on the basis of their past test performance in some subject area. Four students are put on a team, so the class size is divided by four to give the number of teams. A class of thirty-two students would have eight teams (there are special rules for dealing with odd numbers of students). Then the class members are assigned to a team on the basis of their rank ordering so that teams are balanced and equal in terms of the students' achievement level (high, middle, and low).

Teams are given time to review together several times in the days before the upcoming quiz. After the quiz has been completed and graded, difference scores are computed for all students that show their degree of improvement over their baseline level of achievement by which the class was originally rank-ordered. Each team member then contributes his or her difference score to the team total. No points are subtracted for poor performance—only growth counts.

If you use difference scores, slower students who improve contribute more to their team scores than would a fast student who simply matches his or her previous level of performance. In fact, because of the ceiling effect on fast students (there is less room for improvement on high baseline scores), the natural place for a team to pick up ground is by carefully tutoring the slower students. Weekly team standings as well as announcements of outstanding individual achievement and improvement are publicized in a weekly news bulletin in addition to any other form of reward that the teacher cares to devise.

A simplified scoring method devised by Bernice Medinnas and Janine Roberts of the Los Angeles Unified School District Teacher Center does away with the computation of difference scores by simply awarding the scores 6, 4, 3, and 2 to the four members of the top team on the basis of their quiz raw scores. This process is then repeated for each group of four students on the rank-order list. Thus, a low student who did well relative to the other three students at his or her ability level could earn a score of 6 to be added to the team aggregate score.

A variant of STAD also developed at Johns Hopkins is TGT (Teams-Games-Tournaments), a cooperative learning format in which students compete in a weekly tournament as representatives of their team. Students compete with members of other teams who are like them in academic performance. For example, the top four students might be at tournament table 1 competing for scores 6, 4, 3, and 2 as in the previous example. The tournament might cover the material from a given subject for the week, or it might function as a form of test review. Once again, however, the greatest benefits of the team competition are in the peer tutoring and cooperative learning which takes place within the team in preparation for the tournament.

Slow Down for the Humanities

The surest way to kill western civilization study is to reduce it to names, dates, and facts. The information of history is hardly the experience of history. And, unless students experience history in class, they will never come to care about it, much less love it.

As mentioned earlier, when it comes to providing experience to accompany the data of learning, the sky is the limit. Sometimes the only experience readily available is a good animated discussion. For this reason alone the discussion facilitation skills described in Chapter 6 are crucial to the trimodal teaching of concepts, especially in the humanities. And many times the most appropriate means of synthesizing and polishing ideas is through writing, whether in a cooperative learning format or not. For this reason alone every teacher of concepts is also a teacher of English composition, especially in the humanities.

It takes time to discuss a concept thoroughly and write about it. It takes more time still to experience the concept in the form of a simulation activity, a team game, role playing, or a "happening" like the one planned by the teacher who taught the experience of hunger by feeding his class on one fast-food lunch and a bowl of steamed rice.

If you were to reduce the notion of trimodal teaching to its bare bones and simply introduce a manageable bit of conceptual material (3 to 4 minutes), discuss it briefly (5 minutes), and write a short essay about it (5 to 7 minutes), it would take you at least 15 minutes to process one simple idea. Of course, a simulation activity dealing with the same concept might take an entire week, but for now let's think of only 15 minutes for multimodal and kinetic integration. The main difference in the form of a trimodal cycle in dealing with a concept as opposed to a computation is that with concepts the cycles are much *slower.*

Breaking the material into small bits that can be discussed and processed in about 15 minutes has produced what one teacher trainer has labeled "The Rule of Three." The Rule of Three says that if you process manageable bits of conceptual material thoroughly, you can only cover about three such concepts in a typical 50-minute period.

Trimodal teaching, therefore, has some rather direct implications for curriculum. The teacher and, it is hoped, her colleagues, must now examine their curriculum in order to be selective in what they present. You cannot teach the whole textbook well. It is no longer adequate to think of the teaching of the humanities as dashing full speed through daily information overload for an entire semester in order to cover all the material. Covering all the material ultimately becomes a rationalization for the poor teaching which causes so many high school students to describe social studies with one predictable adjective—*boring*! If you were to walk through the halls of almost any high school and observe the teaching of social studies as well as other courses in the humanities, you would typically see a 50-minute lecture by the teacher—a grandiose exercise in information overload and enforced inactivity for students.

Teachers, in order to teach the humanities well, must take control of their curriculum, limit the number of concepts that are being presented to the students, and present the material thoroughly and, more to the point, experientially. It is, after all, better to present ten concepts which are understood than to "expose" the class to 100 concepts that are forgotten. In the words of Madeline Hunter: "If your objective is simply to cover all of the material, you may as well cover it with dirt and bury it because it is dead anyway."

Thus, a direct implication of trimodal teaching in the humanities is: Teach less better.

As soon as teachers of the humanities commit themselves to teaching less better, they are almost always confronted by the dilemma that there is no way that they can cover all the material. At this point I attempt to harden their resolve to teach less better by reminding them that publishing is a business. Publishing companies make more money from large $35 textbooks than they do on small $15 textbooks *much* more money since binding and marketing and distribution costs have already been covered. Publishing companies, therefore, will always put more information into a textbook than a teacher can possibly teach. If teachers are unwilling to take control of their own curriculum and select from the textbooks what they can reasonably teach, the information overload contained in the textbook will be translated into information overload in the classroom.

Teachers who decide to teach less better as a result of training in teaching typically express relief and liberation in the end. One high school social studies teacher recently stated as he reflected on the changes in his classroom:

> The greatest gains are in the bottom half of my class. They do not appear bored any more, and they have told me that they really find the class more interesting and are getting something out of it. The fast students also seem to like it better because they like group discussions and working on research projects better than just listening to me lecture, but their grades are about the same. My test results indicate that the class as a whole is learning more even though I am covering less material as far as the textbook is concerned. I have to be selective now. That is really tough, but it forces me to think about what is really worth getting across. Learning has especially gone up for the kids who used to tune out.

OVERVIEW

Trimodal teaching is by definition active, and at its best it is interactive. It is, therefore, the antithesis of a one-way flow of information from teacher to student. Many of the interactions of trimodal teaching are student/teacher interactions. But trimodal teaching must ultimately go beyond student/teacher interactions since the number of interactions possible for the class during a given lesson will always be limited by the availability of the teacher. We are ultimately blocked by the student/teacher ratio until the students become teachers.

We need to break out of our mold of teaching *to* students. We need to expand our repertoire of cooperative learning methods to transcend what John Goodlad[6] describes as the only two teaching formats used by most high school teachers: seatwork and lecture. We need to regard classroom activity as a *process*—an interaction, rather than a *product* or fact learning created by a one-way information exchange.

Yet we must seek help in our attempts to break free, for experiential teaching is often difficult. The ideas are hard to come by, and the logistics that make it practical and affordable for the teacher are not obvious. Materials are being developed, but many have been developed in the past only to be discarded and forgotten.

Assigning will always be easier than teaching. Talking will always be easier than creating an experience. To counteract these natural forces teachers and faculties and districts and states will have to work at it steadily over a long period of time. But for now some wonderful trimodal formats are available for people who are interested.

As far as the progress of the structured lesson is concerned, good teaching will minimize the need for reteaching. Freed of the need to give frequent corrective feedback and with the help of a performance model to make corrective feedback brief, teachers are finally set free from the exasperation of constantly needing to reteach their lessons to the most needy during guided practice. Now they can perform the proper functions of guided practice, namely, (1) the fine tuning of student performance and (2) quality assurance—the systematic management of diligence and excellence. The final piece of the instructional puzzle will be supplied, however, only when we gain the added management leverage needed to help us deal successfully with student dawdling and sloppiness—the signs of a mediocre level of motivation. The technology of systematically managing diligence and excellence within the classroom is the topic of the next chapter.

REFERENCES

1 Gottesman, Julie M. Peer teaching: partner learning and small group learning. Los Angeles, California: Division of Curriculum and Instructional Services, Office of the Los Angeles County Superintendent of Schools, 1981.

2 The Bay Area Writing Project. Berkeley, California: Dept. of Education, University of California at Berkeley.

3 Gossard, Jenee. Using read-around groups to improve writing. Los Angeles, California. UCLA Writing Project, Department of Education, UCLA.

4 Aronson, Elliot. *The jigsaw classroom*. Beverly Hills, California: Sage Publications, 1978.

5 Slavin, Robert E. Using student team learning. Baltimore, MD: The Johns Hopkins Team Learning Project, Center for Social Organization in Schools, The Johns Hopkins University, 3505 N. Charles St., Baltimore, MD, 21218, 1978.

6 Goodlad, John I. *A place called school, prospects for the future*. New York: McGraw-Hill, 1984.

CHAPTER **10**

MOTIVATION: INCENTIVES FOR DILIGENCE AND EXCELLENCE

When a structured lesson is taught properly, teachers literally work themselves out of a job during guided practice. Few helping interactions are needed, and those positive helping interactions that are needed are brief. Now we will learn to exploit the time during guided practice that has been freed from reinstruction. We will examine ways in which the teacher can best carry out the often neglected tasks of quality assurance and quality control—of holding students strictly accountable for diligence and excellence.

AN ORIENTATION TO INCENTIVES FOR DILIGENCE AND EXCELLENCE

Bringing Motivation under the Teacher's Control

- If I could just get the kids to do the work, I wouldn't have so many discipline problems.
- What good is it to get students to quit fooling around in class if they just end up sitting there like a lump?
- My main problem isn't discipline. It is motivation. How do you make students want to learn?

Motivation is all too often considered to be solely a quality of students, something that they bring with them when they come to school. The reasons for a student's lack of motivation might typically be attributed to either the student's environment or the student's psyche. Thus, when casting about for an understanding of a particular student's academic failure, educators tend to focus either on disorganized home life and cultural deprivation on the one hand or laziness and poor self-concept on the other hand. Whatever the imagined cause, however, the motivation of a student to learn is regarded as a relatively fixed quantity which constitutes the teacher's ultimate limitation in reaching the student.

In spite of this tendency for educators to externalize the causes of student failure, there has always been an accompanying ritual acknowledgement of the role of curriculum and lesson presentation in motivating students. Yet without an understanding of the *specifics* of a clear trimodal lesson presentation and the role of performance models and positive helping interactions in promoting independence and self-confidence, you can find little of substance that could serve as clear-cut causes of student failure when you analyze the presentation of a structured lesson.

Instead, curriculum has been analyzed in terms of its relevance, lessons have been analyzed in terms of their interest level, and the failure of a particular student in a particular class has been attributed to a personality clash. With such vague and fuzzy categories representing the teacher's input into a student's failure, it is not surprising that the diagnosis of failure has stressed causes which are concrete, observable, and external to the classroom.

The behavior modification revolution of the 1960s created the basis for a new mindset for analyzing one of the most prominent "causes" of academic failure—lack of motivation. For the first time student achievement was viewed as a variable largely controlled by incentives for academic productivity. Basics of the technology of incentive management were described, and the teacher was placed squarely at the center of causality as the chief incentive manager in the classroom. The power of incentives was repeatedly demonstrated in what has become an extensive technical literature describing successes with the most intransigent of nonachievers.

"Behavior modification," however, has had almost no appreciable effect on regular classrooms. It has instead been viewed by most educators as a tool for special education. The reasons for the failure of incentive management to penetrate regular classrooms are many, but two of the most prominent are that (1) most teachers know next to nothing about the technology of incentive management and (2) what little introduction they may have had to B-Mod programs stereotyped them as costly, short-term, failure-prone, applicable to only one problem behavior at a time, and suitable mainly for special-education or primary-aged children. Most teachers, especially secondary teachers, avoid incentive management because they see it as a potentially endless progression of individualized programs with rubber spiders and candies for rewards, which ultimately add up to a great amount of extra work in exchange for a limited impact on the class as a whole.

For incentive management to be acceptable to regular education, it must be applicable to many students at a modest cost. It must appeal to a wide range of students and use learning as the main form of reinforcement. To be usable, incentive management for academic productivity must be like incentive management for good behavior—cost-effective, powerful, and mechanically simple. The nature of advanced incentive management for academic productivity is the subject of this chapter.

To Manage or Not to Manage

Most teachers feel that they have the choice of operating or not operating incentive systems for academic productivity in their classrooms. That perception, as it turns out, is an illusion.

Teachers provide consequences of one kind or another for diligence and excellence. Those consequences either strengthen or weaken both diligence and excellence within the classroom. Almost everything teachers do within their classroom produces an incentive system for something. There is no such thing as a neutral classroom environment. A teacher's only real choices are to knowingly reward the behavior he does want or to inadvertently reward behavior he does not want.

A Review of Basics

The technology of incentive systems has been explained in considerable detail in *Positive Classroom Discipline* (Chapters 8 and 9). As a review, simple incentive systems are relatively straightforward applications of "grandma's rule." You have to finish your dinner before you get your dessert. Grandma's rule is simple, but it is *strict.* The work has to be done *right* before you receive *any* reward.

When studying classroom discipline, however, we became highly familiar with complex incentive systems which utilize the additional components of bonus and penalty. Complex incentive systems are typically required for effective group management of cooperation and good behavior because reward cannot be delivered to the group until everyone is behaving properly. To keep the few from ruining reward for the many, penalty must be used to suppress disruption so that reward may be delivered. Much care is taken in the design of complex incentive systems, however, to minimize the probability of the abuse of penalty.

Although incentive systems for good behavior tend to be complex, incentive systems for good schoolwork tend to be simple. A simple incentive system, grandma's rule has only the three basic parts: (1) the task (dinner), (2) reward (dessert), and (3) accountability. Both reward and accountability are cost factors for the teacher since they require planning and effort. By far the most costly part of a simple incentive system is accountability. Thus, in order to understand incentive systems for academic productivity in terms of cost effectiveness, we must acquire a thorough understanding of the nature and cost of accountability.

Accountability, Diligence, and Excellence

Strict accountability defines "diligence" on any job since it measures how much of the task has been completed. If you will accept a half-finished job, then a half-finished job you will get unless the worker has personal reasons for doing more. Strict accountability also defines "excellence" on any job since it defines how well the job has been done. Thus, the first rule of quality control is: *The standard of excellence on any job is always established by the sloppiest piece of work that will be accepted.*

If shoddy work is accepted, then shoddy work is by definition *acceptable*. Some workers, of course, out of their own conscientiousness, may exceed this standard. But if they do so, they do it on their *own time* for their *own personal reasons*. As far as incentive management goes, the sloppiest piece of work which is accepted is obviously good enough.

Accountability for the *quantity* (diligence) and *quality* (excellence) of work produced in a classroom boils down to (1) quality assurance—checking and correcting the work as it is being done, and (2) quality control—checking and correcting the work as soon after it is completed as possible. In incentive management for academic productivity, the age-old admonition regarding accountability and quality control that defines the school teacher holds as true as ever: *We are just going to keep doing it until we get it right.*

The Cost of Strict Accountability

Accountability is typically the most *expensive* part of an incentive system for work productivity, be it in a factory or in a schoolroom, because strict accountability requires the constant monitoring of the quantity and quality of work being done. Constant monitoring can be difficult and time-consuming, far more difficult and time-consuming than delivering the reward in most cases.

Reward, the second cost factor in a simple incentive system apart from accountability, is relatively simple and easy to deliver once you know who deserves to be rewarded and how much reward they deserve. In the classroom most rewards for achievement will take the form of academically rich *preferred activity time* (PAT). Therefore, reward represents an extension of a familiar methodology which costs almost nothing in academic learning time.

The cost of the systematic management of diligence and excellence in the classroom, then, primarily boils down to the cost of accountability. If teachers cannot afford *strict* accountability because the labor of work check is too great, they cannot afford to systematically reward either diligence or excellence. In fact, if teachers cannot check every student's work for diligence and excellence as it is being done or minutes thereafter, they will probably reward the exact opposite.

The Three Management Options

The dilemma of having no choice but to systematically reward diligence and excellence is difficult for someone to appreciate who does not have a background in incentive management. It is easy for the novice to imagine that systematic incentive management for the *entire class* is an option that he or she can refuse at no cost. This section spells out your management options more clearly in order to dispel any notion that you can just forget the whole thing without sacrificing most of your direct leverage over the quantity and quality of work produced by many of your students.

To illustrate the teacher's options in dealing with diligence and excellence in the classroom we will look at one of the most common and difficult incentive dilemmas of classroom management—controlling the quantity and quality of work being done by the students who are "working independently" while the teacher's attention is absorbed in small group instruction. As an example, we will examine perhaps the most common everyday incentive management disaster in elementary education: the reading circle. Whether you teach reading in circles or not, let it stand as a prototype of small group instruction for purposes of demonstration since almost all teachers at all levels do at least a part of their teaching in small groups and since small group instruction so clearly presents our management alternatives for *all* lesson formats.

Option 1 Do your work and hand it in as soon as you are done The teacher plans to work intensely with a subgroup of the class while the rest, it is hoped, stay on task and work hard on a separate assignment. For management option 1, the lesson transition might sound something like this:

> Group! Let me have your attention. I would like the first reading group to join me at the reading table. The rest of you have folder work to do at your seats. Do not come up here and bother me at the reading table. When you are done, place your folders on my desk. You are then excused to read your library books or to go back to the interest centers.

This incentive system looks like grandma's rule at first glance. The students must first complete their folder work (dinner), and when it is done, they may read their library books or go back to the interest centers (dessert). However, one part has been left out—accountability.

When a teacher permits students to have access to a reward such as a preferred activity without first checking their work to make sure that it is all correct, she or he inadvertently designs what is known as a "speed incentive." Any student with a brain in his head knows that the sooner he hands in his work, the more time he has to pet the hamster. The offering of a reward without strict accountability for the quality of work that is done systematically rewards fast, sloppy work.

Thus, when teachers receive sloppy handwriting, incorrect answers, random numbers for math problems, or some other such academic farce, they are only getting what they systematically rewarded. They have inadvertently committed a large-scale reinforcement error. Without strict accountability the offering of a reward does more harm than good.

Yet, in spite of incentives which reward fast and sloppy work in a great many classrooms, some students in these same classrooms persist in working conscientiously and correctly. They turn in good work because their own internalized criteria of diligence and excellence are higher than those implied by the teacher's incentive system. They have values and standards, and the discomfort of violating those standards is greater than the pleasure to be gained from extra preferred activity time. They will do good work in spite of the existing management system, not because of it, and they will do so for their own personal reasons and on their own time. Thus, the student's internalized incentive system of self-reward based on excellence will be strong enough to override the speed incentive for sloppiness inadvertently offered by the teacher.

The fact that some students consistently produce good work in spite of the flaws in our incentive systems tends to blind us to those flaws. A teacher will typically look at the range in quality of work produced by her or his class and conclude logically enough that some students care while other students simply do not care. The prime locus of motivation is placed within the student, as usual. In fact, the locus of motivation is within only those students (typically the minority) who have strong enough internalized standards of conscientiousness and excellence to override the external speed incentive. For the rest of the students the locus is external, and consequently only *they* will respond to the incentive system exactly as designed by the teacher.

Most teachers, however, being innocent of the technology of incentive management, believe what they see, and what they see is the obvious contrast between some students who try and some students who do not try. Since they do not see the incentives being offered much less the effect, it is logical for teachers to attribute sloppiness to the laziness or cussedness of the student rather than to some controlling variable of some unknown and unseen incentive system.

Option 2 Do your work carefully and I will check it to make sure it is *correct* before you hand it in We have learned our lesson about strict accountability and standards of excellence from the previous example. We will no longer allow a student to hand in any old thing and think that she has completed the assignment. We are going to adhere to grandma's rule as grandma intended it, and we are going to make sure that the work is completed *to our standard* before any reward is made available. "We are just going to keep doing it until we get it right."

The lesson transition by our teacher with the reading circle who has been chastened by the description of speed incentives might now sound something like this:

> Group! Let me have your attention. I would like the first reading group to join me up here at the reading table. The rest of you have folder work to do at your desks. When you are done with your folder work, bring it up to me and let me check it over. If there are any mistakes, I will excuse you to go back to your seat and make the corrections. When everything has been done correctly and I have checked your work, you may place it on my desk. You may then read your library book or go back to the interest centers.

Now it becomes more clear as to why the most expensive part of an incentive system is always accountability. When the teacher holds the students strictly accountable for excellence in this situation, for doing their folder work *correctly* before handing it in, the teacher must check all the students' work as soon as it is done.

If the teacher actually tried to hold the students accountable, he or she would be interrupted every 30 seconds by some student asking, "Is this right?", "Would you please look at my paper," or "Would you check this so I can be excused?" The teacher would be bugged to death and would never have the opportunity to teach reading! He or she would soon be forced to introduce a new classroom rule: Class, let me have your attention! I do not want *anyone* coming up here and bothering me during reading circle! I'll look at your work later.

So much for strict accountability! In this example accountability seems unaffordable. Therefore, operating any kind of incentive system would seem unaffordable. If it is the judgment of teachers that they cannot afford accountability, they may well conclude that the only constructive option open to them is to have no formal incentive system whatsoever. Although they may not be able to create a good reason for the average student to seek diligence and excellence because of the cost of work check, at least they will not be committing any reinforcement errors such as the disastrous speed incentive described in the first example. Or so it seems.

Isn't it logical that no incentive is better than a bad incentive? Unfortunately, such a perception is an illusion. There are only two options open to us; good incentive management or bad incentive management. There is no such thing as a neutral classroom environment.

Option 3 Since accountability is unaffordable, have no incentive system in order to avoid any blatant reinforcement error When a teacher decides to have no formal incentive system to promote diligence and excellence, she or he is forced to settle for time on task or, more accurately, the *appearance* of time on task. Since she or he will not be able to check the quantity or quality of work as it is being done, the teacher will have to settle for everyone's *looking busy.*

The lesson transition for the teacher who attempts to manage academic productivity without formal incentives may sound something like this:

> Group! Let me have your attention. I would like the first reading group to join me at the reading table. The rest of you have folder work to do at your desks. I expect you to stay busy until we are done with reading at eleven o'clock. If you get done with your folder work early, you may work on your writing assignment from yesterday or on your spelling words. Remember, I expect you all to be busy until eleven. Do not come up and bother me at the reading table.

By not implementing a formal incentive system with strict accountability by design the teacher has implemented an informal incentive system by default, i.e., one which is an inadvertent by-product of classroom routine. What is the reward for diligence? If the student follows the teacher's directions, diligence is rewarded only by more work. Some students will actually do more work thanks to their internalized standards, but many, if not most, will not.

The apparent lack of any formal incentive system, therefore, leaves a reinforcement vacuum which is soon filled with incentive management of a different kind—disincentives. For diligence the disincentive may be stated as follows: If you are diligent, you get more work. But if you are not diligent, you get only one assignment.

Such a disincentive for diligence translates into an incentive for dawdling. The teacher has created an incentive structure which teaches students to expand the work to fill the time available.

For excellence, as for diligence, the abdication of management by formal incentives produces management by disincentives as the reinforcement vacuum is filled by punishment through default. Formal management of work productivity will typically be by negative sanctions for poor and sloppy work: either the threat of poor grades to suppress nonperformance or the nagging typical of reprimands from a seated teacher to suppress overt fooling around. Consequently, poor management of motivation often precipitates poor management of discipline. In the final analysis we either systematically *reinforce* the behavior we *do* want, or by default we are forced to *contain* behavior that we *do not* want.

A Review of Management Options

It becomes clear as we examine incentive systems for academic productivity that there are really only three management options:

I Do it right: reward and strict accountability
- implement *your* standards for the entire class
- create excellence and diligence
- pay the price of strict accountability

II Do it wrong: reward and no (or poor) accountability
- abdicate any systematic implementation of your standards
- eliminate the cost of accountability
- create a speed incentive
- reward fast and sloppy work

III Don't do it: No reward and no accountability
- abdicate any systematic implementation of your standards
- eliminate the cost of accountability
- reward expanding the work to fill the time allotted
- enforce the appearance of time on task with negative sanctions
- create an incentive for dawdling

Our incentive options for managing academic productivity in the classroom are fewer than we may have imagined. Indeed, in our example of the reading circle it seems as though teachers are damned any way they turn. They cannot afford adequate accountability on the one hand, and the students can ill afford the poor learning habits that result from inadequate accountability on the other hand. What is cheap for the teacher, therefore, is most costly for those students with poorly internalized standards of excellence who are most in need of help through systematic incentive management.

So what about the teacher with his or her reading circle? Is it possible for you to enforce standards for the group during small group instruction? Yes you can, but some changes will have to be made first. To begin with, you must *move*. You can neither give corrective feedback nor check work efficiently for the entire class while sitting on your behind. The discussion of movement patterns related to "praise, prompt, and leave" in Chapter 5 provides a partial answer. Beyond that we must take an entirely fresh look at the way in which we teach reading.

For now we must simply be aware of the logistical hurdles which must be overcome for us to succeed with the systematic management of diligence and excellence in the classroom. There will be incentive management of diligence and excellence in the classroom in all lesson formats either by design or by default. And our ability to do it properly is largely governed by our system of accountability.

The notion of giving rewards in the classroom in the hope that something good will come of it has been oversold in behavior modification over the past two decades, especially to elementary teachers. The result is a lot of sloppy incentive management. Because of high cost, accountability is the part of an incentive system that is most often omitted or discarded by a teacher. But beware. *There is no such thing as a halfway incentive system.* You must either do it right or it blows up in your face. You do not have the option of doing an incentive system sloppily or partway, and you certainly do not have the option of omitting one of the three basic parts of a simple incentive system such as accountability!

You cannot avoid incentive management, and you cannot shortchange it. You have no constructive option but to find a way to do it right. This dilemma gives us little choice but to master the technology of incentive management for academic productivity in the entire classroom and to master the cost problems implicit in accountability for all students. Our analysis has focused our attention, however, on the main logistical barrier to the effective, systematic management of diligence and excellence within the classroom—the cost of accountability. The widespread use of formal incentives for academic productivity is ultimately limited by the cost of checking work as it is being done or soon thereafter in order to make sure that it has been done and done right.

THE PAPER-GRADING TRAP

The time invested by teachers in checking and grading papers must be small enough so that most of it can be done while the class is working on the assignment (quality assurance) and so that the remainder can be done quickly before the next period starts (quality control). But most teachers, lacking an adequate technology of either quality assurance or quality control, either fail to check the work at all or take it home to grade it—the time-honored tradition of the conscientious teacher.

Cold Potatoes

The school day is so packed with activity that little time for work check is available. So most teachers grade papers after school hours if they grade them at all. Papers are typically handed in the day they are completed, checked by the teacher after school or at home that evening, and handed back the next day. Conscientious teachers, by investing what often amounts to hours in work check daily, have definitely gone the extra mile in an attempt to give the students meaningful feedback for their efforts. They can only hope that their conscientiousness will somehow translate into learning.

What do students usually do with the papers that you spent your evening grading when you hand them back the next day? Typically, the highly motivated student takes the paper home, and the average student puts the paper with the mediocre grade into the circular file, not to be given another thought. The time and effort spent by the teacher in providing corrective feedback is literally thrown away and trashed!

The Inefficiency of Going Over It Again

Some teachers become discouraged at seeing so much effort on their part produce so little learning; so they finally quit grading most papers. Other teachers, however, remain convinced of the importance of individualized corrective feedback and remain committed to making their efforts at work check pay off. These teachers frequently structure learning exercises during the following day which utilize the graded papers for purposes of reinstruction.

Though a variety of methods for going over the papers again exist, the most commonly used are going over the exercise again as a group or helping students individually. Unfortunately, both of these methods tend to be highly inefficient.

If you go over all the problems of a math assignment with the *group,* for example, you all but guarantee a high percentage of wasted time and student boredom. If, for example, only five of thirty students missed Exercise 1, and if each student who missed the exercise is dying to learn how to do it correctly, the maximum teaching efficiency will be approximately 5 in 30 or ⅙. The students who got Exercise 1 correct are, for the most part, "on hold" waiting for you to get to a problem for which they need feedback. By the time a student is on hold for 5 or 10 minutes, she has probably lapsed into a coma for the rest of the period.

If, in contrast, you attempt to give corrective feedback to students *individually,* you face the slowness, the negativism, and the generation of dependency indigenous to the universal helping interaction since you typically are dealing with a large chunk of incorrect work rather than a single step of a performance sequence. Although the positive helping interaction may make feedback quicker and more supportive, these skills do not exist in the repertoire of most teachers now. And even if a teacher were trained to give positive helping interactions, she or he would be hard pressed to meet students' needs rapidly enough because she or he would be "picking up pieces" rather than coming off a well-taught structured lesson.

Immediacy Is Potency

The problems inherent in grading papers after school and handing them back the next day are even more acute when we consider the incentive properties of delayed feedback and delayed reward. To put it simply, one of the most powerful variables affecting the potency of a reinforcer in an incentive system is *immediacy of delivery.* The longer feedback and reinforcement are delayed after the work is done, the weaker is the influence of the reinforcer in motivating future work. The weakening inherent in delaying a reinforcer is more severe the younger or more immature the students since their capacity to wait and delay gratification is markedly less than an adult's. Rewards offered tomorrow for work done today typically have only a fraction of the power to motivate students—particularly those in need of external motivation—as they would have were they delivered immediately on task completion.

Personal Reorientation

For a reward to be delivered quickly on the completion of work, accountability must be accomplished quickly, and therefore the extra time and effort invested in work check must be small. By one means or another teachers must get laborious and time-consuming work checks off their backs. To many teachers, this message will be greeted with cheers because they hate taking papers home and wasting evenings doing clerical work. To other teachers, however, reducing the time and effort invested in paper grading produces some discomfort and disorientation. Some of the most conscientious teachers naturally pride themselves in their conscientiousness—in their willingness to invest the extra time to go over the work carefully, to document the students' areas of need, and to give the students feedback the next day. The investment of time in paper grading represents a reaffirmation of a valued aspect of self-concept. Malaise may come from two directions.

- If I don't take home papers and grade them, I won't feel as though I know my students' work well enough to pinpoint their areas of need.
- If I don't grade papers, what do I do to signify to myself that I am a careful, conscientious teacher?

Whatever emotions might come from the imperative to get cumbersome work check off your back, the imperative remains the same. Work check must be accomplished *quickly* in class as the work is being done or immediately thereafter not only because quick paper grading is a precondition to the immediate delivery of rewards for diligence and excellence, but also because paper grading at home is, for the most part, a *waste of time*. Because of the weakness of delayed feedback and delayed rewards, hours spent grading papers at home simply do not efficiently translate into learning.

In addition, conscientious paper grading after hours may actually be counterproductive. There is far too little time available for teachers to plan lessons as it is. You need your planning period and any other time you can get to prepare lessons with careful task analyses and clear performance models. To cannibalize planning time with paper grading replaces our highest level job function with our lowest level job function—clerical work.

METHODS OF WORK CHECK

Since the speed and cost of accountability represent the practical limitation to the widespread use of incentive systems for academic productivity within the classroom, the expansion of our use of such incentives must focus on the technology of work check. There are many methods of work check which may be used separately or together. Some are old and familiar, and some incorporate new ideas. The following descriptions are intended to expand the teacher's range of options rather than to provide a prescription or final answer. Brainstorming with colleagues will provide a much expanded range of options in any curriculum area.

Methods of work check are organized under two major headings: (1) "Quality Assurance": checking work and reinstructing while the work is first being done and (2) "Quality Control": checking and correcting work as soon as possible after it has been completed. As in any workplace, it is cheaper to fix a product while it is being built and to instruct the worker at the same time to prevent subsequent defects than it is to take the product apart at the end of the assembly line to repair it.

Quality Assurance

Having come to understand both the function and necessity of quick and accurate work check as a precondition to the systematic reinforcement of diligence and excellence, it may come as something of a relief to realize that we have spent the previous six chapters learning how to do it. Rather than being a complex and separate management program, quality assurance is for the most part a by-product of positive classroom instruction. Diligence and excellence only become unaffordable when you attempt them *apart* from the procedures already described in this volume.

Work Check during Acquisition Trimodal teaching will, in many lesson formats, give the teacher the opportunity to monitor the quality of performance as the task is being done one step at a time. Corrective feedback is given quickly and supportively—exactly as it would be given during guided practice. True to the objectives of quality assurance, we will assure that the piece of work is built right in the first place—exactly as designed.

The amount of quality assurance for each student, of course, varies depending on the subject, the teaching format, and the class size. Mobility in conjunction with teaching one step at a time maximizes the teacher's opportunities for work check during acquisition. But the teacher is only human and can still be only one place at a time.

In order to increase the efficiency of quality assurance during acquisition we will operate multiple quality assurance programs simultaneously. Where possible we will utilize peers as a second quality assurance system to provide continuous monitoring of performance. The previous chapter provided examples of peer teaching, and additional examples are provided in later sections of this chapter.

Work Check during Guided Practice As mentioned in previous chapters, the effective teaching of a structured lesson eliminates most corrective feedback during guided practice. Trimodal teaching with adequate structured practice will greatly reduce the *frequency* of helping interactions, and the positive helping interaction with the aid of performance models will reduce the *duration* of helping interactions. The teacher will now be free to circulate among the students primarily for purposes of work check and quality assurance.

If teachers mark on the paper as they give corrective feedback during guided practice (see "Praise Subskills" in Chapter 5), they will be checking work as a by-product of working the crowd and praise, prompt, and leave. Work check during helping interactions takes no extra time, provides rapid feedback, and requires that sloppy work be done and redone "until we get it right."

As part of working the crowd, the teacher will usually be checking the work of the students in the bottom half of the class who most need help and who typically lack internalized standards of excellence. Consequently, the students most likely to goof off, play helpless, get stuck, or do sloppy work are those who are continually held to account by the teacher.

Even if the teacher cannot check all the work of the poorer students, by focusing especially on checking the first *part* of the assignment the teacher can still establish a standard of excellence for these students. That portion of the assignment not checked by the teacher can be taken care of by other methods of work check to be described under the heading "Quality Control."

Paper checking will eventually replace helping interactions as the primary type of teacher-student interaction during guided practice. With work being checked as it is being done, teachers can deliver rewards for diligence and excellence immediately on completion during guided practice. With the help of some procedures described in later sections of the chapter, even the checking of complex work can often be completed during guided practice.

Quality Control

Take the Work Home Quality control procedures are used in lieu of quality assurance when we are unable to get all the work checked as it is being done. In our quality control we attempt to check work as soon after it is completed as possible in order to (1) have feedback be a meaningful part of the initial learning experience and (2) allow us to provide reinforcement for diligence and excellence as soon as possible.

Sometimes grading papers yourself is unavoidable. For example, going over papers yourself may be the only way to assess students' performance on an English composition. In any case, however, regard grading papers at home as a *last resort*! Learn to exploit other methods of work check to get most of the job done in class. Peer checking may be used, for example, to check grammar, leaving you free to check composition. In any case, plan to minimize clerical work after school so that you may have more time for lesson preparation.

Have the Students Do It If you cannot get all students' work checked as you circulate during guided practice or as a by-product of praise, prompt, and leave and if you do not wish to take the papers home to check them, having the students check their own papers is usually the next best bet—if you can keep them *conscientious* and *honest*. Teachers have had students grade their own papers since time began, but there have always been problems with sloppiness and cheating that have limited the use of peer checking.

When viewed as a necessity for consistently implementing standards of diligence and excellence in many situations, getting students to conscientiously and honestly check their own and each other's work takes on added significance and defines a challenging area of management methodology. We will explore ways of using student checking as a way of assuring high standards and rapid feedback for all kinds of assignments.

How do you train your students to check their own and each other's papers carefully and honestly at the conclusion of the work period so that rewards can be made immediately available and so that you do not have to take the papers home to grade them? Two areas of methodology immediately spring to mind: (1) self-check and (2) peer check.

1 ***Self-Check*** Self-check is a matter of trust. Different teachers can trust their students to check their own work fairly and accurately to differing degrees. If you can trust them, let them do it. Self-check is one of the most economical methods of work check and should be exploited insofar as possible. Careful monitoring by constantly walking among the students as you would during seatwork can greatly increase the utility of self-check. Thus the *room arrangement* and *movement pattern* of the teacher serve accountability along with corrective feedback and discipline management.

2 ***Peer Check*** The methods of peer check are many and varied. Many have been around much longer than we have. The following list is far from comprehensive but offers some approaches to cost cutting that keep the accuracy of work check high.

a *Exchanging papers with a neighbor.* Exchanging papers with a neighbor is extremely quick, cheap, and efficient if you can trust the honesty and accuracy of the checking. The two main problems to be dealt with in exchanging papers are: (1) honesty and (2) dealing with complex work. Management systems to ensure honesty will be dealt with shortly, whereas dealing with complex work is the subject of the next section.

b *Exchanging papers with spot checking.* Many teachers grade papers themselves because they simply cannot trust the students to do a good job. If the students are not particularly conscientious or honest, incentives can be arranged which will help train them to be conscientious and honest.

After the papers have been checked and returned to their owners, the teacher may simply call for five papers at random and immediately double-check them. For every error in paper grading, the *class loses* a minute of their next preferred activity time as a part of responsibility training (see *Positive Classroom Discipline*). But if there are no errors in the checking, the teacher can add an automatic bonus to the next preferred activity time. The teacher does not take into account who did the checking or who made what errors when delivering penalty to the group.

c *Team checking.* Peer checking is often made more reliable and dependable by having students check work in pairs so that each is under the surveillance of the other. Often the students are excused to go to a "check table" where they grade their work with an answer key and then either hand their work in or go back to their seats to correct their mistakes. If check teams are used, observe the following three guidelines:

- Do not pair good friends.
- Supervise intermittently.
- Spot check as an option.

d *Team checking as a part of team games.* An extremely effective means of motivating students to work hard during skill drill is to use team competition. Not only can team games be used to motivate students, but work check can also be thrown in for free if the teams are seated in rows so that each student is sitting beside a person from another team. Give a fixed amount of time to complete a given problem or exercise, and at the end of the work interval have all students exchange their papers with the student sitting next to them for work check. When such pairs of students are on different teams, peer checking becomes extremely quick and honest if the following procedure is used:

• When the work interval is up, have all students exchange their papers with their neighbors (from another team).

• Give the students the answer and instruct them to mark their neighbor's work as either right or wrong.

• Return the papers to their owners.

• Ask the students from each team in turn to raise their hands to indicate whether they got the problem right or wrong (the teacher can tally hands raised on the board as points for that team).

Peer checking using this format is honest because (1) a student on one team will not cheat for a student on another team by saying an answer is right when it is not, (2) no student will let someone on another team misgrade his or her paper, and (3) a student on one team will not allow her neighbor who is on another team to raise his hand to say that he got the problem right if he did not. The whole routine of exchanging, grading, and returning papers should take under 20 seconds in most cases. A half hour of such a team game does the same work as may be presented in a textbook practice set or a "deadly ditto," but in this format it is a pleasant activity which can even serve as a PAT, with work being checked for free.

e *Peer checkers.* Students who finish early often like to grade papers to help the teacher. Let them! Younger students especially like to grade papers if they get to use a rubber stamp to make marks on the papers they are grading. The checkers also learn as they check. Do not allow yourself to be limited to thinking that you are wasting the time of the peer checkers by having them do your job for you. Having the students help the teacher within appropriate limits is an acceptable way of increasing the teacher's overall effectiveness.

Have Anybody Else Do It If you cannot check the work as you move among students as a by-product of working the crowd and praise, prompt, and leave, and if you cannot conveniently arrange for the students to check their own work, have *anybody* else do it rather than you—utilize parents, aides, or work-study students. Unless aides have been trained in instructional skills, work check to free the teacher for instruction is a far more appropriate use of their time than is the role of "second teacher" working with small groups of "helpless" students.

Don't Do It Do not think that you must check every practice exercise, especially at the elementary level. And do not be apologetic to parents because you cannot. Rather, inform them of your work-check policies as part of your program of sending work home in a weekly folder (see Chapter 4 of *Positive Classroom Discipline*).

Checking Complex Work

Checking work rapidly as it is being done becomes more difficult the more complex the work. You may quickly see what to praise and prompt in a simple addition problem, but what about the visual complexity of a quadratic equation or a geometry proof? Both the positive helping interaction and quick work check become difficult when the work is so visually complex that it is difficult to discriminate correct from incorrect portions of the task. And students may be able to check language arts workbooks or the grammar in a written exercise, but what about English composition?

Although work check by students and others can pick up the slack in a teacher's quality control efforts, the primary burden of quick and meaningful feedback for work in progress is always borne (1) by continuous work check during acquisition and (2) by continuous work check during guided practice when effective teaching has made helping interactions a rarity. This section will help you get at least some of the checking of complex work done quickly and easily.

Check Masters Let's use intermediate level math as an example. How long does it take you to see exactly what has been done right so far in the following piece of work, and how long does it take you to know exactly what the student has to do next?

$$
\begin{array}{r}
276 \\
\underline{\times 598} \\
2208 \\
2484 \\
\underline{1370} \\
164048
\end{array}
$$

Teachers soon experience visual overload as they scan a complex piece of work such as this. In addition, much valuable time is lost if you attempt to do the calculations in your head, and you just may do it wrong. Yet, unless you can quickly tell right from wrong, you will be blocked in your attempt to check work and to give a positive helping interaction. Rather, you will be reduced to the use of a universal helping interaction as you inform the student that the answer is wrong and that it is up to him to do the whole problem over as he looks for the cause. Some students will look, but all will feel discouragement, and many will quit.

As soon as a student's work becomes so complex that you cannot quickly scan the work to tell what the student has done right so far, you will need "check masters." Check masters allow you to quickly check complex work part by part so that you can tell the student *exactly* what he has done right so far and *exactly* what needs to be done next. A check master is a sheet of paper with the work done correctly *in its entirety.*

If we use the mathematics problem above as an example, the check master would have the problem done correctly in its entirety. A check master is distinguished from an answer key in that an answer key usually shows only the answers but not all the parts of the problem. The answer key of a typical teacher's manual is literally predicated on an understanding of corrective feedback as the universal helping interaction since answers alone without the rest of the work permit only a deficit diagnosis of the student's work.

To use a check master, look at the student's work and then look at the same problem on the check master in your hand and scan horizontally for match and mismatch. Each *match* is a praise statement. The first *mismatch* produces your prompt. The entire interaction takes only a few seconds.

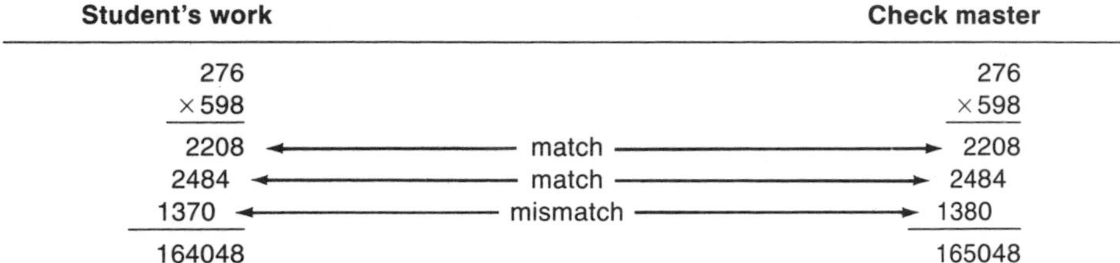

Student's work
Check master
276
×598
2208 match 2208
2484 match 2484
1370 mismatch 1380
164048
276
×598
165048

Positive helping interaction

You have multiplied your 8 and 9 correctly. Double-check your 5 multiplication and then re-add.

Optional statement (additional work check)

These [other] problems are correct [mark them as you talk]. Keep going, and I'll be back around in a few minutes to see how you're doing.

But where do you get all those check masters? The publishing company rarely supplies them. Do you make the check masters yourself using valuable planning time after school? Perish the thought! Remember the rule that governs student chores within the classroom: Never do anything for students that they are perfectly capable of doing for themselves.

Simply confiscate (with full honors, of course) the paper of the brightest kid with the best penmanship who has already completed the assignment. If you have math groups, the fastest group (which does not really need a check master) will make the masters for everyone else. If everyone is together and you have no check master for tomorrow's assignment, offer some bright kid extra credit for doing the assignment today in class or tonight as homework. There is usually a kid with 6 million extra credit points who would die to get a few more. File the check master carefully with copies of your performance model and the practice set so you will have them for the future.

Checking English Composition The most radical change in the work check of English composition teachers comes when they substitute quality assurance for quality control. With brief positive helping interactions during acquisition and guided practice, they can help a student build a high-quality composition rather than having to repair a poor one after the fact. Brief positive helping interactions usually focus on the development of a good topic sentence, for example, or the clear expression of a thought while the student is composing. Much grammar can be taught on the wing as the teacher deals with sentence development.

Yet not everything can be done on the wing even with brief positive helping interactions aided by a performance model. The remainder must be done either by the students at the end of class or by the teacher at home.

When you check English compositions, you are forced to go two different directions at once. You must check both the grammar on the one hand and composition on the other. When you're giving feedback to students, one job gets in the way of the other.

If you grade the grammar, you typically mark all over the paper with red ink and hand back a "bleeding paper." Once students see all that blood on the paper, they are not terribly receptive to the notes in the margin about composition. In addition, grading a paper for grammar often consumes more time than grading it for composition.

Much of the checking of grammar can be done by students. The most straightforward method of exploiting peer check is to have students exchange papers after the compositions have been completed so that a peer can check the paper for grammar, at least in a preliminary fashion. Pair students as you would for peer teaching during a structured lesson (you would probably use the same pairs) so that weaker students have their papers checked by a stronger student. Marking the papers may be done with light pencil markings next to the errors, or you may train the students to use the notations common in professional editing.

After the corrections have been indicated on the paper, it is returned to its owner so that changes can be made. Then the paper may be passed to a second peer for proofreading. Two pairs of peers make a "study square" for the purpose of double proofreading. Following the second proofreading, the marked paper is once again returned to its owner so that grammar can be corrected. Only then are the papers handed in to the teacher.

English composition teachers using this system, whether it be in fifth grade or college, find that much of the grammar will have been taken care of so that their work check can be focused on composition. The bleeding paper is avoided and the students are still held responsible for correct grammar. In addition, the process of peer checking is a valuable learning experience in its own right.

Quality Control and Study Groups The role of student pairs or dyads was described in Chapter 9 as an important means of structuring verbal output and skill performance by students as part of the trimodal cycle. In addition, student team learning was discussed briefly as a means of structuring research. The pairing and grouping of students can be extended not only to peer teaching and research but also to the areas of motivation and quality control. Indeed, the more efficiency-minded teachers become, the more they will find themselves driven toward exploiting peer groupings as a highly cost-effective means of delegating authority and responsibility for tasks ranging from learning to classroom chores (see Chapter 4 of *Positive Classroom Discipline*). A few brief examples may serve to stimulate exploration in the area of student study groups and quality control groups.

Study Groups When students know exactly what they are supposed to learn, you can hold them more responsible not only for learning it but also for teaching it. A Spanish teacher in southern California who was trained as a coach in the Classroom Management Training Program decided to organize her class into study groups of four to six students with a strong student in each group as a leader who was responsible for drilling group members on the vocabulary and grammar skills for the week. The decentralization of the process of teaching immediately produced a heightened degree of student involvement. Then, to heighten motivation even more, the teacher added an element of team competition into the process. Remembering that group rewards promote cooperation whereas individual rewards promote competition, the teacher rank-ordered the study groups at the end of each week on the basis of the group's *aggregate* score on a weekly exam. Higher-scoring groups then had longer access to a highly desired enrichment activity on Friday.

Having greatly increased peer teaching and mild peer pressure toward excellence, the teacher decided to exploit her peer groupings for paper grading. The teacher reported:

> I used to dread grading the students' Spanish notebooks which contained their daily work and special assignments. It would take hours. Finally I got smart and made performance models for checking each type of assignment that we typically did in class. Then I taught the class to do the checking using the performance model as a guide. Then I had the study groups exchange notebooks for grading to provide a double-check on accuracy. It was all done in 7 minutes!

Research Groups If a teacher can provide a *clear performance outline* for a class research project, she can then organize the class into research groups typical of student team learning as described in Chapter 7. This organization of learning into a cooperative problem-solving process based on a clear structuring of both academic and behavioral tasks is beneficial not only for improving the structure of expected performance but also for quality control. The mechanism of peer accountability for individual performance on a portion of a task for which the group is interdependent and for which the group is judged tends to aid the weaker student disproportionately.

The exploitation of peer groupings to provide incentives for diligence and excellence and to aid in quality control while enriching instruction is in its infancy. But one basic rule of group incentive management still applies: students will do things for peer affirmation that they would never do for their teacher or their parents.

CRITERION OF MASTERY

Once you can check work as it is being done, you must ask yourself, "when *is* the student done?" Any incentive system for work productivity must have a well-defined *end point* to the assignment so that the students have a clear performance goal. One reason for an unmotivated student to hustle is to get done early so that he or she may have the opportunity to do a preferred activity. Once you can do work check for the sake of excellence, you will need an end point for the sake of diligence.

Although the end point of an assignment seems quite simple at first—such as completing all the problems in a given work set—such an end point often supplies an incentive for dawdling. It would be far better to have a separate "criterion of mastery."

A criterion of mastery tells a student how many of the problems or exercises have to be done *correctly in succession* before the student has adequately demonstrated mastery of the skill. Ask yourself how much is enough. Must the student do all twenty problems regardless, or is ten in a row a clear and adequate demonstration of mastery? Criteria of mastery for complex learning tasks usually range from five in a row correct to ten in a row correct—a sensible ballpark figure for classroom use.

If the teacher can check papers efficiently while the students are working, the teacher can excuse students from an assignment as soon as they have demonstrated mastery. A criterion of mastery, therefore, greatly increases the strength of the incentive for diligent work while reducing the likelihood of boring students who have clearly mastered the task. And our criterion of mastery underscores the classroom standard by which we define a completed assignment—that it be done *correctly*.

SPONGE PREFERRED ACTIVITIES

Madeline Hunter has coined the term "sponge activity" to describe any learning activity that can "soak up" slack time in order to use it for learning. An example of slack time that is typically wasted is the time an elementary class stands in line at the door waiting for the recess or lunch bell to ring. If the students have to wait more than a few seconds, someone will soon be getting into trouble pushing or roughhousing or making noise. The teacher is subject to one of the basic rules of discipline management: If you do not structure time for learning, the students will structure it for their own amusement.

The sponge activity, in contrast, soaks up such time which so often generates discipline problems, and structures it for some type of enrichment exercise or skill drill. The teacher may drill the students on math or history or general information facts or play a quick learning game. Minutes soaked up for learning can add up over the weeks while reducing the teacher's stress level.

In an incentive system for diligence and excellence the preferred activities or rewards must be *sponge* preferred activities. Like sponge activities in general, the time set aside for sponge preferred activities soaks up leftover time while structuring it for both learning and reward. Sponge preferred activities must be of variable length because students finish their work at different speeds and at different times. The amount of time remaining for a student to engage in a preferred activity after she or he finishes one assignment before the beginning of the next assignment in class is unpredictable. Thus any well-planned assignment is really three different activities that answer three different questions:

1 The directions (What do we do?)
2 The task itself (How do we do it?)
3 The sponge preferred activity (What do we do if we finish early?)

All three activities must be structured in advance and must follow each other in rapid succession, or the teacher will lose a portion of the class to confusion or goofing off at each step.

Scheduling Sponge Preferred Activities

The scheduling of sponge preferred activity time (sponge PAT) as the reward part of an incentive system for work productivity usually (1) takes place immediately following a specific assignment or (2) is delayed until a series of assignments has been completed. A series of assignments followed by a sponge PAT is typically referred to as a "work contract," and it is more common at the secondary level. Thus, for example, a high school class might have five or six assignments to complete during a given week, and the teacher might excuse students to work on their sponge PATs as soon as all the assignments have been completed to the teacher's satisfaction.

Planning Sponge PATs

The teacher must have preferred activity options available to the students when they finish an assignment or work contract. Sponge PATs must, however, require minimal planning, no setup time, and almost no effort and distraction to the teacher during instruction. Optimally, sponge preferred activities surround the students and are continually available to them whenever they complete an assignment *to the teacher's standards* with time to spare. Effective incentive managers will have a large number of sponge PATs at their fingertips.

What are some of the activities that you can surround students with in order to provide sponge PATs at the drop of a hat? Many enrichment activities that may serve as reward options for responsibility training (see Chapters 9, 10, and 11 of *Positive Classroom Discipline*) can do double duty as sponge PATs for your academic incentive system. Projects that set students free to be creative are ideal sponge PATs. Thus your capacity to utilize a criterion of mastery because of rapid work check can be a major antidote to the boredom experienced by many bright students when faced with repetitive skill drill during guided practice. Rather than dawdling when they lose interest, all students now have a reason to strive to achieve the criterion of mastery in order to have access to higher-interest learning activities.

By organizing the PATs in advance a teacher can have *individualized* sponge PATs while avoiding the distractions during guided practice that come from getting students set up and started on their special projects. A primary teacher, for example, might have each student bring a project box (a shoebox) in which supplies for special projects can be kept. A time might be set aside periodically for students to plan projects and collect the materials needed to carry them out. With each student having a box on a shelf with her or his name on it and a project inside, the teacher can excuse a student to work on her or his own sponge PAT as soon as she or he has completed a piece of work without any setup time required from the teacher.

Many enrichment activities, however, can be ever-present and available to all students with very little ongoing time and effort required of the teacher. I can remember as a child the sponge PATs that formed a predictable and enjoyable part of everyday classroom life. There was always a tempera-paint mural across the chalkboard at the back of the classroom in elementary school where students could paint if they finished their work early. I can still see the fall, halloween, and Thanksgiving scenes and the Christmas mural. I can remember the social studies units emblazoned almost life-size—the wagon train moving west, the *Mayflower* landing, prospectors panning for gold, the Vikings, and even the signing of the Magna Carta. I can also remember the class plays that various committees of students would work on in their spare time and the displays at the science table that we had prepared.

Any enrichment activity that students can initiate with little immediate help from the teacher is fair game for a sponge PAT. Interest centers, learning games, science projects, or special projects of any kind can serve beautifully as rewards for diligence and excellence. Stained-glass windows made from colored cellophane and electrician's tape may seem like kids' stuff to secondary teachers, but high school students love to have the chance to have fun with learning as much as they ever did. The teachers, however, may be a bit rusty.

Responsibility Training for Good Work

The main prerequisites of sponge PATs is that they be enjoyable, available, and cheap. The main prerequisite for their appropriate use as work incentives, however, is that *accountability* for the quantity and quality of the work be strict, quick, and cheap. It is easier to deliver sponge PATs than it is to deliver strict and quick accountability. Without strict and quick accountability, sponge PATs will only produce speed incentives.

When used properly, however, sponge PATs in conjunction with strict accountability and a criterion of mastery comprise a type of responsibility training for good work that automatically eliminates both dawdling and sloppiness. PAT begins as soon as the task is completed properly and ends at a predetermined time. If students dawdle, they consume their own preferred activity time since completing the assignment takes longer. If they become fast and sloppy, they automatically penalize themselves because they must go over the work and do it again until it is correct. The only way to maximize reward is to do the work *as rapidly as possible consistent with doing it right the first time*. A student is continually locked into an optimal incentive structure for work productivity whenever the following four elements are present:

1 Assignment of a finite amount of work in a finite amount of time
2 Preferred activities available as soon as the work is completed
3 A criterion of mastery
4 Efficient work check so that the student may be excused from the assignment to do a preferred activity on correct completion of the task

OVERVIEW

Formal incentive systems for work productivity provide clear and systematic rewards for diligence and excellence. Only by experiencing an environment which consistently demands and supports such effort will students learn conscientious work habits. *Without* effective incentive systems for diligence and excellence, students inadvertently learn that they can be excused from the work as soon as they tire of it, regardless of quality. In lieu of them, a teacher must rely on the internalized incentives or *values* that students bring from home, in conjunction with their capacity to inspire students, to produce diligence and excellence. Such values within the general population of students and such skills within the general population of teachers are unpredictable at best.

We have learned that the avoidance of incentive management is an illusion. Without explicit rewards for work productivity, the teacher constructs an incentive for dawdling which inadvertently leads to reliance on negative sanctions as disincentives for poor or incomplete work. Yet quick and easy rewards without strict accountability produce speed incentives. A learning environment must be consciously structured to effectively reward diligence and excellence or, by default, teachers will naïvely relinquish much of their power to produce a consistently positive and productive learning environment.

A thorough understanding of incentive systems is not a luxury or frill for a teacher—it is a necessity. Effective teachers and effective parents have always used incentives to their great advantage whether they could explain what they were doing or not. Without incentives teachers or parents will repeatedly find themselves wanting a child to do something but with no clear way to get him to do it. With no clear answer to the question *Why should I,* both parents and teachers will forever be backed into the two remaining options of (1) nag, threaten, and punish or (2) kiss it off and lower your standards.

With no understanding of the expensive obligation of accountability that accompanies the use of incentives, however, many teachers have gone to a lot of effort offering rewards to students, only to fail. To know the workings of a few pretested and prepackaged classroom incentive systems is not enough. The multiplicity of behavioral objectives that a teacher must accomplish and the multiplicity of student needs in any classroom require that the teacher understand incentives well enough to be able to improvise, customize, and invent with a high likelihood of success. Furthermore, teachers must be able to succeed at a low cost to themselves in planning time and setup time and work check or else the frequent use of incentives becomes unaffordable.

However, in spite of our understanding of incentives for diligence and excellence and our desire to use them, our ability to implement such incentives on a broad scale will always be limited by more basic instructional skills. Quality assurance, if it is to be strict, quick, and cheap, must be done during acquisition and during guided practice while the work is being done the first time. The luxury of spending guided practice in quality assurance is bought at the price of (1) good discipline, (2) trimodal lesson presentation with a clear performance model, and (3) mastery of praise, prompt, and leave. Without such prerequisite skills, talk of high standards of diligence and excellence will forever remain in the realm of unattainable goals and professional platitudes.

With systematic rewards for work productivity, however, teachers can systematically construct and maintain a value system within the class that may ultimately become internalized by many individual students over the course of their schooling. Excellence can become a way of life, but first a student must live in an environment that continually supports excellence and causes it to become both a habit and a constant expectation.

SECTION FIVE

CREATING CHANGE IN EDUCATION

CHAPTER **11**

TEACHER TRAINING

Positive discipline and positive instruction dovetail to form an integrated methodology for managing both discipline and academic productivity. The effectiveness of any innovation, however, is limited by the accuracy with which it is reproduced during dissemination. When proper teaching methods are used to train teachers, learning occurs and a solid foundation is laid for professional growth and change. However, any technique, no matter how effective in the hands of a well-trained teacher, can fail in the hands of a novice who only "knows about" it. To the extent that good teaching practices are abridged during teacher training, the success of any teacher training program is undermined and change is thwarted.

CHEAP CURES AND COSTLY ILLUSIONS

With each passing year, more administrators, no matter what their perspective on staff development, are becoming increasingly aware that they have not been getting much for their staff-development dollar. Money spent on one-shot, in-service presentations and money spent in compensating teachers for accumulating additional college credits rarely translate into improved classroom performance. Whereas the expenditure for in-service presentations may be regarded by some as a one-time loss, college credits usually advance teachers on the pay scale so that the compensation for a single summer course may amount to thousands of dollars by the time of retirement. School boards, administrators, teachers, and even parents are increasingly asking themselves, "Is this getting us anywhere?"

Yet over the years the successful dissemination of innovation within education has been blocked by a combination of naiveté and an unwillingness to allocate resources for teacher training on the part of colleges, school boards, administrators, teachers, and especially the general public. Educators and the people they serve have all been partners in accepting a set of beliefs about the way in which teachers are trained that is both cheap and easy.

Two Types of Learning

The teaching profession acts as if there were two fundamentally different processes of instrumental learning and skill development: child and adult. We can accept that young people need to be held by the hand as they go through the steps of a structured lesson. Kids, of course, need careful explanation, modeling, and performance practice one step at a time as well as extensive repetition and drill. Such care is needed because they have not yet grown up and become smart.

We treat teachers, in contrast, as though they were all one-trial auditory learners who can take a simple explanation from a one-shot, in-service presentation and translate it into effective classroom practice. Do not worry about learning skills one step at a time with lots of practice and precise corrective feedback. If you are an adult, you only need to be exposed to new ideas.

This widely held belief in the efficacy of "exposure" might be labeled "The Viral Theory of Learning." The viral theory of learning assumes that the process of acquiring knowledge is akin to the process by which we acquire chicken pox. A virus can be acquired through mere exposure to it, and so too can teaching skills if one were to judge from the prevailing methods of teacher training and staff development. Viral teaching, the concomitant of viral learning, is extremely common within the education profession. It's the preferred mode of instruction for higher education, social studies, and teacher in-service.

Viral learning is distinct from the processes of instrumental learning or operant conditioning, which are appropriate for children, in that viral learning does not require practice. This attribute has been a great asset to adult education in cutting the cost of skill building in favor of the far quicker and easier teaching formats of lecture (talking to fifty or more) and seminar (talking to fifty or less). In terms of "bang for the buck," you just cannot beat the efficiency of describing some new teaching method to the faculty of an entire district packed into the high school auditorium.

If we are unable to teach ourselves well as professionals, how can we expect to do much better when teaching our classes? If exposure passes for professional development, then it is only a matter of time until exposure passes for teaching in the classroom. Indeed "assigning" rather than teaching is rapidly becoming the norm, especially at the secondary level, with work going home for independent practice that has never been mastered in class. Foolishness on such a broad scale cannot have small consequences.

BASICS OF SUCCESS

Good Learning Requires Good Teaching

Complex skills are not easily learned—especially the skills of managing an entire classroom full of young people so that they all simultaneously forsake the joys of goofing off in favor of the rigors of learning. Unless we know how to consistently produce time on task and independent learning across the many settings and needy personalities of a typical classroom at low stress to ourselves, the odds are perpetually stacked against both our well-being and our students' success. We have few satisfying options apart from the careful and systematic mastery of these complex teaching and management skills.

Skill training is at its core a series of carefully taught structured lessons. *Positive Classroom Instruction,* therefore, provides a manual for successful skill building during teacher training as well as during instruction within the classroom. Good teacher training is good teaching—no more, no less. There are neither magic formulas, quick cures, easy answers, nor panaceas. "Knowing about" is quite different from "knowing how to," and "knowing how to" requires the thorough mastery of correct skill performance that has been properly taught. With teachers, just as with their students, the mastery of skills is learned one step at a time through clear explanation, careful modeling, and practice, practice, practice.

Consequently, the success of the implementation of any innovation within education will be primarily a function of the delivery system through which change and innovation are disseminated. Without a quality delivery system, all innovation within education will die the same death. Procedures poorly implemented tend to fail regardless of their intrinsic merit or quality. Careful training by highly skilled trainers and plenty of follow through are required to implement procedures properly. Both cost money. For teacher training to succeed there is no shortcut.

The Trainer-of-Trainers Imperative

In the beginning of the first volume of this work, *Positive Classroom Discipline,* I briefly recounted my rather rude awakening to the necessity of using proper teaching methods the first time I tried to train a group of teachers to use limit-setting. Success in teacher training occurred only when kinetic, performance-oriented methods of training were employed. During the years since that first learning experience in 1969, the methods of *Positive Classroom Discipline* have evolved steadily, and during that same period our methods of teacher training have grown apace. The experiences of teacher training, in fact, have served as the laboratory for the refinement of many of the instructional methods described in the present volume. Thus two separate technologies have been continuously growing side by side: (1) skills of classroom instruction and discipline management and (2) skills of teacher training and staff development in the field.

Yet as early as 1970, it became apparent that teacher training with proper instructional methods would always be prohibitively expensive. As one might predict, the bottleneck occurred at guided practice. Taking limit-setting as a prototypical skill, (*Positive Classroom Discipline,* Chapters 5, 6, and 7), I had to coach each trainee individually through several management dilemmas of increasing difficulty before performance became fluid and before the trainee got a sense of mastery and self-confidence. Structured practice could not produce the self-assurance and poise that came from performing "on your own" during guided practice. With each practice trial during guided practice, the simple motoric performance of a portion of the skill sequence became automatic and receded from foreground to background in the eyes of the trainees. Finally they could focus on the behavior and feelings of the student rather than on their own anxiety about what to do next. Only with the self-confidence born of adequate guided practice did teachers consistently risk using the new skills of limit-setting in their classrooms. Only with adequate guided practice did they perform both confidently and correctly.

Research and development took two directions as a result of our being confronted with the amount of time which was required to properly coach a trainee through the guided practice of limit-setting and, subsequently, of other skills as well. First, I attempted to increase my efficiency during training, and second, I began exploring the feasibility of training teachers to be trainers without loss of quality. The first line of work led to the understanding of a structured lesson as a trimodal exercise and an appreciation of the central role of structured practice during the initial phase of skill acquisition. The second line of work produced the first hard research to explore issues of quality control with a trainer-of-trainers methodology in the field.[1]

During these years it became apparent that a first-rate job of training could be done by teachers in the field if (1) they were properly taught to teach the lessons of the staff development program and if (2) implementation occurred within a framework of continuing review, collegial sharing and support, and systematic problem solving. It also became clear, in fact, that such training would have to be done by professionals in the field or it would never be done at all. Districts could afford to have me train some of their personnel as trainers, but they could not afford to have me train all their teachers directly.

The scope of our teacher training program has expanded over the years as dilemmas of classroom management and teacher training have been addressed by us one by one. As our classroom management and staff development methods have matured, a fairly comprehensive program for training teachers to perform the basic skills of their profession has come into being. That program is known as the Classroom Management Training Program (CMTP), and a portion of the skills and procedures contained in that program form the content of this book.

A thorough description of the procedures of the Classroom Management Training Program would take a separate volume, but a synopsis will be presented in this section as a model for creating growth and lasting change in schools and school districts. In program implementation, however, it is the proper execution of the *specifics,* the nuts and bolts, which ultimately spells success or failure. Fifteen years in the school of hard knocks has taught us a lot about the specifics of creating lasting change. For our present purposes, however, a few chapters highlighting major emphasis will have to do. I hope this brief treatment will alert those interested in implementing the procedures of *Positive Classroom Discipline* and *Positive Classroom Instruction* to some of the rigors which are the price of success.

Creating a Network of Support

During the 1970s it became apparent from experience in the field that more advantages could be gained from a trainer-of-trainers program than simply cost effectiveness through the multiplication of my efforts. Trainers at a school site or within a school district form an "expertise hierarchy" which greatly aids the continuing dissemination, quality control, and longevity of the training program. The trainers would lead *continuation groups* that met regularly to review and reteach skills, share ideas, and solve problems of implementation. In-house trainers could also retrain their colleagues periodically, conduct "back to school" brush-up workshops in the fall, and train new staff members so that a trained faculty would not be diluted by staff turnover. Just as important, the trainers became resident advocates of quality staff development and often prevented the watering down of the program by administrators less familiar than they with the conditions necessary for successful dissemination.

The positive influence of the coaches is greatly enhanced, of course, if they work in collaboration with administrators knowledgeable about the program and committed to both active participation in, and continuing support for, quality staff development. For this reason we never train faculty at a school site unless the administrators not only go through training but also become members of a training team along with key faculty members. Dissemination is further aided by adequate district support and coordination, which is the subject of the next chapter. Administrative support and teacher training expertise must grow together so that gradually a staff development network is constructed within the district.

The Classroom Management Training Program (CMTP) deals with the entire context of change within the district and school site in addition to teacher training in order to maximize the likelihood of successful program implementation. The skills and procedures of CMTP have two objectives: (1) optimal training to ensure initial mastery of basic skills and (2) the creation of a network of teachers, administrators, and even parents and school board members to provide support for an ongoing process of professional growth, change, and renewal within each school site. The objective of CMTP in the simplest terms is *lasting* growth and change—the hallmark of any successful staff development effort.

Mechanisms of Success

The three criteria of success for any systematic staff development program at a school site are: mastery, penetration, and longevity. "Mastery" refers to the precision with which new skills are reproduced during initial dissemination of the program. "Penetration" refers to the percentage of the faculty and administration who choose to be trained and who remain actively involved at a given school site. "Longevity" refers to the duration of active faculty participation in program implementation and related areas of professional development at the school site.

Mastery and Methods

Guided Practice with Individuals versus Structured Practice with Groups Guided practice is the methodological watershed of quality skill training, for it creates both *precision* through practice with corrective feedback and the *confidence* that can only come from being able to perform correctly on your own. Guided practice also irons out idiosyncratic errors of application and understanding on the part of individual teachers. But guided practice is also the watershed as regards cost. Guided practice requires expert coaching of one trainee at a time by the experts produced by a quality trainer-of-trainers program.

Training the highly skilled experts of a successful trainer-of-trainers program is a slow and careful process. Although structured practice can produce tentative mastery with a large *group* of trainees, guided practice requires *individualized* feedback on the fine points of performance. Structured practice can be carried out in a relatively brief period of time by someone newly familiar with the program, whereas guided practice requires a much greater understanding of the skill being taught, the errors typical of the new learner, the fears and defensiveness typical of colleagues, and especially, advanced skills of giving corrective feedback.

No "Quick and Dirty" Guided Practice Amateurish attempts at providing guided practice within the context of a trainer-of-trainers program can easily backfire, producing defensiveness, resentment, and "bad-mouthing" of the program among colleagues. There is no quicker way for a trainer to raise the ire of a colleague than to use the *universal helping interaction* during the guided practice of a teaching skill. Implied criticism produces instant defensiveness and revenge aimed at both the trainer and the program.

Trainers in a trainer-of-trainers program must, therefore, be taught to teach every major skill in the program perfectly in order to maximize efficiency (time is precious) and in order to minimize defensiveness from strong and weak colleagues alike. For this reason alone it is cost-effective to combine discipline skills (*Positive Classroom Discipline*) and instructional skills (*Positive Classroom Instruction*) into a single training program since the trainers must be taught to use correct instructional methods with discipline skills anyway. In addition, trainers must be given many advanced and specialized instructional skills unique to CMTP which have not been dealt with in this volume but which are critical to specific training exercises.

Beyond Guided Practice Having placed the importance of guided practice into proper perspective, I must qualify this emphasis somewhat lest the whole notion of implementing a quality trainer-of-trainers program appear financially exorbitant. When guided practice is needed it is crucial, but it is only needed for key skills which have a major performance component. Much of CMTP has to do with awareness, raising the level of concern, concept explanation, and generalization—parts of a structured lesson that resemble any other quality workshop. We do not spend all our time in guided practice.

Yet the *key* skills of classroom management are *new* skills and typically involve not only new learning but also the breaking of old habits. The two most prominent and most difficult such skills are "limit-setting" in *Positive Classroom Discipline* and the "positive helping interaction" in *Positive Classroom Instruction*. Teachers will spend the rest of their careers mastering component skills of these two procedures because they have such a strong affective component and because they have such strong negative transfer from old teaching habits. Although such key skills live or die on the basis of adequate guided practice during acquisition and periodic retraining in the months following initial training, other parts of CMTP can be much more readily grasped and implemented. Mastery of the parts of CMTP that do not rely so heavily on guided practice can be greatly enhanced by well-developed software and video. The integration of skill practice with media to produce maximum learning at minimum cost will constitute a continuing area of growth and development for CMTP.

The Trainer-of-Trainers Fad "Trainer of trainers" has become a buzz word in education. It has been linked through research to effective staff development. Everyone, it seems, is suddenly doing trainer-of-trainers programs.

Trainer-of-trainer programs in the field range from the sublime to the ridiculous. Few programs train trainers carefully, and many are simply dressed-up traditional workshops and seminars which are designed to familiarize large numbers of teachers with new methods rapidly. Explanation and demonstration typically dominate with some "walk through" and no guided practice.

Yet training trainers slowly and carefully, in contrast, creates specialists who will pay back the initial investment in their training many times over as they serve their schools and school districts by training large numbers of colleagues and by maintaining their colleagues' effectiveness over time. A trainer-of-trainers program, therefore, is a long-term investment which implies a systematic, programmatic approach to staff development on the part of the sponsoring agency.

Penetration and Volunteerism

Skimming If a staff-development program trains those teachers and administrators who first volunteer for the experience, it will repeatedly reach those who are most eager to learn, to grow, and to change. It *skims* the most active, involved, and competent teachers and administrators in the district and leaves the rest behind. Contrary to the needs of the district, it always helps *most* those who need help *least*. How do you get the rest of the teachers and administrators to want to grow and change?

"Penetration" refers to the capacity of a staff development program to reach beyond the top teachers and administrators and pull the rest of the staff into an active involvement in mastering new skills. If a training program can draw nearly all administrators and faculty into full participation in a training program, it has succeeded to a far greater extent than a program which only skims the top 20 to 30 percent of district personnel.

Success Based on Volunteerism Achieving penetration is tricky because of the necessity of building a quality staff development program on "volunteerism." The desire to change and grow must come from *within* because change requires effort and risk and constant attention to proper skill application both during training and later while on the job. All this required effort can be withheld at will.

When administrators *mandate* attendance at a training program, they create the resistance to wholehearted participation which will all but guarantee half-hearted and short-lived implementation on the part of the coerced participant. They get exactly what was required and no more—attendance.

If volunteerism is so important, where does it come from? Since volunteerism is so rarely present in the teachers who need training most, a successful program must produce much of its own volunteerism. The methods of producing this volunteerism are part of a successful trainer-of-trainers program. Without such mechanisms, training may take place on a broad scale, but change will be spotty at best.

Volunteerism among the bulk of the faculty grows gradually and informally over the long run, largely through word of mouth. Trained teachers will talk enthusiastically to each other about their experiences and success with "the program." Teachers who are experiencing stress or frustration ask their friends who have been trained about the program. Has it really helped? Do you really have fewer problems and less stress? Trained teachers in sharing their feelings and experiences sell the program. We refer to this predictable phenomenon as "the teachers' lounge effect."

But the teachers' lounge effect rests squarely on the consistent efficacy of the training program. If the training program were not making a big difference in the lives of the trained teachers that more than justified the time and effort that went into training, the program would die in the teachers' lounge. Thus a successful training program must indirectly sell itself to teachers who are reticent to volunteer. Selling rests on success, which rests on proper training and implementation. If the program could not sell itself, the administration could not implement it if their lives depended on it. There is no cheap way.

Yet no program sells itself entirely. Selling is first done by an impressive introductory presentation, typically by CMTP personnel, which produces the volunteerism needed to recruit the trainers and the first few rounds of trainees. Selling is subsequently done by administrators in addition to the spontaneous enthusiasm of trained teachers. Administrators, therefore, must carry out a carefully designed support role in order to establish professional growth as a prominent, permanent, and highly valued objective at each participating school site.

The principal's role in producing volunteerism ranges all the way from being part of a training team along with teachers to selling the program in faculty meetings to sharing his enthusiasm with individual teachers. By observing the principal investing time in the staff development program, teachers are able to see concrete evidence of school site and district commitment. Although teachers' skepticism about staff development is strong, that skepticism is based on reality—the farcical and time-wasting in-service programs of the past—rather than an indifference to receiving help in doing their job. If a respected principal is steadfast in his or her commitment and if a "critical mass" of respected colleagues is actively involved in, and enthusiastic about, a new program, most teachers will be drawn toward volunteerism out of enlightened self-interest.

Yet the negativisitic and burned-out teachers often remain recalcitrant. How can you get the teachers who need it most to buy it? There is no final answer to this dilemma, but experience indicates that the best hope of success lies along any or all of the following three paths: (1) a personal and sincere appeal by the principal, (2) a personal and sincere appeal by respected colleagues, and (3) a requirement that the faculty make an all-or-nothing commitment to the program. Even if the negative few are outvoted, at least their participation, however half-hearted, will be the result of a peer process rather than an administrative mandate! Though less than perfect, whole faculty participation based on a peer-group decision-making process has the advantage of producing an entire faculty that at least speaks the same language. If, however, this strategy seems unworkable, the principal can use supervision procedures for individual teachers described in the following chapters.

Building on Strength It should be noted that the requirement for total volunteerism runs counter to the instincts of many administrators—even the most involved and well-intentioned. Their vested interest, out of the best of motives, often is to train the weakest teachers first since they are doing the most damage in the classroom. Though well-intentioned, this instinct is ultimately self-defeating.

In order to spread, a training program must produce a *critical mass of success.* It must be seen by the majority of the faculty as highly successful in the hands of their most esteemed and trusted colleagues. Only on the basis of demonstrated efficacy will most teachers ultimately volunteer for an extensive training program that calls for lasting commitment. To produce this critical mass of success, the very best and most respected teachers who volunteer should be recruited as trainers or coaches, and the next strongest teachers should be trained in the initial rounds of training. Trainers should be:

- Excellent teachers
- Liked and respected by peers
- Eager to coach
- Good communicators

Longevity and Follow Through Even if a program succeeds in involving an entire staff in training and even if it produces immediate success and enthusiasm, it is a questionable investment if 2 years later it is out of sight and out of mind: Are you still doing any of the what's-its-name program in your classroom? To be truly successful, change must be lasting. Lasting change, however, is far more difficult to produce than initial change.

Some rather depressing realities concerning teacher training need to be appreciated if the barriers to long-term change are to be fully understood. First, any skill that is mastered during training but is not implemented in the classroom within 48 hours will probably never be implemented. Second, there is no way to implement all the skills of a sophisticated methodology for doing anything within 48 hours. And third, even if you could implement all the skills within 48 hours, they would probably be gone or half forgotten by next fall. Please keep in mind that the *only predictable result of learning is the immediate onset of forgetting.* Atrophy is the eternal enemy of a good training program.

All the above-mentioned problems are predictable consequences of a good training program unless an additional follow-through program is implemented to systematically combat atrophy. Such a program must create a process of continuing skill practice, problem solving, support, and the sharing of professional expertise that becomes a valued part of the fabric of professional life at any participating school site.

Central to the process of continuing mastery in CMTP is the formation immediately following training of *continuation groups* in which retraining, problem solving, and sharing systematically occur. Continuation groups should have roughly six to ten participants—a team of trainers and the colleagues they worked with during the previous round of training. Small *training* groups permit adequate guided practice during the initial training, and small *continuation* groups preserve the intimacy, camaraderie, and safety of the training group while ensuring that problems and personal concerns can be addressed quickly as they arise in daily classroom experience.

Since continuation groups are small and intimate, a given school site may have several ongoing continuation groups after the entire staff has been trained. These continuation groups have four basic functions: (1) review, (2) problem solving, (3) sharing, and (4) support and enjoyment.

Review During the 3 months following initial training, the entire program must be systematically retaught. Thus a minimum commitment to CMTP training includes not only participation in the initial training but also 3 months of follow-up participation in a continuation group.

Integration of new skills into a teacher's skill repertoire and classroom routine is a gradual process. An analogy might be the folding of recipe ingredients into a cake batter. You need to work one ingredient into the batter at a time so the batter will remain smooth. If you throw all the ingredients in at once and stir, you get lumps. Teachers need time to gradually mix the ingredients of the training program into their classroom routines, or they will take a lot of lumps. They need careful review of each major skill just before classroom application to ensure success.

Continuation groups also provide a thread of continuity from year to year. Skills decay greatly over the summer, and without some practice before the students show up in the fall, teachers may get off to a wobbly start with their classroom management. Commonly, continuation groups spend at least a day in the fall in formal retraining, which can be provided by the CMTP coaches.

Problem Solving To imagine that every skill of a training program will work perfectly the first time it is used by all trainees is to live in fantasyland. Techniques will bomb on occasion because of sheer inexperience. In the first 3 months following training, when new ingredients are being added to their classroom routine, teachers make mistakes typical of inexperience and take some lumps in spite of careful review. During this shakedown period, problems are either solved quickly in a continuation group or else valuable techniques are unceremoniously dropped by a disillusioned teacher.

In order to ensure that a valuable classroom technology is not aborted following training, there must not only be a peer support group from which to get help, but there must also be (1) an expectation that glitches are perfectly normal and (2) a process of problem solving within the group that is both effective and supportive. If teachers feel that failing is a sign of personal inadequacy, they will probably not seek help. And if seeking help causes them to feel embarrassed or humiliated, they will do it only once. Members of the continuation group must be trained to use sophisticated group problem-solving skills so that they can help each other without generating the defensiveness which is typical of advice giving.

Sharing A group of twenty teachers have among themselves enough experience and professional wisdom to solve a great many classroom management dilemmas even without training. Yet professional wisdom rarely passes from one classroom to another. One of the prices we pay for practicing our profession behind closed doors is that we deprive ourselves of each other's insights and creativity. In continuation groups the collective wisdom of the group is systematically shared. In so doing we exploit what may be education's largest untapped resource.

Two common forms of sharing during continuation meetings are (1) peer teaching of PATs and (2) shared lesson design. Typically members of the continuation group will take turns opening the meeting by teaching the group a favorite PAT. Over time teachers at a school site or within a district will collect a "PAT bank" for common use. Joint lesson planning becomes a major activity of continuation group meetings after the first 6 weeks posttraining since discipline management will have largely become old business by then. Teachers from the same department or grade level typically share in the design of good performance models at this time.

As joint lesson planning becomes a major activity of the continuation group during the second month after training, the continuation group begins a formal "peer observation program." Teachers typically pair up to design a lesson with the understanding that one will teach while the other observes. The role of the principal in the peer observation program is to provide coverage for the observer's classroom. Peer observation is followed by a conference of the two participating teachers later in the same day to discuss the lesson. Such observation is nonevaluative and provides a wealth of professional sharing, incidental learning, and enrichment for everyone as well as providing help for teachers who are reticent to ask for it in the continuation group meetings.

Enjoyment and Support Continuation groups often continue for years after training, becoming a permanent part of school life. To be so highly valued, however, groups must be a source of fellowship, friendship, and support in addition to their professional development function. For longevity's sake the group must plan to have fun together. And for longevity's sake the group must rally to the support of a member in need, be it anything from problems with a difficult student or a difficult administrator to personal tragedy.

The mix of personalities within any group is highly variable, of course, but in some form the group members must be the source of their own nurturance and their own PATs. In our work lives we often forget to plan for enjoyment. Better to meet at someone's house with food or to have a party every fourth meeting than to let the group become grim.

METHODS OF DISSEMINATION

In staff development long-term success or failure ultimately rests not so much with the cleverness of the innovation as with the quality of the delivery system. Within an organization, lasting and meaningful change based on shared expertise, high morale, and cooperation will always be limited, therefore, by the sophistication of the methods used to instigate change. Consequently, it is important to understand the basic types of delivery systems and to be able to predict the type of change produced by each.

Dissemination Formats to School Districts

Consultants are at best teachers who travel and at worst nonteachers who travel. As one might well conclude from the preceding section, the quality of a delivery system can be judged by the thoroughness of the teaching which it employs. Since a great many consultants have employed viral teaching to expose tens of thousands of teachers to tens of effective techniques during recent decades, consultants have produced teacher *disillusionment* at a record rate since techniques that are poorly taught rarely work.

Of course such consultants have only been doing what was asked of them by administrators who wanted a brief presentation to expose their faculties to new ideas. According to Fredric J. McDonald, a researcher in teacher training,[2] as a result of this collaboration between naïve consultants and naïve administrators, teachers have learned little from staff development over the years except to be skeptical of anyone bearing new programs. Thus consultants have been vilified as someone who "blows in, blows off, and blows out" or as almost any turkey with a briefcase and a plane ticket. Observing consultants at work, therefore, reveals a great deal about what they regard to be teaching while providing a user's guide to staff development formats.

Introductory Presentations In past decades almost all professional staff development has followed the "blow in, blow off, and blow out" format. In the business such presentations are sometimes referred to as "dog and pony shows" or "hot bath treatments" (invigorating while they last, but as soon as they are over you cool off rapidly). Some consultants or presenters, of course, can give a masterful show, which keeps the audience in stitches. It had better keep the audience in stitches or the presenter will receive a high percentage of negative evaluations because "the seats were too hard." The seats being too hard is educational jargon for the fact that most teachers have lost their patience with shows. They know from experience that the content of the presentation does not magically translate into skills which help them in the classroom. So, to be tolerable, the presentation had damn well better be entertaining. As a result, many presenters, not being dummies, go heavy on the jokes and cute anecdotes while going light on substance.

If it sounds as though I hold introductory presentations in contempt, I have failed to make myself clear. What I hold in contempt is the *overselling* of one-shot presentations. No institution is going to hire an outside person to conduct a quality staff development program until they have become familiar with the program and feel comfortable with the person. Almost all quality training programs begin with a good show. Introductory presentations, however, are good for only two things: awareness and marketing.

The importance of a good show should not be minimized. Owing to the intense skepticism regarding in-service programs that has been generated among teachers by one-shot presentations over the past several decades, overcoming skepticism is the first order of business. Thus overcoming the built-in resistance of a faculty to a new program and replacing that skepticism with enthusiasm and volunteerism is the beginning of any successful long-term staff development effort. The antipathy to in-service programs is particularly strong at the high school level, and unless the faculty can be sold during a 1- to 2-hour presentation, dissemination will probably go no further. Thus, ironically, a dynamite dog and pony show is a prerequisite for the dissemination of any quality trainer-of-trainers program.

The critical question about an introductory presentation is not so much how good is it but, rather, what comes next. Is there a first-rate training program to come that can translate newly introduced concepts and initial enthusiasm into a process of change within the institution? If not, is awareness all you are after? If so, then you are probably indulging yourself in the magical expectations characteristic of viral teaching.

Workshops, Seminars, and Institutes Staff development programs which fall short of systematic teacher training but which go beyond introductory presentations are typically referred to as "workshops," "seminars," or "institutes." By their titles these formats promise more than awareness and marketing. If there is more, it should take the form of more parts of the structured lesson rather than more time. An institute in which you simply sit, observe, and take notes for an extended period of time is just a long dog and pony show (or a short college course). In order to provide more in the way of teaching, a workshop, seminar, or institute should at least add structured practice to modeling. You should get on your feet or get your hands on materials and actually *perform* the skills as part of a group.

Seminars, institutes, and workshops can provide an effective learning experience if there is an ample number of practice exercises which are close analogs of everyday classroom situations and if structured practice is well done. Such training experiences, however, are for the individual rather than for the school site. That is to say, seminars, institutes, and workshops typically represent skimming with limited administrative involvement and no systematic support-team building. Naturally, such training experiences help the highly competent teachers most since the lack of guided practice puts a premium on preexisting motivation, strong readiness skills, and quick learning. Weak teachers, in contrast, desperately need the retraining and support of the continuation group to minimize the misapplication of basic techniques.

Workshops, seminars, and institutes have an important function in the overall picture of staff development, of course, as do introductory shows. Districts need to know about a program in considerable detail before they can become sold on the idea of systematic teacher training. Workshops, seminars, and institutes, which are usually of 1 to 3 days duration, give administrators, staff development specialists, and key teachers a chance to see up close the program and the people representing it.

Like dog and pony shows, however, workshops, seminars, and institutes suffer from frequent oversell. Even highly competent teachers are quickly overloaded. It is the extremely rare individual who can internalize even a single complex skill with the help of rapid notetaking and frequent review after they get home.

Perhaps more damaging, workshops, seminars, and institutes often profess to make *trainers* out of their participants. Fliers frequently announce that participants will be able to "take these ideas and procedures back to your home school districts." Such oversell is heavily influenced by the viral theory of learning, to say the least. Such pronouncements assume that once you have seen or walked through a skill once or twice, you can magically translate that experience into a successful training program. Such a quick and dirty approach to dissemination usually produces little more than the highly imperfect reproduction of only a portion of the workshop for all the folks back home.

Systematic Teacher Training The dividing line between workshops, seminars, and institutes on the one hand and systematic teacher training on the other hand is (1) the development of trainers at each school site, (2) guided practice of skills, (3) the development of a supportive network of actively participating teachers, administrators, and school board members, and (4) continuation groups and peer coaching to provide follow through in the form of an ongoing growth process at each school site. Sowing seeds is cheap, but bringing in a crop to harvest is careful, hard work over the entire life cycle of the crop. Change comes at the price of good teaching, but lasting change requires ongoing support from all levels of the profession.

Principals as administrators have an explicit role to play in both preparation for training and follow through after training. They go through the full coaches' training so that they may thoroughly understand the program while clearly demonstrating its importance by serving as a member of the training team. Following training the administrators keep the program continually on the "front burner" at the school site by (1) talking the program up and arranging for the sharing of success stories at faculty meetings, (2) arranging for class coverage so that peer observation and peer coaching can take place, (3) supporting the continuation group process by setting aside school time for teachers to get together and by never cross-scheduling that time, (4) visiting classrooms and dropping by continuation group meetings to gain a sense of the health of the program and the needs of participating teachers, and (5) helping to organize new rounds of training and ensuring that coaches have adequate time to prepare for them.

The existence of the continuation group also gives principals an important mechanism for quality control as they attempt to help a weak teacher. If, for example, the principal's observations indicate that a particular teacher is having difficulty with some aspect of teaching or program implementation, the teacher and principal can simply pinpoint that area as an important growth objective for the teacher at the present time. The principal then recycles the teacher back through the continuation group where the teacher's peer group can do the retraining. The teacher who is experiencing difficulty merely makes a contract with the principal to request a particular type of training at the next continuation group meeting. Since the coaches are available at the school site, retraining can be carried out when needed and as often as needed with no special fanfare.

As more school sites become involved, more coaches need to be trained within the district. It is not uncommon, for example, to train elementary, junior high, and high school coaches within a district during three successive years. As district personnel watch the growth of their coaches, teachers, and administrators, the investment in the training of coaches usually makes increasing sense to the school board. Over a period of years an *expertise hierarchy* is constructed which includes not only a clearly defined cadre of master teachers but also a significant percentage of the teaching staff within each participating school site in addition to administrators, all capable of carrying out their respective roles properly.

Ideally a third level of the expertise hierarchy will be built over a period of years if the district is large enough and has adequate resources. The amount of coordination, quality control, and retraining of coaches is easily underestimated by a district entering into a long-term staff development program for the first time. Ultimately a full-time coordinator will be needed if training is being carried out at many school sites. In addition, CMTP coaches forget just as their trainees forget, and there needs to be a higher level of expertise available to give them periodic review, updating, and practice. In most cases CMTP trainers of trainers do that job, but that is more by default than by plan. It is best in a large district for there to be a staff development institute which is staffed by several full-time people who are highly sophisticated in staff development. Such people typically have had experience as trainers in several quality staff development training programs and can serve as coordinators and master trainers for the coaches.

Classroom Management—A Course of Study At this time many districts simply cannot or will not afford systematic teacher training. There must be staff development options for districts with limited funds which are less expensive than systematic teacher training but are more helpful than the typical workshops, seminars, and institutes. How can much of the explanation, modeling, guided practice, and continuing growth which is built into the systematic teacher training and continuation groups occur in many districts at a reduced cost?

One obvious answer is video. With the rapidly increasing availability of videocassette recording (VCR) equipment within education, it is possible to put a great deal of video training footage into a relatively inexpensive format. Color videotape is a fraction of the cost of 16mm film, more easily transportable, more flexible, more easily used, and not subject to the breaking and problems of rewinding which cause so many teachers to mutter oaths under their breath when the film snaps and goes flippity-flippity-flip in the projector. Extensive portions of the Classroom Management Training Program could, in fact, be put onto videotape training films in which actual practice exercises are portrayed much as they would occur in live training sessions.

Although much of the future belongs to the VCR, it would be easy to abuse such a medium. It is not possible to send away for a stack of videotapes and train your faculty through the magic of TV. If we show video, we are back to the old dog and pony show with a TV screen substituted for a live performer. Rather, it is critical to have *trained trainers accompany the videotape* and use the videotape as a vehicle for real training. A trainer-of-trainers program, therefore, is still needed although the number of trainers might be reduced.

The greatest economy of video, however, would be the packaging of training into segments that could be done after school or in the evening, thus eliminating the greatest cost of training—substitutes. Videotape is also an excellent vehicle for quality control within the context of a systematic teacher training program since even coaches and members of a staff development institute can review skills periodically from videotape.

Universities are increasingly turning to video as a teaching medium not only as a means of reducing the cost of higher education but also as a means of presenting sights and sounds and experiences within the classroom that could not be produced live. Over the last several years a format known as the "telecourse" has evolved in which 15 hours of video are used as the basis for the presentation of a 3-hour college course. Such courses typically meet twice a week for an hour and a half per class period with each meeting containing a half hour of video and an hour of presentation or interaction with the instructor or professor. The telecourse format can be an aid to rapid, high-quality dissemination of teaching innovations within higher education as well as in the field as long as video is accompanied by adequate performance practice carried out by skilled trainers.

Product versus Process and the Pipeline

It is difficult for districts without experience with systematic teacher training to justify the expense of training trainers to work at each of their many school sites just as it is difficult to appreciate the importance of continuation meetings. Perhaps the clearest way to contrast the benefits of systematic teacher training with more typical staff development formats is to think in terms of process versus product.

Creating a Process The objective of CMTP is not simply to produce a product—a group of trained teachers—but, rather, to produce a *process* of continuing professional growth and renewal that can become a permanent part of the social fabric of each school site. Creating a process, however, is relatively difficult and expensive compared to merely training a group of teachers since it requires:

- long-term planning
- administrative involvement at all levels
- training principals
- training selected teachers to such an extent that they can be trainers, leaders of continuation groups, and peer coaches
- follow through after training with adequate coordination, administrative involvement, and continuous retraining
- organizing calendars around training and continuation group meetings

Obviously, creating a viable process is labor-intensive and therefore costly in training days, substitute costs, and consulting fees. But, perhaps more important, creating a process ultimately changes the organizational structure of the district so that professional growth and change becomes institutionalized. New roles are created and old accustomed ways of "running the shop" are altered.

Yet the investment has profound long-term implications that far outweigh the initial costs if excellence is the goal of the district. A process of professional development which is decentralized to each school site creates more than a support structure for continuing growth, renewal, and change. It creates a *pipeline* for the dissemination of innovation for as long as the pipeline is kept in repair. Thus, although coaches may be trained at each school site by CMTP, those coaches have the training skills to disseminate other programs as well.

For example, a CMTP coach might attend a conference in Chicago in which he or she hears a talk about some valuable innovation in instruction or classroom management. If no training program is available to disseminate the innovation, the coaches could collaborate to construct a training program consisting of well-designed, performance-oriented structured lessons. This core group could then train the rest of the coaches, and the coaches could train the members of their continuation groups as part of the group's normal sharing and retraining process. Thus innovation might spread from a convention in a faraway city to classrooms throughout the district in a matter of weeks.

Without a pipeline there is no way to disseminate innovation in the form of well-practiced skills. Rather, innovation remains forever at arm's length or passes through town in the form of another dog and pony show.

Creating a Product The product of a teacher training program is, to put it most simply, a teacher who has been through a teacher training program. There is certainly nothing wrong with a good product as long as one's expectations are realistic. Training programs tend to profit the most gifted teachers most and the least gifted teachers least. Whatever gains are made begin to atrophy as soon as the training program is over except for the gifted few who have the capacity to rapidly internalize, generalize, and innovate with a new skill.

Staff development as a product rather than as a process is not only far cheaper but also requires less involvement and change on the part of board members, administrators, and teachers alike. It is easier to mandate, and it requires very little active and ongoing leadership. It typically has a district focus rather than a school site focus, and follow through is typically nonexistent. Yet a product is all that most school districts will receive in the foreseeable future. It is all that they are prepared to accept, and it is all that they are prepared to afford.

Problems with Staff Development Specialists

Ironically, one of the most consistent blocks to quality program dissemination is local staff development specialists. At best a specialist in staff development within a state department of education, county office of education, teacher center, or local school district will want to become a partner in the process of change and collaborate in carrying out a quality program. Typically such individuals appreciate that the training process of a quality program is its greatest asset—a methodology developed and tested during years of use in the field. Such individuals are willing to collaborate because (1) they have a primary concern for the process of the training program and want to see it carried out properly, (2) they are personally open to collaboration and look forward to learning from the training methods of the program as well as contributing to them, and (3) they have the freedom to carry out the program correctly because they have the backing of local administrators.

At worst a staff development specialist or local consultant is a cut-and-paste artist—a gleaner of the content from many programs intent on designing a curriculum of her or his own but with little appreciation for the rigors of quality training. Such individuals, since they often tend to focus on content rather than process, characteristically bypass the careful training needed for successful program dissemination. Thus they often dissect a quality program by focusing primarily on concepts while cutting corners in training in order to reach a large number of teachers quickly.

The propensity for disseminating concepts rapidly rather than carefully developing skills comes from many directions including naiveté, defense of one's territory, budget constraints, or administrative pressure. A combination of all these factors is most characteristic of state departments of education, county offices of education, and large city school districts in which in-house experts have a defined territory to defend and in which the pressures to reach everyone with new ideas quickly on a low budget is great. These pressures can all but preclude quality staff development. This pattern of methodological mediocrity is averted only when there is a semiautonomous staff development institute or teacher center with a clearly defined mission of excellence in staff development and political checks against pressures to reach everyone rapidly.

Staff development specialists either actively protect the integrity of a quality training program or they are instrumental in destroying it. They either actively educate those around them concerning the importance of using proper teaching methods and of building a support network to achieve lasting change or they end up doing the opposite. Unless they model excellent teaching they will probably model viral teaching.

OVERVIEW

I wish that systematic teacher training were easier and cheaper. I have tried to economize in almost every imaginable way over the past 15 years to help districts with inadequate funds learn about positive classroom discipline and positive classroom instruction. As a result, I have made almost every mistake imaginable and watched my program achieve only partial success or fail altogether more times than I would like to remember.

The description of systematic teacher training contained in this chapter is not pie in the sky but, rather, simple necessity. Though it may seem elaborate to someone unfamiliar with staff development, the descriptions contained in this chapter represent, in fact, bare minimums. I would love to have more time to work with the coaches and more time for the coaches to train the teachers, and I would love to come back to the district to retrain more often than I typically do. I want to include skills that I do not even touch on in training. A colleague of mine who has served as a coach in the Classroom Management Training Program put it simply a year ago when he made the following statement:

> You know, Jones, when I first went through this program, I was a little overwhelmed by all of the new concepts and teaching skills that I was being given. I sorted it out over the next year or two thanks to being a coach and to the continuation groups, but it still seemed like "high-tech" teaching. But now that I have coached it several times and used it for two years it has gotten to be second nature. Now I've been able to go beyond it, look back, and see what the Classroom Management Training Program really was. It was boot camp! It was the

basics—nothing but the basics—the bare necessities of surviving and succeeding in the classroom. If you don't have that stuff, you'll work yourself to death and never understand why you're so tired and why so many of the kids still are not learning.

REFERENCES

1 Jones, F.H., Fremouw, W., and Carples, S., Pyramid training of elementary school teachers to use a classroom management "skill package." *Journal of Applied Behavior Analysis,* 1977, *10,* 239–253.

2 Toch, T. Inservice efforts fail a system in need, critics say. *Education Week,* September 29, 1982, 10–11.

CHAPTER 12

THE LEADERSHIP ROLE

A staff development program that grows within a district must sell itself to a considerable degree by its own success with participating faculty serving as ambassadors. Yet, though much of the program support must come from the bottom up, the rest must be supplied from the top down by administrators and the school board. To the extent that administrators with the help of the school board perform their leadership role wisely, growth and change will take hold and thrive. To the extent that the district leadership fails to grasp its role in creating and maintaining growth and change, any staff development program, no matter how well designed and implemented, will be seriously undermined and its impact limited.

THE FOCUS OF CHANGE AT THE SCHOOL SITE

One of the primary emphases of the preceding chapter was that deep and lasting change must not only reach the majority of teachers at a school site, but it must also involve those teachers in a lasting growth process that is supportive, instructional, and enjoyable. The school site is the primary functional unit of change in any school district because it is the primary social unit of any school district. Its members are physically close enough to each other to see each other on a regular basis, to share ideas readily, and to offer support on a daily and weekly basis. Since the school site is the social unit that will impact most directly on the teacher's daily life, the leader of the school site will therefore be the main facilitator or inhibitor of change.

The Importance of the Principal

Recent research has pinpointed the principal as the primary determiner of the success in any staff development effort at a given school site. Yet the principal is usually neither the one who disseminates the program directly nor the one who uses it within the classroom on a daily basis. The principal, however, determines the program's long-term life or death by the nature of his or her participation.

To understand why a principal has such power over the fate of staff development we must keep in mind two key factors.

1 *Penetration and longevity.* The short-term success of a staff development program may be determined by the relevance of its content, the charisma of the presenter, and the degree of skill mastery achieved during initial training, but the long-term success is measured in terms of penetration and longevity. Although principals may not determine the content, style, or methods of initial training, they do determine penetration and longevity to a large degree by the nature and extent of their ongoing support for change at the school site.

2 *Change is not easy.* On a good day 20 percent of the human race enjoys and seeks the stimulation of change, 30 percent are ambivalent, and 50 percent find it downright threatening and aversive. To bring the middle 30 percent, and ultimately the lower 50 percent, into involvement in a process of change, they must be actively and consistently affirmed and supported for their efforts and given extra help along the way. Affirmation and support for change that elevates a staff development program to a position of lasting prominence at a school site comes mainly from the principal.

It is the principal of the school site who is the gatekeeper for change since it is the principal who determines what is important and what is not important at the school site. From among the dozens of urgent imperatives coming at teachers from all directions—all the way from the national government to an upset parent—it is the principal who determines what is on the *front* burner and what is on the *back* burner. The *rule of the stovetop* states that things on the front burner get done, and things on the back burner do not.

Change must be kept on the front burner in clear sight for an extended period to achieve program penetration and longevity. Half the faculty is hoping that they will not have to participate in the program; and history has taught them that if they ignore the program long enough, it will dry up and blow away. School districts in general have compiled an abysmal record of staff development implementation and follow through over the years, and teachers who find comfort in the status quo are banking on history to repeat itself. The less involved 50 percent of the faculty will simply keep a low profile until the initial enthusiasm blows over (which usually engages the chronically eager top 20 percent of the profession), and then they will chalk it all up to just another false alarm. The middle 30 percent of the faculty is the swing group that can be pulled into a good program or pulled by the bottom 50 percent away from a program that is not properly sold. Apart from introductory presentations by CMTP personnel and the "teachers' lounge effect," selling is largely the job of the principal.

When the principal is one of the bottom 50 percent, there is in effect a silent conspiracy of do-nothingness among the majority of professionals at the school site which will also pull the middle 30 percent into business as usual. With change safely on the back burner, any staff development program will ultimately fall victim to limited volunteerism and the natural forces of atrophy. Consequently, innovation eventually dies of neglect at the school site—save for the top 20 percent.

Two Types of Principals

When it comes to enjoying change, principals are distributed pretty much like teachers and the rest of the human race—20 percent like it, 30 percent are ambivalent, and 50 percent find it aversive. The middle 30 are a swing group that can be pulled toward growth or nongrowth depending on the prevailing priorities of the district, and the bottom 50 percent need a lot of help. Yet regardless of which way the swing group swings, in the final analysis the principal is either part of the problem or part of the solution. As regards staff development and institutional change, principals can be characterized as operating to various degrees in accordance with two contrasting styles: (1) instructional leaders and (2) plant managers.

Instructional Leaders One of the most useful descriptions of a leader is a person who *maximizes the performance of everyone over whom he or she has direct responsibility.* The leadership role of the principal would therefore tend to focus on facilitating teachers' job performance, professional growth, and morale. Thus, although principals may not be the direct agents of change in most cases, they must be expert to the extent that they are able to aid teachers in selecting growth objectives, and they must collaborate effectively in providing professional development opportunities. Above all, the principal as instructional leader is a *process* person whose role in professional development calls forth skills of communication, problem solving, team building, morale building, and quality control.

Communication, Problem Solving, and Team Building Only when administrators and teachers work together toward some overriding goal which expresses shared values does problem solving become consistently constructive. At the beginning of systematic teacher training, such teamwork rarely exists at a school site and must, therefore, be built as a by-product of training. Team building occurs at many levels; it begins with the ironclad rule that training will never occur at a school site unless the administrators are trained as trainers right along with their selected faculty members. Although the faculty members carry most of the weight of program dissemination in the long run, it is vital that the rest of the faculty view their administrators as clearly committed, informed, and involved.

Team building progresses as "continuation groups" are formed immediately following training. Each continuation group contains at least one trainer or "coach" to provide retraining and to guide group process, and the principal has a support role to carry out that is clearly structured.

Morale Building Morale building and professional development are far more intimately connected than is usually appreciated. A person's relationship to his or her career functions according to the laws that govern all relationships. Like a marital relationship, for example, a person's relationship to his or her career is either growing or dying. There is no lasting equilibrium or homeostasis because life always upsets equilibrium by presenting problems to be solved. You must constantly cope to stay even, and to cope you must solve problems and grow. To remain the same is to allow problems to grow unresolved until they finally assume overwhelming proportions. Unless you work at growing together, you finally grow apart; the relationship atrophies until it finally becomes a burden.

The *methods* of teaching are the *teacher's craft,* and it is through growing in the skills of one's craft that teachers keep their relationship with their profession alive. To fail to grow is to face the same classroom every day with the same subjects to teach in the same way. The dynamics of the profession is missing, and instead of the challenge of growing and the pride in getting better there is only repetition.

Antonio Stradivari built violins from his apprenticeship in adolescence until his death at the age of 93 (1644–1737). It is recorded that in his fifties he remarked that he was finally beginning to understand the woods. History tends to prove that statement accurate since his "Golden Period," so named because of the great number of masterpieces that were produced, spans the years 1700 to 1730—from age 56 to 86. To one who does not understand the nature of craft, Stradivari would seem to have had a repetitive job indeed—one violin after another with an occasional cello for nearly 80 years. But one who understands the nature of craft also understands the challenge that keeps a craftsperson alive and growing. For an instrument maker no two pieces of wood are ever the same, and producing consistently excellent tone calls for constant variation in design and the utmost skill in execution. For a craftsperson such as Stradivari something about design is learned from each instrument, and coping with the perniciousness of each new piece of spruce or maple provides a constant challenge. These challenges kept the master alive and growing in his chosen craft for eight decades.

Teaching too is a craft that, in order to stay alive, must continually *grow* through the development of the skills of teaching, and the craftsperson must continually *change* to adapt to the needs of the raw material—the students. Professional growth provides the enduring yet ever-changing focus that is the natural antidote to boredom and spiritual burn-out. If teaching long division is primarily content rather than process, then boredom is foreordained since long division will be about the same from one decade to the next. But if creating learning and social maturation in students is our craft, then we can look forward to the continuing mastery of our craft for as long as we teach. Thus, good teachers are "process people" first and "content people" second.

The alternative to growing in one's chosen craft is the boredom, tedium, and negativism typical of most teachers' lounges. Such negativism feeds upon itself to produce a destructive cycle that can ultimately undermine morale and job performance at an entire school site. Grow or die is the imperative of all relationships.

Quality Control Principals have as part of their job quality control—the evaluation of strengths and weaknesses of teachers and the development of a professional growth plan for every teacher. A teacher training program, however, can be viewed as a threat by teachers if the skills embodied in the program immediately become criteria of evaluation.

As mentioned in the preceding chapter, however, quality control and team building are linked through the vehicle of the continuation group. Continuation groups consistently place the principal in a supportive, nonexpert role in relation to meeting the special needs of the team and its team members. Most problem definition and problem solving occurs as part of a peer-based growth process, usually in the principal's absence. Sometimes, however, the principal may collaborate with the teachers who are experiencing special difficulties by helping them pinpoint areas of need and by allocating resources for whatever program of help is most advisable.

Principals, in summary, have two very different roles: (1) supporting excellence in the classroom and faculty morale on the one hand and (2) managing the plant. Helping to build instructional excellence at the school site is the process part of the principal's job which focuses on the relationship of teachers to their own careers and the relationships of teachers to each other. Insofar as principals are committed to and skillful at their process role, teachers will experience the continuing stimulation and renewal of a profession that is alive.

Yet not all principals are comfortable or skillful or even committed to looking after the process portion of their job. Indeed, many find the process role of the instructional leader foreign and uncomfortable. Often, therefore, principals find it preferable and in most districts relatively easy to retreat from the ever-changing role of the instructional leader to take comfort in the concrete and more easily manipulated tasks of managing the plant.

Plant Managers In lieu of professional growth there is little left but to manage the plant—to open it up in the morning and look after the details of keeping it running. I have an assistant superintendent friend, very savvy in staff development, who refers to most of his principals as "3B principals." The three B's are (1) beans (the cafeteria), (2) buses (transportation), and (3) budget. The three B's comprise most of the leadership role of the traditional principal, with crisis management and dealing with parents consuming the rest.

In schools run by 3B principals, teaching is clearly a profession practiced behind closed doors and so also is the principalship. Administrators and faculty often agree that this is the way things should be. The teachers run the classroom by themselves, and the principal runs the building while occasionally subduing outrageous students and keeping obnoxious parents at arm's length. Everyone goes their separate ways until they burn out.

The prototypical 3B principal is definitely not a "process person." His human relationship skills were often learned on either the drill field or the athletic field, and his capacity to put people at ease and to facilitate professional growth as a part of clinical supervision is equaled only by his familiarity with the positive helping interaction. Instituting change, therefore, tends not to be seen as a long-term growth endeavor which is shared by teachers and administrators. Rather, change is typically seen as a product rather than a process—a matter of policy to be mandated. Leadership is viewed as dealing with concrete entities, such as keeping the plant running as smoothly as possible. Comfort with and tolerance for the ambiguity and open-endedness of the processes of relationship building and career building are typically quite limited.

A Shared Enterprise

Not too surprisingly principals who divorce themselves from the affairs of the classroom have a very different view of classroom management than do teachers and parents. For example, the 1982 "Fourteenth Annual Gallup Poll of Public Attitudes toward the Public Schools"[1] showed that school administrators see discipline problems as "absenteeism, vandalism, and similar problems," whereas parents, like teachers, see discipline problems as "obeying rules and regulations, classroom control, and respect for teachers." Parents share the perspective of the teachers because their children live in the world of the classroom where discipline problems mean the moment-by-moment hassles that destroy both the teacher's patience and time on task. The principal's world is typically so divorced from the world of the teacher that to him discipline is all but synonymous with solving problems outside the classroom. Living in different worlds, teachers and administrators ultimately acquire viewpoints and concerns so distant and unrelated that communication about basic concerns becomes difficult if not impossible. Instead of experiencing support in their instructional efforts over the years, teachers often feel estrangement which easily turns to alienation.

Research is increasingly showing that effective schools differ from ineffective schools primarily by having a shared way of doing things that is the result of a long-term collective focus by teachers and administrators alike on the instructional process. Research by Michael Rutter and Associates[2] in inner-city secondary schools of London with comparable populations but with differing levels of student achievement showed that success was primarily related to the "internal functioning" of the schools—to shared and agreed-upon ways of doing things that were under the control of staff rather than "external realities." The most prominent differences centered around the "organization of school life"—factors as disparate as:

1 Teachers working together in groups to plan curriculum and deal with behavior problems
2 Teachers' work being observed by senior staff with ample feedback
3 Responsibility being stressed in class, with jobs and posts assigned to many students and care of books and equipment stressed
4 Concern for students being expressed in many ways, from the frequency of outings to the flexibility of counseling
5 Emphasis on teaching and learning being ever-prominent through high expectations for exams, the assignment of homework, keeping careful records, and displaying students' work

In all these particulars, one gets a strong sense of coherence—of a faculty working together with clear goals, careful planning, and coordination of effort. The sense one gets from the less successful schools is that of drift—of a group of teachers without instructional leadership in which everyone goes his or her own way with no rallying or focusing force.

When the principal assumes the role of instructional leader, operating a school becomes a shared enterprise. The principal provides the organizational coherence to promote everyone's pulling together in a common direction.

All too often, however, teachers and principals go their separate ways. To our detriment, our professional training programs prepare us to go our separate ways with degree programs and credentialing procedures which provide little overlap in skills and concerns between administrator and teacher. Excellence, in contrast, results from a shared sense of purpose that comes from teaching as part of a team rather than alone. Excellence develops as principal and teachers join forces.

DISTRICTS THAT GROW

The Superintendent's Role

Some districts are designed for professional growth, but most are not. Whether professional development exists as a basic priority for a district can usually be gleaned from a quick inspection of its organizational chart. Where are the personnel to carry out systematic, long-term staff development? If you cannot see them on the organizational chart, then staff development is probably "nobody's baby" and receives little emphasis from management.

Districts vary greatly in their understanding of the process of professional growth, change, and renewal. Most districts, however, have never experienced a systematic and sustained teacher training program with any built-in quality control or follow through. In most districts there is literally no mechanism by which systematic staff development can be implemented should the desire arise.

The Superintendent Sets the Priority Perhaps the most clear-cut characteristic of a school district that sets high staff development goals and achieves them is clear and consistent leadership from the superintendent. The superintendent defines the criteria by which the job performance of assistant superintendents and principals will be evaluated. But perhaps more important, the superintendent sets the priorities and professional tone of the district. If superintendents are preoccupied with budgets and politics and personnel matters to the exclusion of instructional excellence, then they convey a plant-manager mentality to all district personnel. If, however, the achievement of instructional excellence and the establishment of a staff development mechanism by which to achieve excellence is ever-prominent within the district, then staff development may live and thrive.

Districts with a strong, in-house staff development program typically have people at the top—at the superintendent and assistant superintendent levels—who are highly knowledgeable about the means and ends of staff development and who are thoroughly committed to implementation. They then amass the budget and staff to implement quality training while bringing the principals along gradually with the teachers. Over time a staff development institute or teacher center of some type evolves with full-time, highly trained leaders who direct and coordinate the efforts of teachers training teachers in many specialty areas.

When sophistication at the top is missing, clout is missing and staff development goes perpetually begging. Enthusiastic principals, of course, can do much for their school sites through their own personal leadership aided by the failure of other principals to actively compete for staff development funds. But the district as a whole goes nowhere.

Districts that are going nowhere in staff development tend to develop a management perspective over time that actively thwarts growth and change. If most of the principals are plant managers and if the superintendent is the head plant manager, then management soon becomes a "good ol' boys" club. Change does not live because there is no ongoing process which focuses on the practice of teaching. Consequently, change is seen in only the most concrete of terms—adopting a new curriculum or text, responding to a state or federal mandate, raising funds for a new building, or negotiating a new contract. Teachers' needs are responded to with quick, cheap, in-service presentations that are rarely coordinated toward any long-term goal.

The Mandate Mentality If you do not know how to create change, you mandate it. Mandates are the prime example of seeking to produce a product without a process—of decision making without laying the groundwork for implementation. Mandates, in fact, actively undermine implementation by separating policy formation from policy implementation. Rather than viewing leadership as a process of team building in which the people who are to carry out the policy are enfranchised in the development of the policy, the mandate mentality views leadership as solely responsible for policy formation.

Having to be right all the time by devising correct policy isolated from the input of those closest to implementation in the field is a stressful, impossible, and unnecessary burden. But it is not as difficult as trying to get a bunch of people to implement a policy that they don't give a damn about. The fruit of disenfranchisement is alienation. The people in the field lack commitment to mandates, and the leader then resents the apathy and resistance of the subordinates. It is the prototypical top down leadership of a plant manager. To say that such a leader does not understand how to create either (1) the skills to execute the plan or (2) the desire to execute the plan is an exercise in understatement.

Naïve superintendents and their subordinates tend to deal with change by relying on mandates and policy directives. And, predictably, they tend to become frustrated when policies are "screwed up" or simply not carried out. Like any teacher who teaches poorly, these administrators lay the blame on the learner. When superintendents teach by mandate, the teachers who are supposed to change are often viewed as either stupid or unmotivated like any poor student. Now the fact that teacher and administrator live in separate worlds on so many levels finally bears its full fruit—open antagonism.

The mandate mentality is concordant with, and even requires, the viral theory of learning. In lieu of a common enterprise of growing in the profession of teaching along with one's staff, plant managers must disseminate as best they know how. For internal policy there are announcements and bulletins, and for professional development there are one-shot presentations.

Ultimately we must come to realize that lasting change is a result of *process and method*. You can mandate compliance, but you cannot mandate excellence. Ultimately

THE ORGANIZATIONAL FRAMEWORK FOR OUR OBJECTIVES

The achievements of an organization are the result of the combined efforts of each individual in the organization working toward common objectives. These objectives should be realistic, should be clearly understood by everyone in the organization, and should reflect the organization's basic character and personality.

If the organization is to fulfill its objectives, it should strive to meet certain other fundamental requirements:

FIRST, there should be highly capable, innovative people throughout the organization. Moreover, these people should have the opportunity—through continuing programs of training and education—to upgrade their skills and capabilities. This is especially important in a technical business where the rate of progress is rapid. Techniques that are good today will be outdated in the future, and people should always be looking for new and better ways to do their work.

SECOND, the organization should have objectives and leadership which generate enthusiasm at all levels. People in important management positions should not only be enthusiastic themselves, they should be selected for their ability to engender enthusiasm among their associates. There can be no place, especially among the people charged with management responsibility, for half-hearted interest or half-hearted effort.

THIRD, the organization should conduct its affairs with uncompromising honesty and integrity. People at every level should be expected to adhere to the highest standards of business ethics, and to understand that anything less is totally unacceptable. As a practical matter, ethical conduct cannot be assured by written policies or codes; it must be an integral part of the organization, a deeply ingrained tradition that is passed from one generation of employees to another.

FOURTH, even though an organization is made up of people fully meeting the first three requirements, all levels should work in unison toward common objectives, recognizing that it is only through effective, cooperative effort that the ultimate in efficiency and achievement can be obtained.

It has been our policy at Hewlett-Packard not to have a tight military-type organization, but rather to have overall objectives which are clearly stated and agreed upon, and to give people the freedom to work toward those goals in ways they determine best for their own areas of responsibility.

Our Hewlett-Packard objectives were initially published in 1957. Since then they have been modified from time to time, reflecting the changing nature of our business and social environment. This booklet represents the latest updating of our objectives. We hope you find them informative and useful.

David Packard
Chairman of the Board

William R. Hewlett
Vice Chairman of the Board

John Young
President and Chief Executive Officer

September 1983

FIGURE 12-1
The organizational framework for our objectives. (*The Hewlett-Packard Company.*)

learning and personal growth on a large scale are the result of an insistence by district leadership on proper teaching and careful follow through. Effective leadership, indeed, is inseparable from the production of organizational growth and change. The leader who produces the most change in the desired direction with the highest morale leads best.

A History of Frustration Unfortunately, many administrators who may have wished to achieve educational excellence over the years have been blocked by the sheer lack of programs which could deliver. Thus, both they and their teachers have often been stymied in developing a plan for professional growth that could succeed.

Until administrators have at their disposal a program that really works, they are powerless to deliver convincing results and, not surprisingly, to get the financial backing of the school board. Thus, in most cases both the teachers and their administrators must at some point become jointly sold on the merits of a particular program and experience short-term success before long-term commitments can be made. In a successful staff development effort, everyone typically grows together over a period of time. Although some superintendents have seen what quality staff development can do and are committed to it in advance, most superintendents and their school boards will proceed cautiously and skeptically.

The School Board's Role

A Statement of Purpose One of the characteristics of well-run and successful corporations both at home and abroad is a clear-cut and prominent value system that continually reminds all personnel of the overriding goals and objectives of the organization.[4] Such a statement of purpose is more than a collection of platitudes, for it sets clear priorities in production and personnel matters that shape decision making at all levels. It provides the basics that people go back to when decision making seems blocked or at loggerheads between conflicting viewpoints.

In high-tech industries there tends to be an overriding concern for the development of the skills of the individual and the health of the work group as necessary preconditions to corporate success. This is not surprising in a sector of industry that thrives on creativity, teamwork, and up-to-the-minute knowledge of the field.

Since the means to excellence are clearly people rather than machines, these corporate statements of purpose are documents which reflect the organization's understanding of *staff development*. An example from the Hewlett-Packard Company is most enlightening—especially its emphasis on participation in "continuing programs of training and education" as the first fundamental requirement toward fulfilling its corporate objectives. See Figure 12-1.

Teaching, too, is a rapidly emerging hi-tech profession. Its methods are increasingly based on both a solid empirical foundation and an advanced understanding of professional practice that is a quantum leap beyond the folklore of the past that led the public to view classroom teaching as little more than glorified parenting. This book attempts to accelerate this metamorphosis of teaching from common sense as perceived by the general public to full professional status.

Every school district needs to reassess its accustomed goals and practices in this time of rapid change to see if they are helping to create a new and better future for teaching or are, instead, simply echoing the past. Is there even a coherent statement of purpose? If so, does it deal with platitudes about what we want for our children, or is it a practical document that defines the form of the interrelatedness of the *adults* in the organization? The district payroll is made up of adults, not children, and as in a marriage, until the adults get their relationship functioning constructively, the children will be perpetually deprived.

The Basic Policy

There is one school policy which must be clearly affirmed by the school board in order to give the superintendent a strong hand in facilitating staff development throughout the organization. This basic policy, which I refer to as "the professional development imperative," states that:

> Professional growth is a basic and fundamental part of professional life. In order to stay alive and vital within the profession of teaching, all teachers need to be continually working on

> some focused goal of professional enrichment and development. Without such a focus and without such an effort, the practice of one's profession becomes routine and sterile and goes stale over a period of years.
>
> All teachers within the school district will have a personal goal or objective for professional growth which is selected and defined in conjunction with their school site principal. The school board and the administration are obligated to provide resources to allow teachers to actively pursue their professional development goals.

This policy, like the broader statement of purpose, is as much a statement of values and priorities as it is a statement of procedure. It clearly affirms up front that teachers must be learners—that we are all students. If we do not live the learning that we try to sell to kids, will they not see through our hypocrisy by the time they reach the age of reason? All who participate in this profession must be continually reminded of one simple notion: There is no credential that says growth is no longer necessary.

The Deficit Model of Staff Development When defining professional development as a natural part of school life, the school board at the very beginning opts out of a "deficit model" of staff development. A deficit model of staff development views staff development as remedial, something needed by a teacher who is having a problem. Such a deficit model of staff development so stigmatizes the process of staff development that personal pride and professional respectability almost require everyone to claim that they do not need it.

Structuring the Role of the Instructional Leader Having sidestepped the issue of whether or not any individual needs staff development, the board places in the superintendent's hands the leverage to require every principal to define as major aspects of their job: (1) consultation with their teachers concerning the selection of staff development goals and (2) the organization of resources so that teachers have an opportunity to progress toward their goals.

Thus the "professional development imperative" kicks down the chain of command so that the job description of school site administrators is defined to a significant degree in terms of their active participation in professional development. Until the job of the principal is defined in terms of professional development, staff development programs will always be an add-on obligation which will be seen by many as interfering with their real job, which is to manage the plant.

Building the Foundation for Collaboration The message from the top down that staff development is basic to professional life typically produces a sympathetic response from most teachers. Teachers know that they need to select a professional development goal, and they have to specify what they want. They will also have a reason to take their choice of goals seriously since the professional development imperative implies the allocation of resources.

The principal will be asking the teachers, "What do you want to do with your money?" The teachers on the other hand will say to the principals, "I have some money coming. These are the things I want to do." The administration is thus placed in the role of the benevolent dispenser of resources, whereas the teacher is placed in the role of the adult responsible for using those resources.

Unless, however, the school board puts enough money behind the professional development imperative to provide quality professional growth opportunities, its policy is nothing but claptrap—another mandate with nothing backing it up. With adequate resources, the school board, along with county, state, and federal agencies, is literally putting its money where its mouth is: creating an opportunity for excellence rather than a hollow mandate.

THE ADDICTION TO FADS AND THE QUICK FIX

Systematic teacher training is a slow, gradual process that focuses on the careful development of professional skills of teachers and administrators alike. It uses proper teaching methods, and it creates a supportive interpersonal network in which growth and change are nurtured over time. It focuses consistently on *process* and *method* and is preoccupied with quality control, productivity, and morale both during training and at the school site thereafter.

Fast Results

Administrators and school boards who do not understand the process by which lasting change is created within an institution often see the investment of the time and resources required for lasting change to be exorbitant and unjustifiable. If the objectives of the training program are not appreciated, then the expense provides the reason for not proceeding. But if the objectives of the program are *partially* appreciated, an even more alarming prospect rears its head—the strong desire for *fast results*. The first type of administrator or school board may ignore a program to death; the second type may implement it to death.

With wide-eyed enthusiasm, a high-level administrator newly converted to a staff development program may say, "Let's train all our high school teachers this year" or "Let's go countywide!" Although closure has been reached as to the content of change desired, we still have a long way to go with process.

How can you go countywide with a quality trainer-of-trainers program this year? How can such large numbers be reached so fast if we are carefully training people rather than simply "exposing" them? We are still confronted with the viral theory of learning. "We'll really turn this district around!" can be the battle cry to oblivion.

Once a program is embraced at the content level, the next problem is to make sure it is embraced at the process level. Although the first objective of dissemination requires getting teachers and administrators to want specific instructional methods in their schools, the second objective of dissemination is to get administrators to take the process of change seriously. When administrators experience a rush of enthusiasm over the improvement promised by a quality staff development program, it is necessary to repeat the following advice over and over:

- Slow down.
- Think small.
- Build gradually.

Quality does not come with a rush. It is built incrementally with a large investment in training quality people as trainers before dissemination to other staff is even possible. Quick quality on a large scale is an illusion.

The importance of implementing a worthwhile program properly is put into focus by one simple fact regarding program dissemination: You get only one chance. Once teachers have been through a program, as far as they are concerned, they have "done it." You will rarely get them back again to do it right if you did it sloppily the first time.

Shifting Focus

A concomitant of our tendency to embrace innovation as fad and to approach change as a quick fix is our tendency to shift focus frequently so that change efforts are robbed of adequate follow through. Educators are not used to making 5-year plans for staff development. A 2-year commitment is usually about all that the imagination will allow. A long-term, systematic approach to staff development is still a novelty in most districts, and a long-term commitment to a specific program and a specific consultant can be downright frightening. In addition to fears that the consultant may be a turkey, questions also arise as to whether the district wants to focus on any particular method to such a great extent.

Indeed, when change is carried out properly, you must choose your change objectives carefully because you will be living with them for a long time. And when energy is invested in real change, there will not be enough energy for many change programs. In general a school site can invest in only one major change effort at a time in addition to the normal change of curriculum and class assignments. If training is to be carried out properly, we can no longer employ a scattergun approach to staff development. We must choose our programs and our objectives carefully and maintain a coherent vector over time.

Actually the reduction of choices inherent in careful training is more a helpful antidote to fragmentation than a real limitation. There are really only about five major dimensions of staff development in education: (1) classroom management skills and the development of school standards, (2) instructional methodology, (3) communication, problem-solving, and counseling skills, (4) curriculum, and (5) leadership and quality control. There is no end point for professional development in any one of these areas (add a sixth if you like). Rather, it is more useful to think of staff development as a *continuous process* in which teachers and administrators cycle through one of the five areas each year always reentering an area at a higher level than before. Thus a district with a strong staff development apparatus would constantly be operating programs in all five areas at several levels on an ongoing basis. Obviously, some high-level, in-house expertise is required to operate such a focused and multidimensional staff development enterprise. For most districts, it requires considerable growth and maximum effort to do just one program well.

Business As Usual

Some of the strongest built-in forces which can undermine quality staff development at the school district, county, state or national levels are the forces of political necessity. Politically oriented leaders typically need to show splashy results in order to enhance their leadership positions. In politics the best results tend to be the quickest results.

The best way to illustrate the workings of political expedience at cross-purposes with staff development may be to give some concrete examples. Each of the following vignettes is not only true but rather frequently true.

An Election Coming Up I received a call from a university professor colleague familiar with my program; he said he had been approached by the State Department of Education to develop a staff development program for school discipline that would be disseminated throughout the state. My colleague was told that there would be a lot of support for training in school discipline coming from the State Department of Education and that the State Superintendent of Education was going to earmark special funds for the training.

Although such a message might sound like a staff development specialist's dream come true, I have learned to be cautious. I told my colleague to get as many specifics as possible on (1) the time frame for training, (2) the dissemination network, and (3) political pressures which might be operating at the state level.

In a week my colleague called back and, speaking with far less enthusiasm than the week before, described the picture. It seems that the State Superintendent of Education was an elected position in this state, and elections were one year away. A recent poll financed by the State Department of Education pinpointed school discipline as the number one concern of the citizens regarding education. The state superintendent had decided to run for reelection and had decided to make school discipline one of his major platform issues. He therefore wanted to put together a "very visible program" on school discipline that would have statewide impact the year before the election.

The State Department of Education had already put out a fair amount of publicity to the press regarding their discipline program, but the specifics were hard to find. The reason, of course, was that people in the state department did not know a great deal about school discipline, had not had time to paste together a curriculum, and had no dissemination network for skill development on a statewide basis. Preliminary plans, however, targeted ten large school districts (those with the most voters) to receive state funds to carry out a trainer-of-trainers program to help local districts deal with problems of school discipline.

When pressed further by my colleague the head of professional development at the state level said that they hoped to put together a curriculum in the next few months and to use State Department of Education employees to travel out to the school districts to put on the workshops. The workshops were to be of 1 or 2 days duration aimed at administrators and department heads. These people were then to take the information (no mention of *skills*) from the workshop back to their local school sites.

After nearly two decades of staff development, my reaction to the preceding scenario is that it's the instant replay of a bad dream. "Quick and visible" are the real objectives of yet another ill-conceived in-service program designed not so much to produce actual staff development as to show a constituency that "we are doing something!" As usual, a curriculum was to be slapped together in a short time, and the notion of mass dissemination through a "trainer-of-trainers program" overlooked the necessity of carefully training the trainers, using the skills in real classrooms, supervising the process of training, supervising the trainees after training, and setting up a support or continuation program at each school site. It was viral teaching on a statewide basis—another glorified, warmed-over, one-day wonder.

No Backing from the Top The most common dilemma of a staff development specialist attempting to implement a quality training program is the lack of support from the top until the program is a demonstrated success. At that point the support is typically verbal with a showy display in front of the school board as business in the district proceeds in its typical fashion.

I have developed over the years a criterion for estimating the depth, breadth, and longevity of a staff development effort within a school district. When I first visit the school district, if I get on the plane to leave without having spoken at length with the superintendent about long-term staff development goals and methods, we are in trouble. Surprisingly often, superintendents are thoroughly unavailable for such discussions.

I will provide a composite case history of a "limited success" to give you the flavor. I'm contacted by a director of staff development (whose title includes a half-dozen other responsibilities) who has heard about my work at a conference. I am to speak on a district "in-service day." The head of staff development is the only woman assistant superintendent in the district—newly appointed and having very little clout—or a teacher on special assignment having no clout. She is, however, extremely competent and savvy about instruction and staff development, having been in the classroom for many years. During my visit to the district there is very little conversation about staff development initiated by any of the other administrators, but the director of staff development and I swap ideas like crazy over lunch.

After the presentation there are teachers pounding down the doors of their respective principals wanting training. A dozen principals are then on the phone to the director of staff development wanting to know what happened. Of those twelve principals, four are happy that there is a good staff development program available whereas the other eight are annoyed at having their lives disrupted.

The assistant superintendent in charge of staff development goes to the superintendent for money to carry out a trainer-of-trainers program at the school sites of the four interested principals. She is immediately turned down, but the superintendent and board agree to reconsider when they are deluged with requests from teachers and after several fired-up teachers give a testimonial and a brief demonstration in front of the school board. Who can say no to a roomful of teachers who want a professional development opportunity—particularly when they won't leave until they get it?

The trainer-of-trainers program proceeds over the following months until the coaches and the first round of trainees are trained. Word reaches the top that the new trainees are highly enthusiastic, as are the trainers, and plans are made for an additional round of training at the participating school sites. So far so good.

The missing element in this scenario is involvement from the top. The superintendent does not come to the training, the other assistant superintendents do not come to the training, nor do principals from school sites not involved. The teachers at four school sites and their administrators are not connected to a district network in which innovation and enthusiasm spread, because there is no network. Nor is staff development a district priority. After all the rave reviews are in, I finally get the meeting with the superintendent that I have been lobbying for, and I do my best to explain what I know about making staff development work.

On the way to the airport I am told that the superintendent will probably not ask for any money because, of course, there isn't any money and he does not want to upset the board. The superintendent, in fact, was very clear about there not being any money during our earlier conversation. On the way to the airport I am also told, however, that the district has decided to build a new field house for the high school, which was passed unanimously at the last board meeting on a voice vote without discussion.

Implementing the Program to Death After having given a workshop for staff development specialists in an eastern state, I was contacted by the staff development people from a particular county who were lobbying to get the county interested in the Classroom Management Training Program. They also demonstrated some of the classroom management skills at a school board meeting in order to rally support. The superintendent liked what he saw, but in order to get the money from the school board for the training program, he promised the board rashly that everyone in the county would be trained during the following year.

It seems as though each district must learn about quality staff development while experiencing it for the first time regardless of what is said in advance. Only when we had trained the first round of trainers and the first round of trainees and only after I had had several long conferences with the various levels of administrators did it finally dawn on people that the process was slow and methodical and could not possibly reach every teacher in the county during the next year. Various compromises in the program were suggested by the top administrators and rejected by me since I knew and explained why each such compromise would eventually produce failure.

Nevertheless, attempts were made during the following year to have coaches train teachers from *different* school sites only to have many of the continuation groups falter due to lack of leadership within the building. A year later we regrouped and the county decided that the program was worth doing and they would do it right because they could now see that tampering with the structure of the program was causing it to produce results that were noticeably inferior to the school sites in which the program had been properly implemented.

We have now been working together for over three years and we are now back on track, but there is still a problem of speed. We have trained the junior high teachers and have started with the senior high teachers. The senior high principals who were not initially included in the program are impatient, and the elementary school principals feel left out. The county wants to speed up the process, but they hate to spend any more money. Is there any way we can change the program to train more teachers quicker? Sounds familiar.

The Money's Gone I was asked by a school district to give an introductory talk on their staff development day. Thc cnthusiasm was high among the teachers, but at dinner afterward the administrators told me that they had already spent this year's staff development funds, and the state would probably cut all such funds for next year.

"What did you do in staff development this year?" I inquired.

"We conducted a needs assessment," they said.

"How was it done?" I asked, ever curious about such things.

"We hired a consulting firm to come in and conduct a formal survey, tabulate the results, and prepare a formal report."

"What did they find?"

"Well, the main concerns according to the teachers were classroom discipline, time on task, and the noise and mess in the halls, cafeteria, and playground with several teachers mentioning burn-out."

"No kidding," I responded, trying to stifle my amazement. "How much did you spend for the needs assessment?"

"Twelve thousand."

"What do you plan to do with it?"

"Nothing. We're out of money."

"Why did you do it? Every needs assessment in the country in the last 10 years has said almost the same thing."

"We know. But you can't get state or federal money without first showing thorough documentation of a needs assessment. We did that part, but we didn't get the grant. So now we're high and dry."

"How about using your own money?"

"Are you kidding?"

I was at another district which had recently spent $30,000 to hire a consulting firm to do a "trouble-shooting report" on problems at the administrative level. The report, which took 6 months to prepare and included in-depth interviews with key personnel at all levels of management, focused on deep-seated problems of communication and morale. It seems that administrators and program coordinators at all levels felt powerless and disenfranchised from policy development, and they felt that many policies were not practical and did not meet their needs.

"What is the district going to do about it?" I asked.

"The superintendent is going to announce his policy next week."

"What about all the people who feel powerless?"

"I understand the new policy will address that."

"Were they involved in the development of the new policy?"

"Not to my knowledge."

"Any money for staff development?"

"Are you kidding?"

Look Out for the Counties I gave a workshop for the personnel of a nearby county office of education in which their staff development people were in attendance and taking notes. We talked enthusiastically afterward about working together with several of the districts in the county that were looking for help with discipline.

Within the year, however, the county's funds were cut by the state. As usual, staff development was regarded as a particularly expendable area. So much for our plans.

Several months ago I heard that the county office was offering its school districts "a discipline program patterned after the work of Fred Jones." I inquired among some friends in the county and found out that indeed the few county staff development people who were left on the payroll were offering such a workshop; it covered "the eyeball technique" (limit-setting, I suppose) and "the stopwatch technique" (which can get rather weird out of context). I asked what form the dissemination was taking, and I was told that it was a half-day workshop at various school sites held usually during the afternoon of a minimum day.

A friend, who is a lawyer, said on hearing about it, "You ought to sue!" I felt that that was a rather self-serving remark for a lawyer to make.

I replied, "Sue for what, using my name indirectly? Listen, my book will be out soon, and all kinds of people will be doing the same thing. You can't sue people for being naive and foolish. There's no law against it."

County offices of education, as well as states and large cities, are particularly vulnerable to pressures from above to water down a trendy innovation and parade it around the territory. It shows how "with it" the county office is and how eager they are to serve. As for proper training and lasting change—well. . . .

Parading Innovation

Short-Term Gain The pressures to go quickly and cut costs are built into the implementation of any staff development program. The tendency to water down programs is particularly strong among educators because of their general inexperience concerning the implementation of a successful professional development effort. These pressures are compounded by the short-term political gain to administrators for *parading innovation.*

Converting innovation into deep and lasting change may turn heads slowly, but it does not cause necks to snap. It takes a lot of time and effort, with the major investment up front. Parading innovation, in contrast, is flashy and creates publicity. Yet parading innovation, and the watering down of training that inevitably accompanies it, is the prime killer of innovation since innovation poorly implemented never works.

Is It Over Yet? One of the strange and final ironies of implementing a quality staff development program within a district is the tendency for administrators and board members to think of all staff development programs as time-limited rather than as continuing. They keep asking, "When will it be over?" or "How much longer do we have to fund this program?"

I attempt to explain to the district that staff development must be a permanent part of professional life. It is the job of the consultant to train people within the district to the point where they can be relatively self-sufficient: able to continue the staff development effort *without* a constant dependence on, and need to pay, an outside consultant. Good consultants should, therefore, systematically work themselves out of a job.

But, though there may not be a continuing need to pay the consultant, there is a continuing need to pay. There is no such thing as free staff development because time is money. The objective is to eventually pay *your own people* and own the program.

In my naiveté I keep expecting someone to say, "Let's set up a timetable for achieving autonomous functioning so that our present level of support for the program can be directed toward enhancing the salaries of our own people instead of your salary." I keep explaining this objective to people, but it always comes as unsettling news. And after I think I've gotten my point across, someone again says, "You know, the board is wondering how much longer we are going to have to support this thing." It reminds me of the middle-of-the-roaders in the typical classroom who keep asking, "Am I done yet?"

Until staff development is understood as a process, I suppose it will just be regarded as a transitory expense. As long as it is regarded as an expense, frugal board members will constantly be attempting to terminate the process. As long as the public and their representatives on the school boards regard teaching as a "job slot" rather than as a profession, professional development will always be an uphill battle.

A LESSON FROM QUALITY CONTROL CIRCLES

Educators often imagine that things are different in the world of business where there is a bottom line and where people are forced to do things efficiently and effectively in order to survive. Such fantasies ignore the highly publicized realities of the bottom line—that productivity in American industry is sagging right along with profits, a decline which is followed closely by loss of morale. It is of no small interest to me, therefore, to observe the process by which American industry attempts to change, grow, and incorporate innovation in this time of stress. One innovation which is generating the most enthusiasm throughout all sectors of industry and which is entirely process-oriented is the "quality control circle" (QC circle)—the so-called secret ingredient of Japanese productivity and product quality.

Quality control circles are working groups of two to ten people within an organization with a common job who share a vested interest in solving problems in production, quality control, and morale. Most QC circles on the shop floor meet 1 or 2 hours per week and are led by a foreman, but the process has now spread through all levels of management. The QC circle membership considers various problems needing attention which are proposed by group members, and the group then selects a limited number of problems to be the object of systematic study by the group over a 3- to 6-month period. Problem solution then leads to suggestions for change in any relevant aspect of production. The average QC circle in Japan produces fifty to sixty implemented suggestions per worker per year.[4]

QC circles have particular relevance to me because (1) they closely resemble the continuation groups developed by CMTP as a vehicle for ongoing growth and quality control, and (2) like continuation groups quality control circles require extensive training on the part of members for the group to function effectively in solving problems. In particular, QC circles represent the process side of business—the investment in increasing the relatively intangible value of the human resources of the corporation. The implementation of QC circles, therefore, serves as a clear test of the methodological sophistication of American industrial management in staff development.

I spoke recently with a former student and colleague of mine who works for a Chicago-based industrial consulting firm, and I asked him what his clients were currently doing with quality control circles. He replied, "Oh, I think that has already peaked and is on the way down. People wanted *results,* and executives are already beginning to complain that they have not realized the benefits that they had projected for the program. They seem to think that any group of workers called together by management is a quality control circle."

My friend's observation of QC circles as an American industrial fad viewed by management as the latest wonder cure is reinforced by a recent statement by W. Edwards Deming, the widely recognized "father of the quality control circle." Dr. Deming stated, "Quality circles only work if management does its job. There are thousands of them in the United States, many because management *can't* do its job and hopes someone else *can*!"[3]

The investment in staff development that management must make to produce successful quality control circles is outlined by Dr. William Ouchi in his best-selling book *Theory Z.*[4] Dr. Ouchi stressed that the average Japanese employee receives approximately *500 days* of training during his or her first 10 years of employment—a monumental investment in staff development. This training focuses on all aspects of job performance as well as statistical techniques for analyzing data collected by the group and interpersonal skills and values which make one a productive member of a problem-solving team. The real difference between American and Japanese management, according to Dr. Ouchi, is the determination of the Japanese to invest in teaching these techniques to production-line employees and then to delegate to them the power and authority to influence the way things are done. The real focus of managerial leadership in Japan is the development of the human side of the organization.

In particular, stressed Dr. Ouchi, QC circles *cannot* be implemented by fiat. Rather, management must create positive conditions and then have the patience to allow effort and morale to grow naturally. QC circles work only if middle and upper management understand the conditions for success and actively support them over time.

It would seem that American management, whether in the public or private sector, is afflicted by an orientation toward the human side of the organization which is shortsighted and simplistic. Our culture for some reason transmits a set of values, expectations, and skills that favor quick cures based on policy rather than people. We have an intolerance for the kind of change which must be bought at the price of slow, process-oriented, long-term professional development. We tend to believe in the spread of change mandated from the top down by management and implemented from the bottom up by people who have been disenfranchised from policy development; change supported somehow magically by morale that has never been fostered and effected by expertise that has never been built. Whether in the private sector, the public sector, or in politics, it is fad upon fad, quick cure upon quick cure, and disillusionment upon disillusionment. Trapped in our "mandate mentality," we chronically fall victim to our own naiveté and impatience.

OVERVIEW

Having presented classroom management as a coherent and humane system which bridges both discipline (*Positive Classroom Discipline*) and instruction (*Positive Classroom Instruction*), I am left with one haunting fear. I worry that the whole effort may die from "exposure." "Positive classroom discipline" and "positive classroom instruction" have grown and matured in the field as a by-product not only of systematic research and observation but also of experience with the Classroom Management Training Program. This is a program of staff development in which skills are imparted to teachers carefully using the teaching methods described in *Positive Classroom Instruction*. Having trained teachers to use these techniques in all kinds of regular and special educational settings, I know how powerful they are in the hands of well-trained teachers. And, since the Classroom Management Training Program is a trainer-of-trainers program, I have seen many teachers other than myself consistently produce mastery and self-confidence in their colleagues. Success, therefore, must be regarded as a by-product of method rather than personality. But I have also seen untrained teachers try to use these methods, and I know how botched and pathetic these techniques can be in the hands of an *untrained* teacher.

When learned poorly, any technique can fail—even in the hands of an otherwise competent individual. When a technique fails for a teacher in front of a classroom full of students, it is quickly relegated to the trash can with the lame but customary assessment that the method "just doesn't work for me." Indeed, skills have a nasty habit of not working for anybody who has not mastered them.

Unless skills are taught well in the first place with careful coaching and practice, followed by retraining, sharing, problem-solving, and support from a healthy support network, the only outcome of any teacher training program will be transitory success at best and failure at worst. Failure then produces disillusionment and cynicism toward the skills, the methods of dissemination, and staff development in general. Innovation of all kinds is killed by improper dissemination, and teachers are left the poorer for their cynicism than they would have been without training.

Within education, teacher training has traditionally exemplified the worst possible teaching methods. At college, students typically receive methods courses via lecture with little modeling and no structured or guided practice. Once on the job, teachers are typically introduced to innovations through either one-shot in-service workshops or quickie seminars. Such exposure is a setup for failure and disillusionment because skill mastery does not come from exposure.

In teacher training and staff development, therefore, method or process is to an extent more important than content. A dated or less than optimal method well taught and well implemented will produce more good than the state of the art poorly taught. At the most concrete level, teachers learn more about teaching from the methods used to teach them than from the content of the presentation. There is no reason to expect better methods from teachers in the field than those which were used to train them. Success, therefore, is ultimately governed by the sophistication of the *delivery system*. The sophistication of the delivery system must match the sophistication of the methods being disseminated or all is for nothing.

Yet experience has taught me to be optimistic. The technology exists for dramatic improvement in classroom instruction and student achievement. And the technology exists for training teachers and for bringing even a cynical faculty into a process of growth and renewal. Sophistication within the education community concerning the need for, and the methods of, successful teacher training is growing rapidly. I have seen the future, and it looks much better than the past. In my work I see most of the "insolvable" problems of education routinely overcome by well-trained teachers and administrators working together.

REFERENCES

1 Mirga, T., and White, E. Poll finds rising concern about school finance. *Education Week*, September 1, 1982, 12–13.

2 Rutter, M., Maughan, B., Mortimore, P., Ouston, J., and Smith, A. *Fifteen thousand hours, secondary schools and their effects on children*. Cambridge, MA: Harvard University Press, 1979.

3 Deming, Edward D. In *Car and Driver*, October 1981, 29.

4 Ouchi, William G. *Theory Z*. New York: Addison-Wesley, 1981.

CHAPTER **13**

NEW STRUCTURES FOR THE TEACHING PROFESSION

In April 1983, the National Commission on Excellence in Education issued its report as an open letter to the American people entitled, "A Nation at Risk: The Imperative for Educational Reform." The task force report created more than a stir within education—it created a major political issue for the 1984 presidential campaign within a month and a half of the report's release. The need for far-reaching educational reform had finally come out of the closet with a suddenness and urgency that caught most educational policy makers and politicians off guard. Since the spring of 1983 the competition among educators and national and state legislators to come up with a cure for what's ailing our public schools has reached the point of clamor.

By June 1983, both the major political parties were issuing policy statements which dealt with topics ranging from the length of the school year and the length of the school day to merit pay for teachers and major new emphases in curriculum. By September 1983, almost all the major news magazines had run upbeat cover stories on the reforms in education citing example after example of state and federal legislation pending or passed that addressed the "rising tide of mediocrity in our schools." Indeed, it would seem that perhaps education's long, hard winter of public apathy, criticism, and reduced support could at last be coming to an end. But the speed of the turnaround was impressive to say the least. If the report of the National Commission on Excellence in Education can be viewed as the first sign of the long-awaited spring, it is amazing that it took only 2 months for the entire nation to come into full bloom.

Although many of the reforms being proposed are accompanied by laudatory rationales and although some of the proposals even have a chance of being successful, it is important to keep three basic realities in mind. First, basic change in an institution as large and inertia-bound as education is slow, costly, and hard-fought. Second, improvement in education ultimately takes place within the classroom. Although effective public policy can add momentum to many constructive trends within education, excellence is not achieved in Congress, in the State House, at the county level, or in the office of the district administration. Whatever legislative policies are passed, the major measure of excellence in education is that teachers learn to teach and manage their classrooms better. Third, presidential, congressional, and state elections are ever imminent, and much of the rush to legislate excellence must be viewed as election-year politicking. If excellence in education is "in," then any politician in his right mind should be staying up late trying to draft an omnibus education reform bill. If omnibus education reform bills could reform education, we would not be in the shape we are in. And if reform could be done as rapidly as a stroke of a legislative pen, it would have been done long ago.

It is understandable that the sudden surge for educational reform will produce an encyclopedia of quick cures. Many may seem to have merit, but none will be as simple as it at first appears. Organizational change is a subtle, difficult, and time-consuming process, and the mandate mentality is no more effective from the state house than it is from the district office. Indeed, many of the most sensible-appearing and straightforward cures for education being proposed at present address extremely complex issues which, if dealt with clumsily, could easily produce more harm than good. The present chapter attempts to deal with some of the most basic issues in the current rush to improve education so that they may be seen within a broader context of staff and organizational development: the delivery of the tools for educational excellence into the hands of the classroom teacher and the district administration.

GOOD TEACHERS AND BAD TEACHERS

There are two related but separate approaches to improving the quality of education quickly (apart from the curriculum) which are the first to occur to most concerned citizens, namely (1) getting rid of incompetent teachers and (2) merit pay for exemplary teachers. It is safe to say that most school board members, administrators, and politicians, to say nothing of the general public, think that having control over these two issues would produce quick and dramatic improvements in teacher performance. Ironically, both of these perennial favorites represent simplistic solutions to complex organizational problems which are, for the most part, doomed to failure.

Weeding Out the Dead Wood

Collaborative versus Adversarial Leadership When an organizational leader expresses his or her leadership mandate by attempting to "weed out the dead wood" as the initial focus of his or her leadership without a major *prior* investment in team building and professional growth, the faculty unites around the attacked colleague irrespective of the issue of excellence. The group will then organize for self-defense and raise as many obstacles to the removal of the attacked colleague as possible. The result is a form of warfare between adversaries with a rapidly increasing cost to everyone, concurrent with rapidly decreasing flexibility on the part of administrators in dealing with weak teachers. The whole thing may eventually end up in court; the district rarely wins and the lawyers take the money. Meanwhile, the leader of this naïve attempt to produce quick reform will have spent a great deal of time and energy with the net result being a polarization of the work group.

Team Building and Professional Growth Ironically, the attack on the weak teacher is not only destructive to organization building in most cases, but it is also an inefficient way to improve the mean level of the performance of the work group. The leaders will produce a much greater increase in the performance of the group if they help fifteen fairly competent teachers to improve than they will by getting rid of one or two incompetent teachers.

The primary focus of organization building for leaders, therefore, should be to build a growth process in which the majority of the group joins in a common professional development effort that substantially improves group performance and morale. It is the job of leadership to build group cohesiveness around the shared focus of achieving excellence rather than to destroy group cohesiveness through adversarial behavior.

As the process of professional growth and the camaraderie which accompanies it become more established, the inept teachers, rather than being the center of social cohesion, will become more and more peripheral to the group process. They will be voluntarily omitting themselves not only from professional development opportunities but also from the extensive social interactions associated with them—a context of working together that is not only rewarding but also associated in the minds of the peer group with being a good teacher.

Supervision and Feedback In addition to team building, part of the principal's job is evaluation and feedback. When, however, it is possible for principals and teachers to live in separate worlds free of the systematic pursuit of excellence, supervision and feedback are for the most part institutional irrelevancies. In years past, plant managers have commonly had teachers fill out their own evaluations, glad to be freed of meaningless paperwork. Mandatory classroom visits once or twice a year by principals rarely produced incisive comments concerning the quality of teaching. To get a negative review there had to be a riot going on, a comatose teacher, or a bulletin board done in shades of gray.

Now the age of the instructional leader is upon us and principals are going in droves to workshops and seminars on "clinical supervision." Such training has done much to give principals a sense of what to look for in a classroom, how to document what they see, and how to give verbal feedback to teachers. Such workshops and seminars, however, are usually fairly brief, large-group affairs that lack the capacity to train principals in high-level clinical skills (as the name would imply). Consequently, principals typically revert to type when giving corrective feedback and lace their remarks with more than a few "yes-but compliments" and "helpful criticisms."

Their skills of clinical supervision all too often degenerate into mixing criticism with enough praise to sweeten some of the resultant bitterness. The result of such clinical clumsiness, predictably, is a considerable amount of awkwardness and discomfort on the part of the supervisor and frequent defensiveness on the part of the teacher.

The most common problem with clinical supervision is that it is typically based on poor instructional practice. To put it simply, it typically employs the universal helping interaction. And why not? The universal helping interaction has been invisible in the classroom up until now, so why should it be any different in the instruction that goes by the name of supervision? The job of the universal helping interaction is to find the problem and fix it. It begins with a deficit diagnosis and proceeds to corrective feedback by way of a prescription for remediation. Even when amply padded with praise, the typical supervisory session often becomes a prolonged, awkward, and often painful yes-but compliment.

In the Classroom Management Training Program there is no differentiation in training between teacher and administrator. Not only must administrators understand the program and visibly support it by being part of the training team, but they must also use it in carrying out their role of instructional leader. They must not only know what to look for in precision teaching and classroom management skills when observing a classroom, but they must use those same teaching skills in supervision. They must always give corrective feedback, and they must sometimes teach a structured lesson from scratch in the process.

An example may be helpful at this point. A particular junior high principal in Virginia had been trained along with several of his strongest teachers to be a trainer in the Classroom Management Training Program. During the following year, all teachers at the school site who wished to participate in the program went through training and participated in the continuation groups that follow training. The principal skillfully put the program on the front burner at the school site and kept it there, producing a high rate of volunteerism. But, predictably, a few of the "chronic bitchers and moaners," to use the principal's words, flatly refused to have anything to do with the program.

Rather than directly confronting this negativistic behavior, which would have only produced more of the same, the principal used his coaching skills within a tutorial context. He visited the classroom of one of his more negativistic male teachers and scheduled a feedback session as was customary. In the feedback session the principal carefully described the strengths that he had observed in the classroom and then made his transition from praise to prompt ("The next thing to do is. . .").

> You know, Henry, one of the things I liked, as I mentioned, was your getting around to different students when they were working independently in order to help them with their work [The actual number was four]. Is there any way we can make that job easier for you by cutting down the amount of walking you have to do—by arranging the furniture so you don't have to walk around so many obstacles to get where you want to go? If we can come up with a room arrangement that allows you to get around easier, I'll talk to Bob, the custodian, so he'll leave it that way.

Some brainstorming produced a much-improved room arrangement, and the principal walked down to the teacher's room to help shove furniture around as the two continued to discuss the subject. During the following week, several brief conversations with the teacher in the hall not only confirmed that the new room arrangement had helped but also kept the whole issue on the front burner. A week or so later the principal visited the teacher's room again and scheduled another feedback session.

> Henry, it looks a whole lot easier for you to get around in there now, and I think you are able to help the kids more often as a result. Today I'd like to focus on a way of getting around even faster so that we can help kids more often and, in particular, get to kids as soon as they feel stuck before they start goofing off.
>
> Here's what I have in mind. Our objective will be to help a kid who is stuck as quickly and efficiently as possible. We'll try to make the interaction as simple as possible so it takes less than a minute. Then nobody will be on hold long enough to get into trouble. Besides, you'll be able to move often enough so that you'll be looking over the kids' shoulders all of the time.

The next several supervisory sessions were spent on the positive helping interaction, and then the focus shifted to illustrated performance sequences. Pretty soon they were talking about limit-setting on the wing and remaining calm when a kid mouths off.

"You know, it took some time," said the principal, "but I got old Henry through almost all the program, and it really helped him. The kids had been giving him a pretty hard time before. And we got to know and trust each other. I actually think he looks forward to our supervisory sessions. In fact he said so once. But he still says he won't have a damn thing to do with the Classroom Management Training Program. That's just Henry. If it looks like the thing to do, he'll do the opposite. But he got it anyway."

Evaluation and feedback are crucial facets of the instructional leader's role. But, unless these functions are carried out within a context of correct instructional methodology, they will be handled within a context that is fundamentally incompatible with psychological support. The result is teachers who see evaluation and feedback as threatening—a perception that ultimately makes the job of instructional leadership difficult if not impossible. The basic skills and the value system inherent in positive classroom instruction must ultimately reverberate to the top of the organizational hierarchy because good supervision and leadership are good teaching. The classroom is not a unique context nor is the principal's role unique. Getting people to do things right with a positive attitude and high group morale pervades all levels of organizational life. It requires not only correct basic methodology but a way of thinking about all people as potential learners.

Facing the Issue of Nonperformance If we can keep staff development from being stigmatized by either adversarial behavior or by the "deficit model" which associates staff development with needing help (see previous chapter), principals will have increased flexibility in dealing with the weak teacher. They will, in fact, spend a larger share of their consulting time with weak teachers since the strong teachers do not need to be continuously held by the hand when working toward professional development goals. With weak teachers a principal may spend a great deal of time clarifying values and objectives, helping the teachers find growth-producing experiences, and evaluating efforts to change. Since the goals and means of professional growth are always a collaborative effort between principal and teacher, the principal can constrain the range of choices to be within the teacher's areas of immediate need.

But, how does a principal get rid of a truly incompetent teacher who either does not try to improve or does not seem capable of improving? Do you get rid of her by "taking her to the mat"? If so, what steps precede confrontation that make the process as humane as possible?

The Accelerating Quality Control Cycle If a teacher needs to leave the teaching profession, it is the principal's obligation to help her or him out—to help with firmness and compassion until the necessity of job change is painfully obvious to all. Helping a teacher out of the teaching profession should be viewed as a matter of due process in which the teacher is given every possible opportunity to grow. Yet, while principals collaborate in providing every possible opportunity for growth, they are also the chief quality control person on the school site, and the buck stops with them. They are both obligated to provide a real opportunity to grow and forbidden to accept incompetence.

In practice, these two tasks of giving help and quality control are expressed for the principal in terms of a cycle of (1) goal setting, (2) staff development, and (3) evaluation—a quality control cycle which simply increases in rate over time in the case of the particularly needy teacher. Goals are set, steps are taken to help the teacher grow, and observation and evaluation follow. This fundamental process of systematic professional growth is no different in form for the weak teacher than for the strong teacher since everyone is always involved in staff development without implication of deficit. Weak teachers are different only insofar as they call attention to themselves by their lack of progress.

Only when no growth is taking place does the *rate* of the quality control cycle increase. Evidence of nonperformance produces a redefinition of goals and a more informed and detailed selection of additional means of growth. Participation in some kind of growth opportunity is followed by more frequent observation which is followed by an additional cycle of goal clarification and goal attainment planning. Over time the cycle accelerates so that much of the principal's and teacher's energies are concentrated on the attempt to achieve growth. With such scrutiny the attainment of growth will be as obvious as the failure to attain growth.

Although the quality control cycle has a cost in terms of the principal allocating time and resources, it has a corresponding cost to the weak teacher who must also allocate time and energy. At some point either the teacher will stop stonewalling, or it will become evident to everyone that the teacher is either incapable or unwilling to grow. When such a realization begins to dawn, the teacher in question will experience pain. That pain may be expressed in a variety of ways, but it is usually evidence of a life crisis that is long overdue.

Existential Choices and the Chickens That Come Home to Roost The choice of one's profession is a profound existential decision, a search for personal meaning through one's work. Staying in a profession in which you are ill-suited and not succeeding is a pain-producing act of existential cowardice. When the chickens finally come home to roost, there will be pain. When the pain becomes evident, it is the principal's role to become counselor, not adversary.

The issue of competence is not negotiable. When avenues of change have been explored and found useless, the agenda is unavoidable. The principal has to say, "It's not working. Classroom instruction is not for you. Where do we go from here?"

Many times the principal begins a process of job counseling that can then be assumed by other professionals within the district. Sometimes they will just take heat from a scared and resentful individual. Sometimes teachers find other roles within the school organization, and sometimes they simply find a doctor who signs the papers that get them disability due to stress. Sometimes the teacher for the first time deals with the fact that he or she made the wrong career choice. In any case, the principal's role is that of counselor within the framework of being the person responsible for quality control at the school site. The buck stops with the principal, but the school board must empower principals to do their job gently, systematically, and humanely. You do not run people out of the teaching profession. You help them out, because anyone who is leaving needs help. Dealing with an incompetent teacher must ultimately be a humane endeavor or the unavoidable pain and associated costs will be multiplied for all parties involved.

Merit Pay for Exemplary Teachers

There are two possible rationales for merit pay: (1) thanking good teachers and (2) providing an incentive system which produces an improvement in performance for members of the profession. Traditional methods of merit pay say thank you to the excellent teachers in a school system, but they typically fail to serve as an incentive system for professional development.

Merit Pay and Incentives for Excellence

Problems of Reward To help understand why traditional merit-pay schemes tend to fail as incentive systems, it may be helpful to consider a common practice—rewarding car salespeople when they win a regional competition for having the most car sales. Imagine, for example, that a major automobile manufacturer offers a trip to Bermuda for the three top salespeople in a given region. Does that incentive improve the performance of the average salesperson? The answer is probably not. Why?

Let's imagine that there are 100 salespeople in the region. To begin with, five or ten of them are not only talented but also chronic workaholics. They have been sharing the top honors for the past several years, and everybody else in the region knows who they are. Before the contest even starts, the vast majority of salespeople have already quit because they have no intention of giving up all their nights and weekends, their spouses, children, hobbies, and sports to try to win a contest that they will probably lose anyway. Thus from the very outset of the contest, the three trips to Bermuda are probably serving as incentives for maybe ten salespeople while everyone else goes about their jobs as they see fit.

In addition, the trip to Bermuda is not until next February, which is 10 months away. Delay in reward greatly undermines its potency. Consequently, the automobile company is asking a typical salesperson to give up dinner with his family tonight and stay until 9:00 p.m. doing paperwork in order to have a chance to earn a reward that won't even be announced for another 10 months. For most people such a reward is simply too distant and too tenuous to be worth the price.

Thus, although the trips to Bermuda might engage the top 5 to 10 percent of the sales force, and although the incentive may be regarded more or less positively by the rest of the sales force as a genuine attempt on the part of the company to say thank you, the incentive does not function to generate different work habits on the part of the vast majority of employees. It is not a motor for behavior change—a functional incentive system for the achievement of diligence and excellence on a broad scale.

To get back to schools and classrooms, if you were to poll the faculty of a school by asking them what teachers on their faculty would probably receive merit pay, they would tell you. They know who is outstanding. There are very few secrets among the members of a school faculty. Therefore, why would large numbers of teachers reorganize the way they teach, go to the effort of learning new skills, spend extra hours in the evening preparing lessons, and change their methods of discipline management for a reward they know they will probably never get?

Problems of Accountability In addition to problems of operating an incentive system that adequately rewards large numbers of teachers, there is the problem of operating an incentive system correctly so that it does not self-destruct. In our discussions of incentive systems in both *Positive Classroom Discipline* and *Positive Classroom Instruction* we have focused repeatedly on the issue of the cost of accountability. For an incentive system to succeed, the assessment of the behavior that is to be rewarded must be strict, accurate, and affordable. It must be viewed by participants as *valid*. If assessment is not accurate and fair, it will not only cause participants to become disillusioned with the incentive system and stop participating, but it will also produce ill feelings among those who did not receive rewards and felt unfairly judged.

Merit pay in its traditional form is consistently opposed by teachers when they feel that the assessment will be quick and dirty, that is, when it will be performed by an administrator such as their principal who in the teachers' minds cannot tell good teaching from bad and who has both favorites and unfavorites on the faculty. Unfortunately, the teachers are all too often right in this perception and will continue to be right for a long time to come. The supervisory expertise and evaluative sophistication needed to operate a straight merit-pay system does not exist in the field now and will not exist for decades even if all the money in the world were allocated to merit pay tomorrow.

Thus, although traditional forms of merit pay may say thank you, they are among the most inefficient ways of altering the way in which the majority of teachers teach. In fact, as mentioned earlier, most of the faculty will not even compete for merit pay. And those few who do compete for it but fail to get it will often feel wronged. Thus, the research shows that merit pay typically generates ill feelings among the faculty and is typically abandoned because it is more trouble than it is worth.

Professional Development and Service Pay

Extra Pay for Extra Work Although it is very difficult to create a meritocracy based on simple money rewards, it is fairly easy to create a meritocracy based on extra pay for assuming added professional responsibilities for which people have been specially trained. Since the extra work of added professional responsibilities is quite tangible, colleagues rarely resent the extra pay that the extra work produces. And, if a potentially large number of teachers can have access to varying amounts of extra pay for extra work, we have the basis for an incentive system that will in fact be a motor for producing widespread behavior change and professional growth.

Although there are many ways for teachers to make a special contribution to the functioning of a district, one of the ways most relevant to increasing professional excellence is to assume the role of trainer in a systematic staff development program which almost by necessity will employ a trainer-of-trainers model. Administrators should in all cases choose their trainers from among their best teachers, and being trained to be a trainer will equip those teachers with special professional expertise.

Initial experience with the trainer-of-trainers program allows the trainers to decide whether or not they enjoy the training experience enough to continue with it, and it gives supervisors a chance to decide whether that person is working out as an effective trainer. During the first year, the reward for the trainer may be the luxury of receiving expensive high-level training for free (at the district's expense) and trying his or her wings in a new role. By the second year in which a teacher functions as a trainer, he or she should be earning extra pay for the extra work. Such pay is, however, service pay rather than merit pay in the traditional sense.

Mentors and Master Teachers Programs presently being proposed, which attempt to reward exemplary teachers while sidestepping the traditional pitfalls of merit pay, are for the most part service-pay systems. In such programs teachers who receive extra stipends for disseminating their special skills throughout the district are usually referred to as "mentor teachers" or "master teachers." The mechanics of such service-pay systems are still in their formative stages, but the major design issues and potential problem areas are plain enough.

1 Who gets to say who is a master teacher, and what are the criteria of selection?

In most programs presently being considered, teachers are typically nominated by a committee of parents, teachers, and administrators to receive added pay for serving as mentors for new teachers or as master teachers who disseminate their special skills throughout the district. This system of "consensual validation" often works quite well when small numbers of teachers are being chosen—teachers whose reputations precede them in the selection process and thereby confer validity upon the selection. The selection process will be held to closer scrutiny and criticized more on grounds of validity as soon as larger numbers of teachers are enfranchised into the service-pay system. In order to create both the substance and appearance of validity of selection, there will be increasing pressure to replace consensual criteria of selection with "empirical validation." At that point the cost of accountability in our incentive system increases dramatically.

2 How many teachers can be mentors or master teachers? Will many teachers be enfranchised, or will there be just an elite few?

One of the most obvious means of cost containment is elitism. Indeed, few of the mentor- or master-teacher programs presently being proposed enfranchise more than a few percent of the total teacher population into the service-pay system. Even such a limited effort can produce large dividends if carried out properly, but the eternal "Why should I?" must still be answered for many if they are to make their special contributions to excellence.

3 What approach to skill dissemination will be used if mentors and master teachers are to train their peers?

The fact that teachers are exemplary in their classrooms does not mean that they can systematically reproduce that expertise. Perhaps the Achilles' heel of all mentor- or master-teacher programs presently being proposed is the naïve assumption that mentor teachers (1) can accurately describe the skills that make them excellent and (2) can convey those skills to their colleagues without making them defensive and resentful. A decade and a half of perfecting trainer-of-trainers methods in the field began with a couple of lessons in the school of hard knocks that I have never forgotten: Exceptional teachers are almost powerless to describe at a high level of precision exactly *how* they manage a classroom and their colleagues get extremely defensive and petty as soon as a "master" teacher presumes to give them advice.

How carefully, then, will the *process* of disseminating expertise be attended to? Will a quality delivery system be slowly and carefully built in which master or mentor teachers can function effectively? Or will we once again simply turn a blind eye toward the most difficult aspect of staff development and hope for the best?

Before service-pay schemes are ironed out in the many school districts across the country interested in such programs, a considerable amount of trial and error will take place. As I travel, I already find effective principals worrying aloud that their less effective administrator colleagues will probably make mentors into assistant principals if given the chance. In some other districts teachers with the most seniority are hinting that they are the natural choice for the role. I find superintendents anxious about dissension and hurt feelings because the criteria of selection are so fuzzy and because the issue of extra pay is already making the composition of the selection committee a political football.

In localities where there has historically been a strong staff development apparatus, however, often in the form of a federally funded teacher center, a state or county professional development center or a staff development institute within a larger district, I find a remarkably smooth and sensible process of evolution developing. In localities where systematic staff development has a history of several years and where many of the best teachers have already served as trainers in at least one and often several quality trainer-of-trainers programs, these experienced trainers are emerging as the natural choices for the mentor- or master-teacher roles. They are the obvious choices because they are in effect already serving as mentors and master teachers and have demonstrated mastery of the complex skills required for successful peer training.

There is no substitute for systematic staff development based on the unhurried development of a district's best talent if a multileveled meritocracy is to be built in education. Without such a planned development process the selection of mentors and master teachers often resembles anointment more than career advancement, with some strange sideshows being created in the process. In contrast to the impatience built into legislative solutions to the "rising tide of mediocrity," excellence must be carefully built rather than mandated.

Built-In Resistance It is ironic, as I travel and train teachers, to repeatedly deal with administrators and school board members who are on the one hand considering merit pay programs in their districts and who are on the other hand unwilling to pay my CMTP coaches extra money for the extra preparation and training time that goes into a quality trainer-of-trainers program. Many districts even have a policy forbidding extra pay for work after hours. Suggesting such an innovation brings dark looks and serious concern over setting a dangerous precedent.

Indeed, the teaching profession has had a long history of exploiting the enthusiasm of teachers who are willing to go the extra mile. Unfortunately, as we have learned in previous sections, in human affairs there is no such thing as a nonincentive system. When teachers do extra work and are not rewarded for it, they are placed on systematic extinction for doing that extra work. Without service pay of some kind, the day will come when the extra work will be done no more.

BUILDING A CAREER LADDER

It is becoming increasingly difficult to recruit the more capable college students into the teaching profession. Apart from inadequate pay and low status in the eyes of the public, one of the chronic criticisms of the teaching profession is that it is a dead end profession with no career ladder—no continuing challenge or widespread opportunity for assuming greater responsibility with pay to match.

Teaching, unfortunately, is not seen as a profession at all by the general public and, in particular, by school boards. Rather, it is generally viewed as simply a job in which you will be doing the same thing the week before you retire that you did the day after you were hired.

Staff Development and Avenues of Enrichment

If money is going to be spent on rewarding excellent teachers, far better to use it not only to reward excellence but also to build excellence—to build a career ladder which provides career development for career teachers, incentives for excellence, and extra pay for extra service. Exceptional teachers should be developed as the primary human resource of the school system. Rather than (or in addition to) being given extra pay for being excellent teachers to start with, teachers should be given special opportunities to grow professionally and demonstrate professional competence. Once that special competence has been mastered and demonstrated, they should be paid extra money for spreading that competence throughout the district.

The concept of service pay, therefore, is closely tied to a conceptualization of staff development within a school district as a long-term, programmatic enterprise worthy of the allocation of considerable resources. Both professional development on a districtwide basis and the development of a career ladder which is needed to attract and keep highly competent individuals within the teaching profession are in fact one integrated program.

Avoiding the "Peter Principle"

One additional advantage of service pay as opposed to merit pay is its tendency to be a natural antidote to the "Peter Principle." Traditionally, the only way to achieve career advancement and increased pay within education has been to leave the classroom and go into administration. Thus, many talented teachers have been siphoned away from the classroom, often into jobs for which they were less enthusiastic, less competent, and/or less prepared. According to the Peter Principle, people rise within an organization until they achieve their level of incompetence at which point they remain. That is, if people succeed at one job, they may be asked to advance up the professional ladder to the next rung. If they succeed at the second job, they may move up the ladder to a higher level and then to an even higher level until they finally do poorly at a job. Once they fail at a job, they are no longer asked to move up. Rather, they are passed over for advancement and remain where they are indefinitely.

Service pay keeps good teachers in the classroom. Indeed, it is inconceivable that a teacher could be permanently *removed* from the classroom to be a trainer of advanced educational skills and remain sharp in the use of those skills. A trainer-of-trainers program all but requires the trainers to stay in the classroom at least part time using the skills, honing their expertise, and solving problems in order not only to stay sharp and grow but also to help colleagues in continuation meetings. There is always a dialogue between the skills and concepts of a professional development program and the experience of handling management dilemmas within the classroom on a day-to-day basis. The result is professional growth quite apart from the formal training of the program proper. In conjunction with continuation meetings, quality professional development produces a process in which day-to-day innovations by teachers are constantly fed to colleagues through "the pipeline."

LENGTHENING THE SCHOOL DAY AND THE SCHOOL YEAR

The time-on-task literature would certainly imply that the longer students work, the more they learn. It is also obvious from a comparison of the numbers of days students in the United States and those in other nations spend in school that we spend fewer days in class. It is a logical conclusion, therefore, that lengthening the school year will produce more learning. Indeed, it should produce more learning as should a lengthening of the school day. Whether the money could have been better spent in other ways, however, is a separate issue.

As a result of teacher training, we have documented a near doubling of academic productivity in the bottom half of a typical classroom,[1,2] and teachers consistently report rapid increases in the rate of learning because of the use of performance models alone. Owing to responsibility training we typically have students in their seats working when the bell rings which saves us 5 minutes at the beginning of every period, and we typically reduce lesson transitions to 30 seconds which saves us over 4 minutes per lesson transition in a typical classroom. Thus by the use of some advanced classroom management procedures, a well-trained teacher is already generating between a half hour and an hour per day of extra instructional time.

The bill for paying teachers to work 20 extra days per year will be in the billions of dollars nationwide, and the lengthening of the school day will not be free in the long run either. Although our school year may be too short, I would hope that we think in terms of quality and not just quantity when looking for cures for the "rising tide of mediocrity." It would create many more hours of learning during the school year for teachers to have advanced management skills at their disposal than it would to just add more days. If legislators are contemplating spending billions of dollars for increased time on task, they might well consider using a few of those extra days for training teachers so that during the following year their investment could produce benefits in the classroom *every* day.

To state my case in somewhat different terms, if we are going to invest in excellence in education in a major way, let us have the wisdom to invest in the *process* of education—to build a delivery system for the teaching of basic subjects that is far superior to what presently exists. Quality staff development can take place on a nationwide basis if there is a predictable market for it that would provide the incentive for the development of widespread professional expertise in that area. Unless such a clear and long-term commitment to quality staff development is made at a national level as well as at the state, county, and district levels, the most predictable outcome of the present enthusiasm over educational reform will probably be a coopting of extra moneys by the educational establishment into more business as usual.

THE ROLE OF HIGHER EDUCATION

In all the discussions of reform within the American educational system and in all the various commissioned reports, one group of educators gets off with amazingly light treatment. Reports inevitably include sentences concerning the need to upgrade teacher training at colleges and universities, but rarely does the specification of reform go beyond this amorphous statement of need.

In juxtaposition to this rather passing concern with the quality of teacher training at colleges and universities is the glaring dissatisfaction with teacher training programs at colleges and universities which is universally expressed by the teachers I train. I will ask a group of several hundred teachers to raise their hands if any of their methods courses ever did them any good once they took a job. No one raises a hand. I ask teachers and administrators to describe the relevance of their methods courses, and the main adjective they use is "Mickey Mouse." Teachers express bitter resentment at having paid thousands of dollars for tuition and expenses to receive a professional degree which ended up having almost no relevance to their professional life. Instead, they walked onto the job with no professional skills apart from the social skills they possessed anyway and "took it in the teeth" until, with a huge expenditure of adrenaline and stomach acid, they finally pieced together over several years' time some semblance of a methodology for managing a classroom that allowed them at least to survive on the job.

How can a profession expect to achieve excellence if the major professional training opportunity is squandered so that teachers walk onto the job with virtually no functional job skills? How can we expect districts to have funds to totally retrain their staffs when the general public assumes that teachers were already trained when they took their first jobs? And how can you easily engage teachers in retooling their professional skill repertoires after they have already spent 15 years in the school of hard knocks? Quality professional development will always need to be a permanent, ongoing part of any living profession. But the first major professional development opportunity is at college, and it is a crime to waste it.

It would, in fact, be easy to make a rather strong case that higher education is one of the major weak links in the entire educational system. Universities have the captive students eager to learn, the financial backing of federal and state governments *and* the students' parents, and the time with which to make teachers, at least in a preliminary fashion, out of nonteachers. But instead they get Mickey Mouse.

Yet undergraduates express no dissatisfaction. They are not informed consumers. They do not know what they are walking into. Only the teachers who have been out for several years express to me the deep abiding bitterness at their methods courses taught by professors who had not been near an elementary or secondary classroom since they graduated from high school.

It is sad and rather ironic that higher education, which holds a near monopoly on teacher preparation, gets such a light rap when the entire nation is seemingly upset with the lack of preparation of its teachers. Perhaps the high-sounding commission reports would sound different were they written by practicing teachers instead of the deans and professors of the very faculties that perpetuate the existing process of teacher preparation.

OVERVIEW

The nation is at a turning point in its understanding of the education process and in its commitment to excellence in public education. Turning points, however, are not only great opportunities but also awesome responsibilities, for they do not come frequently and they do not last long. A turning point missed is at least a decade missed. If our reforms are quick and easy, their effects will be superficial and their legacy will be disillusionment. Yet, if we ask the more difficult questions and seek the more difficult remedies, sacred cows are threatened and howls of discomfort are heard throughout the educational establishment.

I have become convinced in my years of daily working with teachers that they, more than any, resent the mediocrity of public education and, in particular, the institutional structures which produce and foster that mediocrity. They are the victims of a system that ill prepares them to begin with and then stifles professional development and advancement. My sympathy is first with the children; for it is they whose education is lost, and it is their parents whose dreams are eroded by mediocrity in the classroom. Next my sympathy lies with the teachers, for it is they who work hardest, suffer longest, and are least appreciated. There are grossly incompetent teachers who are a blight on the profession, but most teachers want excellence desperately, for a teacher cannot feel successful in a classroom unless her or his students are learning. Teaching can be *therapeutic* for the teacher properly equipped to succeed. But for someone who is ill equipped, teaching will exhaust the body and sap the spirit until there is finally nothing left to give.

REFERENCES

1 Jones, F. H. and Eimers, R. Role-playing to train elementary teachers to use a classroom management "skill package." *Journal of Applied Behavior Analysis,* 1975, *8,* 421–433.

2 ———, Fremouw, W., and Carples, S. Pyramid training of elementary school teachers to use a classroom management "skill package." *Journal of Applied Behavior Analysis,* 1977, *10,* 239–253.

BIBLIOGRAPHY

Anderson, C.S. The search for school climate: a review of the research. *Review of Educational Research,* 1982, *52*(3), 368–420.

Anderson, G.J. Effects of classroom social climate on individual learning. *American Educational Research Journal,* 1970, *7*(2), 135–152.

Aronson, E., Blaney, N., Stephen, C., Sikes, J., and Snapp, M. *The jigsaw classroom.* Beverly Hills, CA: Sage Publications, 1978.

Ascione, F.R., and Borg, W.R. Effects of a training program on teacher behavior and handicapped children's self-concepts. *The Journal of Psychology,* 1980, *104,* 53–65.

Austin, G.R. Exemplary schools and the search for effectiveness. *Educational Leadership,* 1979, *37*(1), 10–14.

Averch, H.A., Caroll, S.J., Donaldson, T.S., Kiesling, H.J., and Pincus, J. *How effective is schooling? A critical review and synthesis of research findings.* Santa Monica, CA: The Rand Corporation, 1972.

Axelrod, S., Hall, R.V., and Maxwell, A. Use of peer attention to increase study behavior. *Behavior Therapy,* 1972, *3,* 349–351.

Bloom, B.S. *All our children learning.* New York: McGraw-Hill, 1980.

Borg, W.R. Changing teacher and pupil performance with protocols. *Journal of Experimental Education,* 1975, *45,* 9–18.

———, Langer, R., and Kelley, M.L. The minicourse: a new tool for the education of teachers. *Education,* 1969, *37,* 91–96.

Brookover, W., Beady, C., Flood, P., Schweitzer, J., and Wisenbaker, J. *School social systems and student achievement: schools can make a difference.* New York: Praeger, 1979.

Brookover, W.B., Ferderbar, G., Gay, G., Middleton, M., Posner, G., and Roebuck, F. *Measuring and attaining the goals of education.* Alexandria, VA: Association for Supervision and Curriculum Development, 1980.

Brophy, J.E. Advances in teacher research. *The Journal of Classroom Interaction,* 1979, *15*(1), 1–7.

Burka, A.A., and Jones, F.H. Procedures for increasing appropriate verbal participation in special elementary classrooms. *Behavior Modification,* 1979, *3,* 27–48.

Carroll, J.B. A model of school learning. *Teachers College Record,* 1963, *64,* 723–733.

Centra, J.A., and Potter, D.A. School and teacher effects: an interrelational model. *Review of Educational Research,* 1980, *50*(2), 273–291.

Chasnoff, R. (Ed.). *Structuring cooperative learning experiences in the classroom: the 1979 handbook.* Minneapolis, MN: Cooperative Network Publication, 1979.

Cooper, H., and Good, T. *Pygmalion grows up: studies in the expectation communication process.* New York: Longman, 1982.

Cooper, M.L., Thomson, C.L., and Baer, D.M. The experimental modification of teacher attending behavior. *Journal of Applied Behavior Analysis,* 1970, *3,* 153–157.

Coopersmith, S. *Antecedents of self-esteem.* San Francisco: W.H. Freeman, 1967.

Cowen, R.J., Jones, F.H., and Bellack, A.S. Grandma's rule with group contingencies, cost-efficient means of classroom management. *Behavior Modification,* 1979, *3,* 397–418.

Cruikshank, D.P. Simulation. *Theory Into Practice,* 1968, *7,* 190–193.

Deming, E.D. In *Car and Driver,* October 1981, 29.

DeTure, L.R. Relative effects of modeling on the acquisition of wait-time by preservice elementary teachers and concomitant changes in dialogue patterns. *Journal of Research in Science Teaching,* 1979, *16,* 553–562.

Deutsch, M. Cooperation and trust: some theoretical notes. In *Nebraska Symposium on Motivation,* Lincoln: University of Nebraska Press, 1962, 275–319.

DeVries, D., and Edwards, K. Learning games and student teams: their effects on classroom process. *American Education Research Journal,* 1973, *10,* 307–318.

Dodson, R., and Dodson, J.S. *Humaneness in schools: a neglected force.* Dubuque, IA: Kendall/Hunt, 1976.

Educational Leadership, 1982, *40*(3), entire issue.

Elkind, D., *Children and adolescents.* New York: Oxford Press, 1974, 105–127.

Finn, J.D. Expectations and the educational environment. *Review of Educational Research,* 1972, *42*(3), 387–410.

Flynn, E.W., and LaFaso, J.F. *Group discussion as a learning process.* New York: Paulist Press, 1972.

Fullan, M., Miles, M.B., and Taylor, G. Organizational development in schools: the state of the art. *Review of Educational Research,* 1980, *50*(1), 121–183.

Gage, N.L. The scientific basis of the art of teaching. New York: Teachers College Press, Columbia University, 1978.

Gall, M.D. The relationship between inservice education practices and effectiveness of basic skills instruction. Final report. Eugene, Oregon: Center for Educational Policy and Management, December 1982.

Gallop, G.H. The 14th annual Gallop poll of the public's attitudes toward the public schools. *Phi Delta Kappan,* 1982, *64*(1), 37–50.

Gibbs, J., and Allen, A. *Tribes.* Oakland, CA: Center-Source Publications, 1978.

Gideonse, H.D. The necessary revolution in teacher education. *Phi Delta Kappan,* September 1982, 15–18.

Good, T.L. Teacher effectiveness in the elementary school. *Teacher Education,* 1979, *30*(2), 52–64.

———, and Brophy, J.E. An empirical investigation: changing teacher and student behavior. *Journal of Educational Psychology,* 1974, *66,* 399–405.

——— and ———. *Looking in classrooms.* Harper & Row, 1978.

Goodlad, J.I. *The dynamics of educational change: toward responsive schools.* New York: McGraw-Hill, 1975.

———. *A place called school, prospects for the future.* New York: McGraw-Hill, 1984.

Gossard, J. *Using read-around groups to improve writing.* UCLA Writing Project, Dept. of Education, UCLA, Los Angeles, CA.

Gottesman, J.M. *Peer teaching: partner learning and small group learning.* Division of Curriculum and Instructional Services, Office of the Los Angeles County Superintendent of Schools, 1981.

Green, T.F., *Predicting the behavior of the educational system.* Syracuse, NY: Syracuse University Press, 1980.

Hall, R.V., Lund, D., and Jackson, D. Effects of teacher attention on study behavior. *Journal of Applied Behavior Analysis,* 1968, *1,* 1–22.

Hanf, M.B., *Mapping: a technique for translating reading into thinking.* Dept. of Education, University of California at Berkeley, Berkeley, CA.

———, **and Boyle, O.** *Mapping the writing journey.* Curriculum publication #15, Bay Area Writing Project, Dept. of Education, University of California at Berkeley, Berkeley, CA.

Hawley, R.C., and Hawley, I.L. *Human values in the classroom.* Arlington, VA: Education Research Associates Press, 1973.

Holt, J. *How children fail.* New York: Dell, 1965.

House, E.R. *The politics of educational innovation.* Berkeley, CA: McCutchan, 1974.

Hunter, M. *Reinforcement theory for teachers.* El Segundo, CA: TIP Publications, 1967.

———. *Retention theory for teachers.* El Segundo, CA: TIP Publications, 1967.

———. *Teach more—faster!* El Segundo, CA: TIP Publications, 1969.

———. *Teach for transfer.* El Segundo, CA: TIP Publications, 1971.

———, *Prescriptions for improved instruction.* El Segundo, CA: TIP Publications, 1976.

———, **and Breit, S.** *Aide-ing in education.* El Segundo, CA: TIP Publications, 1976.

Hyman, J.S., and Cohen, S.A. Learning for mastery: ten conclusions after 15 years and 3,000 schools. *Educational Leadership,* 1979, *37*(2), 104–109.

Insel, O.M., and Moos, R.H. Psychological environments: expanding the scope of human ecology. *American Psychologist,* 1974, *29,* 179–188.

James, T., and Tyack, D. Learning from past efforts to reform the high school. *Phi Delta Kappan,* 1983, *64*(6), 400–406.

———, **and Johnson, R.** *Learning together and alone: cooperation, competition, and individualization.* Englewood Cliffs, NJ: Prentice-Hall, 1975.

———, **and** ———. Cooperative, competitive, and individualistic learning. *Journal of Research and Development in Education,* 1978, *12,* 3–15.

Johnson, D.W., and ———. *Joining together: group theory and group skills.* Englewood Cliffs, NJ: Prentice-Hall, 1982.

———, **Maruyama, G., Johnson, R., Nelson, D., and Skon, L.** Effects of cooperative, competitive and individualistic goal structures on achievement: a meta-analysis. *Psychological Bulletin,* 1981, *89,* 47–62.

Johnson, J.L., and Sloat, K.C. Teacher training effects: real or illusory? *Psychology in the Schools,* 1980, *17,* 109–115.

Johnson, R., and Johnson, D.W. What research says about student-student interaction in science classrooms. In *Education in the 80's Science.* Washington, DC: National Education Association, 1982, 25–37.

Jones, F.H. The gentle art of classroom discipline. *The National Elementary Principal,* 1979, *58,* 26–32.

———, and Eimers, R. Role-playing to train elementary teachers to use a classroom management "skill package." *Journal of Applied Behavior Analysis,* 1975, *8,* 421–433.

———, Fremouw, W., and Carples, S. Pyramid training of elementary school teachers to use a classroom management "skill package." *Journal of Applied Behavior Analysis,* 1977, *10,* 239–253.

———, and Miller, W.H. The effective use of negative attention for reducing group disruption in special elementary school classrooms. *Psychological Record,* 1974, *24,* 435–448.

Joyce, B.R., Hersh, R., and McKibbin, M. The structure of school improvement. New York: Longman, 1983.

———, and Showers, B. Teacher training research: working hypotheses for program design and questions for further study. Paper presented to the American Educational Research Association, Los Angeles, 1981.

———, and ———. The coaching of teaching. *Educational Leadership,* October 1982, *40,* 4–10.

———, and Weil, M. *Models of teaching,* 2d ed. Englewood Cliffs, NJ: Prentice-Hall, 1980.

Kazdin, A.E., and Klock, J. The effect of nonverbal teacher approval on student attentive behavior. *Journal of Applied Behavior Analysis.* 1973, *6,* 643–654.

Kiesling, H.J. *A study of successful compensatory education projects in California.* Santa Monica: The Rand Corporation, 1971.

Knapczyk, D.R., and Livingston, G. The effects of prompting question-asking upon on-task behavior and reading comprehension. *Journal of Applied Behavior Analysis,* 1974, *7,* 115–121.

Lawrence, G. *Patterns of effective inservice education: a state of the art summary of research on materials and procedures for changing teacher behaviors in inservice education.* Tallahassee: Florida State Department of Education, 1974.

Leithwood, K.A., and Montgomery, D.J. The role of the elementary school principal in program development. *Review of Educational Research,* 1982, *52,* 309–339.

Levin, T., with Long, R., *Effective instruction.* Alexandria, VA: Association for Supervision and Curriculum Development, 1981.

Lortie, D.C. *Schoolteacher.* Chicago: University of Chicago Press, 1975.

McLaughlin, M.W., and Marsh, D.D. Staff development and school change. *Teachers College Record,* 1978, *80*(1), 69–94.

Mirga, T., and White E. Poll finds rising concern about school finance. *Education Week,* September 1, 1982, 12–13.

Murnane, R.J. Interpreting the evidence on school effectiveness. *Teachers College Record,* 1981, *83*(1), 19–35.

———, and Phillips, B.R. What do effective teachers of inner-city children have in common? *Social Science Research,* 1981, *10,* 83–100.

Ouchi, W.G. *Theory Z.* New York: Addison-Wesley, 1981.

Phi Delta Kappan. *Why do some urban schools succeed? the Phi Delta Kappan study of exemplary urban elementary schools.* Bloomington, IN: Phi Delta Kappan, 1980.

Rogers, C.R. *Freedom to learn.* Columbus, OH: Merrill, 1969.

Rosenshine, B., and Berliner, D. Academic engaged time. *British Journal of Teacher Education,* 1978, *4,* 3–16.

Rosenthal, N.R. A prescriptive approach for counselor training. *Journal of Counseling Psychology,* 1977, *24,* 231–237.

Rosenthal, R., and Jacobson, L. *Pygmalion in the classroom.* New York: Holt, 1968.

Rotter, J.B. Generalized expectancies for internal versus external control of reinforcement. *Psychological Monographs,* 1966, *80*(1), whole No. 609.

Russell, D., and Hunter, M. Planning for effective instruction. *Instructor,* September 1977.

Rutter, M., Maughan, B., Mortimore, P., Ouston, J., and Smith, A. *Fifteen thousand hours, secondary schools and their effects on children.* Cambridge: Harvard University Press, 1979.

Sarason, S. *The culture of the school and the problem of change* (rev. ed). Boston: Allyn and Bacon, 1982.

Saunders, R.M., and Hanson, P.J. A note on a simple procedure for redistributing a teacher's student contacts. *Journal of Applied Behavior Analysis,* 1971, *4,* 157–161.

Schmuck, R.A., and Schmuck, P.A., *Group process in the classroom.* Dubuque, IA: Wm. C. Brown Company, 1971.

Sharon, S., and Hertz-Lazarowitz, R. Effects of an instructional change program on teachers' behavior, attitudes, and perceptions. *The Journal of Applied Behavioral Science,* 1982, *18,* 184–201.

Shoemaker, J., and Fraser, H.W. What principals can do: some implications from studies of effective schooling. *Phi Delta Kappan,* 1981, *63*(3), 178–182.

Silberman, C.E. *Crisis in the classroom.* New York: Random House, 1970.

Slavin, R.E. Classroom reward structure: an analytical and practical review. *Review of Educational Research,* 1977, *47,* 633–650.

———, *Using student team learning, the Johns Hopkins team learning project.* Baltimore: Center for Social Organization in Schools, The Johns Hopkins University, 1978.

———. Cooperative learning. *Review of Educational Research,* 1980, *50*(2), 315–342.

———, and DeVries, D.L. Learning in teams. In H. Walberg (Ed.), *Educational environments and effects and productivity.* Berkeley, CA: McCutchan, 1979.

Stallings, J. *How to change the process of teaching reading in secondary schools.* Menlo Park, CA: SRI International, 1979.

Stipek, D.J., and Weisz, J.R. Perceived personal control and academic achievement. *Review of Educational Research,* 1981, *51*(1), 101–137.

Thayer, L. (Ed.). *Effective education: strategies for experiential learning.* San Diego, CA: University Associates, 1976.

Toch, T. Inservice efforts fail a system in need, critics say. *Education Week,* September 29, 1982, 10–11.

Zevin, J. Training teachers in inquiry. *Social Education,* 1973. *37,* 301–316.

[illegible]

INDEX